OPENING
TO SPIRIT

Designed by the author and illustrated by Roxane Aslani.

16-step Ziggurat and the Caduceus

SPIRITUAL BODY

In your body is Mount Meru encircled by the seven continents;
the rivers are there too, the seas, the mountains, the plains,
and the Gods of the fields.
Prophets are to be seen in it, monks, places of pilgrimage
and the deities presiding over them.
The stars are there and the planets, and the sun together with the moon;
there too are the two cosmic forces: that which destroys, that which creates;
and all the elements: ether, air and fire, water and earth.
Yes in your body are all things that exist in the three worlds,
all performing their prescribed functions around Mount Meru;
he alone who knows this is said to be a true Yogi.

Siva Samhita 2, 1:5

OPENING

TO SPIRIT

Contacting the Healing Power of the Chakras
& Honouring African Spirituality

CAROLINE SHOLA AREWA

Thorsons
An Imprint of HarperCollins*Publishers*

Thorsons
An Imprint of HarperCollins*Publishers*
77–85 Fulham Palace Road,
Hammersmith, London W6 8JB

Published by Thorsons 1998
1 3 5 7 9 10 8 6 4 2

Caroline Shola Arewa asserts the moral right to
be identified as the author of this work

Text illustrations by
Peter Cox, Su Eaton and Geoff Edwards

A catalogue record for this book
is available from the British Library

ISBN 0 7225 3726 3

Printed in the U.S.A.
Creative Print and Design (Wales), Ebbw Vale

The information in this book is not intended to replace advice from a medically qualified practitioner.

This book is dedicated with love to Claire Tallett, who returned to the spirit world on 8th May 1994. Claire's encouragement and comforting presence, both before and after her death, have made this book possible.

This book is dedicated with love to Chégianna Newton, who returned from the spirit world to brighten our lives on 21st April 1998. May you never forget the ways of spirit, Chégianna, and always continue to teach us.

CONTENTS

ACKNOWLEDGEMENTS

I give thanks to the Creator for my life, for the Spirit that moves through me and the mysteries of the universe that fill me with inspiration.

Respect, love and thanks to the spirits of my Ancestors for softly but firmly calling me home to the chakras, the centre of my being, so they could guide me.

I thank my parents Clara Akintunji and Rasheed Arewa for bringing me into this world, and blessing my life. Love and thanks to my Brothers and Sisters, Nike, Kunle, Wale, Tayo, Abdul, Bimbola, Bosede, Sade, Shalewa and Akintayo. Love and thanks to my family in York. Special thanks to my sister Dian and her husband John and Mike and Kath. Thanks for all the love you have shown me over the years. Blessings to all generations of my extended family. Peace to Mr and Mrs Hall who are now in the spirit world.

Deepest gratitude to my teacher Swami Joythimayananda of Kalkudah, Sri Lanka who introduced me to all forms of yoga, massage and naturopathic healing. My respect to Swami Vishnudevanandaji, whom I had the good fortune to be a student of when he was alive. I thank Swamiji's close disciples Swami Shankarananda, Swami Mahadevananda and Swami Saradananda for teachings I have received from them and for their devotion to delivering the message of yoga.

I sincerely thank Swami Nischalananda – spiritual director of Mandala Ashram in Wales, for his support and encouragement with this book. Although my work differs from Swami Nischalananda's his openness, breath of knowledge, and wisdom has offered a guiding light.

His support never wavered even when he was extremely ill. I thank him for reading the entire manuscript and offering feedback with love, honesty and humour.

Thanks to Tony Merry for being an excellent teacher and a very special friend. Thank you Tony for all your help and encouragement over the last ten years. I learnt so much just from being in your company.

Thanks to Sara Thomas, Merry Dufton, Merle Van den Bosch, Phil Young, Morag Campbell and Mike Considine.

I thank my students and clients, without whom my work could not have been put to the test. Special thanks to my Brixton yoga students, many who walked with me and supported my work over the years. 'I hope you're all still doing your yoga.' Thanks to my massage and bodywork students who were willing to explore the deeper parts of their souls with only a mere suggestion from me. Thanks to my clients for trusting me and having the inner wisdom to re-connect with spirit.

Special thanks to Dr Femi Biko – scholar in African Studies, Namonyah Soipan – trainer in Afrikan and Native American shamanism, Cynthia Benham and Keith Smith – Black studies tutors. Ivor Jeffors – artist, Charles Oba – writer, Dr Akintunde Oyetade – Yoruba Scholar and linguist, my Uncle, Dr Anjuwon Akinwande and my dear Sister Julia Akintunji. I thank you all for the hours you lovingly spent with me in sometimes passionate, always intense conversations as I tried to repair my Europeanized image of Africa and came to respect, honour and give thanks for my rich Yoruba heritage. I thank you all for your expert knowledge, which you shared with me, as I pieced together some of the history, achievements and suffering of African people. You have all helped me know myself better.

I give thanks to my friends and colleagues: some read parts of the text, others helped keep my confidence from sinking and all offered encouraging words of support. Anne-Marie Khachik, Stuart Taylor, Christene Burgess, Egidio Newton, Gary Chapman, Stephen Tallett, Vanessa and Vinda Sax, Sister Elaine McInnes, Sandy Chubb, Jilly Sliz, Sabel Thiam, Carolyn Pollock, Sue Beere, Rev. June Gatlin and Jackie Holder.

My appreciation for the help of Susan Mears, Claire Harvey, June Dyson, Jane Jones, Charlie Ward, Laura Boomer, Muz Murray, Carole Rudd and Francesca Shaw. Thanks to Rowena Mayell for working tirelessly on the colour plates.

I am especially thankful to Stephen Edwards and Namonyah Soipan who have been closest to me over the years that I have written this book.

Stephen, thanks for being there for me, listening to either endless versions of the same thing or total silence all but the clicking of the keyboard. Thanks for all your encouragement and help with this book and for your love and support through the years.

Namonyah, thanks for your loving friendship and deep understanding of the ways of spirit. Thanks for sharing high moments with me and being there for me when I felt low. Thanks for encouraging and supporting my work and being you.

Thanks to the talented team at Thorsons/HarperCollins. My Commissioning Editor Michelle Pilley, for seeing that this book could work and then supporting it wholeheartedly. Special thanks to my editor Barbara Vesey, Paul Redhead and designer Jacqui Caulton. Thanks for the assistance of Tim Nelson, Anna Grapes and Nicola Graydon.

As I advocate blending the old ways with the new, I had better give thanks to my computers, Hand-held and Desktop, without their help this book would still be in the making. My thanks also to the Òrishà Ogun who moves through them.

The presence of so many wonderful people has graced my life and helped create the energy that nourished and delivered this book, I am ever thankful to you all. Thanks to all the angels and spirit guides in ethereal and human form who have made this book happen and thanks to those who have waited patiently for it to be published.

The author and publishers would like to thank the following for permission to reproduce copyright material: The International Sivananda Yoga Vedanta Centre for the quotes from *Meditation and Mantras* by Swami Vishnu-devananda; Element Books Ltd for the quote from *The Polarity Process* by Franklin Sills; Thames & Hudson Ltd for the quote from 'The Tree of Life' *Image for the Cosmos* by Roger Cook, 1974; David Higham Associates for the quote from *The Temple of my Familiar* by Alice Walker, published by The Women's Press; and Rosenstone/Wender for the lyric by Lynn Ahrens from the Broadway Muscial ONCE ON THIS ISLAND by Lynn Ahrens and Stephen Flaherty. Based upon the novel by Rosa Guy. Lyrics Copyright © 1991 by Hillsdale Music. All enquiries concerning right to play must be addressed to the author's agent, ROSENSTONE/WENDER, 3 East 48th Street, New York, NY 10017.

The author and publishers would also like to thank the following for permission to reproduce photographs: Cherry Gilchrist for the Egyptian Qabalah from the temple wall in Komombo, Egypt (page 56); The Oriental Museum at the University of Durham for the Ancient Yogi (page 55); and Dr NJ Wosu and Bijon promotions for the Queen Mother head from Benin, Nigeria (page 266).

Colour illustrations: designer, Caroline Shola Arewa; Illustrator, Rowena Mayall; Retouching, Charlie Ward. Plate 1: CS Arewa and C Ward.

PREFACE

When I began writing this book I asked for the message of Spirit. I asked my Ancestors for guidance and trusted their wisdom and love would be with me as I listened to the still small voice within. Now this work is complete 'I give thanks'. Since *Opening to Spirit*, the title of this book, was born, I have been guided every single step of the way.

My journey with this book has been long, it has been uplifting and fulfilling, mostly sweet and always revealing. At times it has been painful as I realize our Ancestors suffered so much to keep alive the sacred traditions that now, in this time of need, we are desperately reclaiming. I have battled with anger and prayed for love as I have grieved for our many Ancestors who were killed while their traditions were suppressed. I have felt and remembered those that were forced to believe in what for them was a limited reality. This reality of 'so-called' civilization is now taking its toll on many of us who try to live in its narrow confines. I believe it is time to for us make rapid changes in the way we live. We need to re-evaluate spiritual traditions that have survived for thousands of years and integrate ancient knowledge with the science of our time. We must open the doors of perception and let Spirit in.

As we move forward into the next age the spirits of the ancients are reminding us that we are one people born from the essence of love. We ride on the same wheel of life and are bound by the same laws of nature. The Eternal spirit dwells within us all. We each have a responsibility to make personal changes that will cause peace and harmony to prevail in the world we share. It is time for many of us to reassess our life's and be guided by Spirit.

This book carries a message of unity. The Eternal Spirit unites the human race. The Eternal Spirit knows no boundary between past, present and future. We carry the spirits of our Ancestors into the present and our children will carry our spirits into the future, this is the circle of life. At the centre of this circle are the vibrating energy centres known as the chakras. Awakening the chakras and balancing their powerful energy elevates Eternal Spirit. Elevating spirit at this level can bring lasting healing and transformation. This is because the chakras live on when the physical body dies. My experience of the chakras has led me to believe that we carry the chakras of our Ancestors and our children will carry them into the future. As we heal ourselves through the chakras we heal our Ancestors and clear a path for future generations.

In these turbulent times it is only through looking back and integrating ancient wisdom into the art and science of everyday living that we as a human race will survive. Therefore this book makes the ways of the ancients available for use in everyday life.

I have found both embodiment and enlightenment to be important goals on the spiritual journey. The potential to experience ecstasy in the body is one of the great gifts we have been blessed with. For this reason attention is drawn to embodiment and developing the ability to celebrate our physical bodies as temples of Spirit. We are not only caretakers of our physical temples we are also caretakers of planet earth. At this moment in time we are the guardians of our troubled planet. When we embody spirit and bring it down to earth we also learn to respect the planet, we feel the rhythm of our earthly mother supporting us. The stronger we connect with the earth and build awareness of our sacred bodies the more we are able to soar towards enlightenment.

There have been times on my spiritual journey when I have doubted the very existence of enlightenment or at least my own potential for attaining it. Fearing I would never get close I even tried telling myself enlightenment was uninteresting. My fears and doubts only fuelled my desire to know the Divine essence that moves through me. I have now come to see that we have each glimpsed the Divine Spirit and experienced a short moment of enlightenment. I believe we already know bliss. It is a lasting experience of bliss that we search for as we journey through life.

Working with the chakras is like striding on stepping stones. In order to reach the destination, each step is important. Likewise each chakra has many important lessons and qualities to experience. Enlightenment may be the aim of crossing the stepping stones, but meanwhile the challenge is on the journey. Awareness must become heightened and although the destination remains in sight, full attention must be drawn into every moment. It is this attention that connects us more fully to the everlasting bliss of the Divine Spirit that resides deep within our souls.

Expanded awareness of the Eternal Spirit connects us to life's many dimensions. We can use the analogy of connecting to cable television and gaining the potential to tune into numerous channels where before only interference existed. As we connect consciously to the Eternal Spirit we gain the potential to see and communicate through new channels, many of which are beyond our ordinary reality and the limitations of space and time.

This book offers many ways to fine-tune the chakras and work towards a more fulfilling life. At the sacral chakra we can generate self-love which is a precursor to the universal love of the heart. Heart chakra energy is an important healing force that our planet and our people are literally dying for. If we are to survive then like the ancients we must Open to Spirit and spread universal love. We all have a role to play in positively changing the world in which we live. We each hold within ourselves unique qualities that we brought into this world. Working with the root chakra helps us unfold and honour the precious gifts we carry. These gifts help us see the 'soul purpose' of our existence. With this grounding we can begin a steady ascent towards the crown chakra.

At each chakra you are introduced to various practices and invited to reclaim the sacred art of ritual, the ancients gained much inner knowledge using these techniques. I also offer guidelines for developing personal *rites of passage* that recognize and celebrate the ascent of your spiritual and personal development.

I honour, with love and respect, the wise ancestors of Africa and Asia and the elders who until this day have maintained the sacred traditions in many parts of the globe. Opening to Spirit through the ancient chakra system teaches us to embrace both heaven and earth. The knowledge gained is our spiritual inheritance and we should use it at all times with wisdom and love. This way we too will become keepers of the secret knowledge of the ancients.

18 August 1998

INTRODUCTION

A S I BEGIN WRITING, I WONDER IF THIS TASK IS TOO GREAT FOR ME ALONE. Fortunately I am not alone: I have with me my Ancestors and Spirit Guides. *'I do not stand by myself, but on the shoulders of all the great people who went before me.'* In remembering this African dictum, I realize my task need not be difficult, as long as I remain Open to the Spirit. As I write the words Open to Spirit I feel a sudden surge of energy move right through my body. My entire being comes alive with excitement and enthusiasm. It is as if all my Ancestors have arrived at once, with urgency, to help me. I had only to ask – they provide and now I cannot write quickly enough. And so the title of this book is born, and the first steps on a new part of my journey are taken.

My Ancestors and Spirit Guides make it crystal-clear to me that they are ever by my side. They take my hand and lead me. If it is travel I want, they show the way. If it is people I need, they introduce them to me. If delivering the message of spirit is my task, then I know they will provide me with the words.

Spirit is the creative life-force, the very essence of all things. God, energy and consciousness are some of the many names we use to describe this wonder. This force manifests in different densities, reaching from the subtlest energy to gross physical matter. 'Like air, the creative force cannot be quantified. Air is air; there is not one air or many airs. Likewise there is not simply one or many Gods.'[1] Rather the creative force is a dynamic quality that resides everywhere and in everything.

Spirituality is to maintain an awareness of this quality as it moves through and around your being. It is the practice of utilizing this creative force for the collective good of humanity.

Opening to Spirit is to heighten awareness, extend consciousness and awaken your entire being to the energy which animates and connects you to the universe. Opening to Spirit means to open your sacred body temple and allow the Divine essence to flow with ease, filling you with love, wisdom and understanding. When you truly Open to Spirit, you accept the great **gift of d**ivinity (God) that is your birthright.

Opening to Spirit is a way of being and knowing. It requires an appreciation, awareness, respect and love of your physical body, without being over-attached. Your beloved body will one day fade to dust. It can be returned to the earth to complete the food chain. We eat fruit and vegetables from the earth; they give us life. When the body dies it is accepted by the earth and used as nourishment. Fruit and vegetables receive nourishment from the earth, and so the physical cycle of life continues. Strong attachments to the physical realm and material world often lead to feelings of separation from spirit. This sense of separation causes grief for that which is lost, and longing for something permanent in life. We then try to hold on to possessions and people, but they do not bring the permanent happiness we crave. Although we are deeply angry about our loss, we try to keep our emotions stable, hiding our true feelings even from ourselves. We search for lasting feelings of joy and love, for fulfilling relationships, for satisfaction. When they escape us we experience confusion and despair. We forget that what we really look for is the experience of our spiritual nature that we lost so long ago.

The shock and pain of trauma, illness or approaching death often make us look for something more than the limited life we know. A sense of true worth can emerge, reminding us of our spiritual nature. Pain seems to provide a glimpse at the impermanence of the life we are attached to. Buddha became enlightened only after he saw and experienced suffering. Deep within the centre of pain lies truth. We realize that we have been dulling ourselves through excessive work, sleep, addiction, lies and other tactics we have discovered. As we begin to feel our pain, transformation takes place. The pain holds within it a message, a spiritual message and an opportunity to reconnect consciously with spirit.

Opening to Spirit means accepting pain and limitation and transforming them into gains and liberation. Recognizing the energetic forces that govern you opens the possibility of being guided by those forces. The despair you knew is transformed into a beautiful rainbow. Consciousness extends and your energy field opens to receive a joy and bliss that are beyond words. Transformation is the personal,

alchemical metamorphosis that we reach through profound states of inner awareness and spiritual growth. This book is offered as a tool for transformation.

I write this book for healers, bodywork practitioners and those interested in
spiritual development. I trace the history of spiritual practice to its very beginnings
in Africa, drawing on African spirituality and mythology throughout the book.
I place an emphasis on practice, and to that end provide the reader with numerous
techniques for working with the chakras. There is a chapter on preparing for chakra
work (Chapter 5). This covers among other things cleansing, diet, support and some
problems that may arise if correct preparation is not adhered to. Each chapter on
the individual chakras (Chapters 6 – 12) has an extensive section on ways of working
with the chakra energies. And Chapter 13 focuses on Self-healing and professional
responsibility, raising considerations for those working as practitioners with clients.
The book closes with a comment on the chakras of evolutionary time and their role
in taking ancient wisdom forward into the new millennium.

I write from personal experience and theoretical study. I first heard the word
'chakra' when I began using yoga as a means of stress management. I realized important life changes would have to be made for me to gain optimum benefit from yoga.
I found this difficult at first, and simply took in the seed consciousness of the chakras
and allowed the seed to lay fallow. I continued practice of hatha yoga, pranayama
and relaxation, preparing the ground in which this seed would later grow. The seed
began to germinate when I qualified as a yoga teacher in India.

My training as a yoga teacher exposed me to the diversity of yoga. I began to
realize that yoga is not just about keeping fit, improving concentration and being
relaxed – these are only side-effects. Yoga aims to reunite individuals with the
Divine Spirit. Yoga is a philosophy for living. It has teachings on the questions and
problems we face as we journey through life. Yoga takes us inside ourselves and finds
the colours of consciousness within. My daily programme of intense practice and
study continued from 6 o'clock in the morning to 10 or sometimes 11 o'clock
at night. My resistance to change softened and I continue to be rewarded greatly.
A transformation slowly took place. My whole life as I knew it changed and I allowed
it to happen. Yoga has remained a very important and fundamental part of my personal life and work ever since. Yoga forms the foundation of this book.

When I returned from my years spent in India and Southeast Asia, I felt a need
to ground my spiritual experience. I began an experiential study of psychology and
psychotherapy. This I did within a humanistic framework and with an emphasis on
the body. This study clarified and paralleled a lot of what had been my personal feelings over the past few years. I began to see my experience of travelling and my study
of yoga as a kind of personal therapy. The spiritual and the psychological were to go
hand in hand.

Modern experimental science is beginning to mirror ancient 'in-perimental' knowledge. Dr Sperry's[2] experiments with epileptics and his findings in the late 1970s on the differences between left and right brain function, parallel the ancient yogic knowledge of Ida and Pingala, an aspect of Swara yoga. Swara yoga[3] is a complete yoga, which recognizes the different but complementary functions of the cerebral hemispheres and how the breath can influence them. This information is utilized to bring about balance in the entire organism. The importance of Self, in psychology, such as Maslow's theory of Self-actualization,[4] seems to echo the yogic concept of Self-realization. Responsibility for actions and personal development seems to mirror the yogic idea of karma and spiritual growth. The similarities are many.

As my work has developed to incorporate both the spiritual and the psychological, I have been drawn to work more and more with ritual. Through ritual, I connect with my ancestral heritage. History has masked the spiritual achievements of the African race, whether they be the Africans of the Motherland, such as the ancient Egyptians, or people of the African diaspora such as the early people of the Indus Kush (India).[5] Our African Ancestors were generalists: spirituality, philosophy, mythology, psychology, the arts and healing knew no separation. Being a generalist is sometimes frowned on in Western society, where specialization is often preferred. I have struggled to overcome separation and I try to reflect the path of my Ancestors. They did not divide knowledge pertaining to life, instead they held a holistic view specializing in all aspects of life. Likewise, in their complexity the chakras integrate a diversity of different realms.

When throughout the text I mention ancient people, I speak of the earliest civilizations and nations. I refer to the first people of Africa. I speak of the traditions of the ancient Egyptians (Kemitic) and the people of Nubia[6] who inspired them. The first Africans to inhabit the planet migrated north, peopling Ethiopia (originally named Kush, meaning Black), the Sudan and the Nile valley. Later the Egyptians travelled to many parts of the world. These Africans took with them creativity, wisdom and spirit. Have you ever wondered why people the world over have very similar traditions, beliefs, stories and symbols? This is no coincidence. This is our inheritance from the first children of Africa, the foreparents of all the planet's children.

The guidelines and techniques presented in this book have helped me and the many people I have had the good fortune to work with as teachers and students. Journeying through the chakras helps me to live my life, to embrace the laughter and tears. I have turned to numerous sources for inspiration and have journeyed consciously for many years. In this book I return to the chakras as the organizing principle they truly are. The ancient chakra system underpins the spiritual, psycho-emotional and physical realms. My intention is to present a text that will allow you to explore these realms for yourself. It is my hope that in writing both you and I will come to know more of life's mysteries.

This is for today's seeker, a guidebook for the spiritual traveller, companion for those seeking psychological growth and healing. It comes with maps for exploring your innermost Self. In it you will find suggestions for working with the chakras using meditation, yoga exercises, journal-keeping and ritual.

You are invited to embark on a journey through the chakras, opening to your own unique spirituality. Take time to understand how your energy changes and what patterns you have created in your life. Learn how to transform your life, heal the hurts and become acquainted with the wondrous, creative and beautiful person you truly are.

I

ENERGY

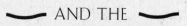

—AND THE—

CHAKRAS

1

CORE ENERGY

GIFT OF DIVINITY

WHAT ARE CHAKRAS?

These seven Chakras are who and what we are, what we feel and how we think and change, they are how we express ourselves and how we create ... The Chakra system is precisely the means by which we gain awareness. It is how we experience life, how we perceive reality, and how we relate to self, others, and the world. It is life itself.

Rosalyn Bruyere

CORE ENERGY IS THE STILL POINT OF OUR VERY EXISTENCE, THE HUB AROUND which the wheels of light known as chakras revolve. This central core links us to every living entity and connects us to our creator. The chakras unite us with our Ancestors, who bestow blessings upon us. The wisdom of past, present and future is revealed to us via the chakras. Through the chakras we find God – the 'gift of divinity' which lies at the very core of each human being.

As human beings we are all part of the greater universe and cosmos, we are the microcosm within the macrocosm. All the same, yet uniquely different. The ancient Egyptians, who are thought to have built the world's oldest astrological observatory 10,000 years ago, observed the heavens and understood our relationship to the cosmic rhythms. From the Egyptian Dendera zodiac we see that the Piscean Age is coming to a close and we are fast approaching the Aquarian Age – the age of Hapi, God of the Nile.

As the planet enters the Age of Aquarius we are flowing together through a time of much change. There is a quickening movement towards understanding the inner Self and searching for spiritual knowledge. Within each of us there is a need that can only be filled by answering this inner calling.

Not so long ago, knowledge and wisdom were the secrets of those who renounced the world. Priests in temples, ascetics living in monasteries or caves, or dwelling in the wilderness and mountains, learned to sublimate (repress, some would say) all things personal – the realm of the three lower chakras (root, sacral and solar plexus). In their spiritual environments they focused on the higher chakras (heart, throat, third eye and crown) until they reached enlightenment.

Today, seekers like ourselves want wisdom and knowledge in the world. We do not want to renounce the personal; instead we aim to integrate the individual Self with the spiritual. This is the transformational age of Anahata (heart) chakra[1] – the Aquarian Age where we have the potential of Hapi, who connects upper and lower Egypt, symbolically uniting the higher and lower aspects of our being. Opening to Spirit and working with the ancient chakra system provide an opportunity to realize this integration.

Hapi, the dual Nile God, is seen here as 'God of the Nile of the south' and 'God of the Nile of the north'. In the centre is the 'sema', a symbol of union. Hapi is uniting upper and lower Egypt. This union also symbolizes the union of our higher and lower selves.

OPENING TO SPIRIT

The Chakras – Position and Purpose

The chakras were named and highly developed in India. However, knowledge of their energetic force appears to reach back to the beginning of humanity. The chakras are known in many diverse cultures.

Chakra means 'wheel' in Sanskrit, and refers to cone-shaped vortices which spin and vibrate within the energy body. Humans are made up of many chakras. We have 7 major,[2] 21 minor,[3] 49 minute and numerous minuscule chakras.

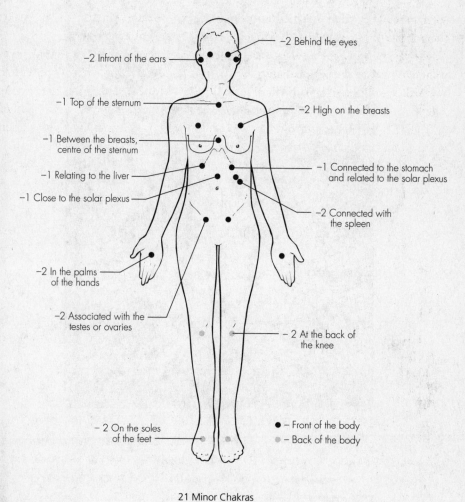

−2 Behind the eyes

−2 Infront of the ears

−1 Top of the sternum

−2 High on the breasts

−1 Between the breasts, centre of the sternum

−1 Relating to the liver

−1 Connected to the stomach and related to the solar plexus

−1 Close to the solar plexus

−2 Connected with the spleen

−2 In the palms of the hands

−2 Associated with the testes or ovaries

− 2 At the back of the knee

− 2 On the soles of the feet

● − Front of the body
● − Back of the body

21 Minor Chakras

The chakras are energy centres. They draw energy in from the universal energy field and distribute it out into the energy pathways – known as nadis in the traditional Indian yogic system, meridians in the traditional Chinese healing system – and from here energy radiates out into the aura.

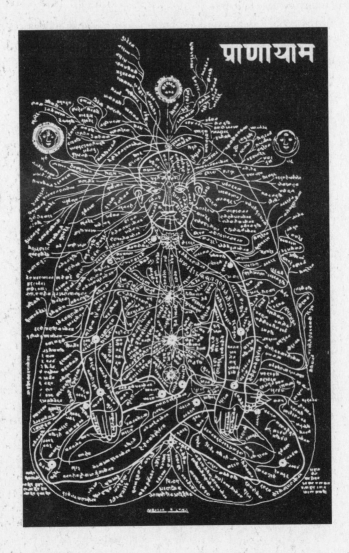

Ancient texts refer to 72,000 nadis as the energy pathways through which the Divine life-force flows. Of these nadis, three are central to chakra work. They are known as Ida, Pingala, and Shushumna. They are also named after the three sacred rivers of India: Ida = Ganga, Pingala = Yamuna and Shushumna = Saraswati.

The energy thrown off by the chakras manifests in different densities. At the most subtle level are the five elements (earth, water, air, fire and ether), the deities, and *ka* – the Eternal Spirit. These energies travel through the nadis and inform the mind, and the nervous system, which works closely with the endocrine glands (hormonal system). The most gross level is, of course, the physical body.

Chakras are responsible for creating and maintaining our very existence. The seven major chakras radiate out from different points along the spine, forming a vertical axis which runs from the base of the spine to the top of the head (see colour plate section). A pathway is produced that can transport us from the individual and personal realms of being to the spiritual and universal.

DIRECTION FLOW OF ENERGY

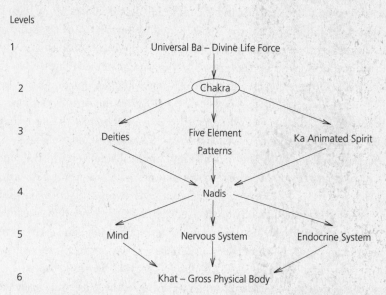

The Divine life-force animates the chakras and directs energy into the subtle vehicles – level 3. Energy then flows through the nadis, fuelling the gross vehicles – level 5 – and sustaining the physical body.

Chakras hold the key to spiritual awakening, psychological well-being and physical health. Each of the seven chakras governs a different stage of psychological and spiritual development, creating various levels of consciousness. The first three chakras – root, sacral and solar plexus – are responsible for survival, sense of Self and inner-power, respectively. The heart centre, which is fourth, is the point of transformation from the inner world, our personal reality, to the universal reality. In yoga terms this transformation starts the movement from darkness into light; the removal of the veil of Isis or Maya (illusion) towards God-realization. The three remaining chakras – throat, third eye and crown – are universal centres, focusing on communication, insight and wholeness.

Physically, each chakra has various body parts under its control. The seven chakras govern seven main endocrine glands, and in this way influence the entire harmony of the body.

How the psyche, endocrine glands and chakras relate is best illustrated with an example. The root chakra is directly linked to the adrenal glands, and grounding is the quality associated with this chakra. The root chakra relates mainly to our connection with the earth, the mother and our feminine/receptive side. The earth provides us with stability, the mother provides security and the feminine aspect which, along with the masculine, creates our full identity. If our sense of identity and feelings of security and stability were disturbed at any time during our foetal life, at birth, or in the first year of worldly existence, or if they are challenged in the present, this will inevitably give rise to a prominence of fear and insecurity. In turn this will affect the adrenal glands. The adrenals have either a stimulating or balancing effect on the organism. Constant fear causes constant stimulation, resulting in an excess of chemicals being released into the system. The body responds by remaining continually alert and 'on guard'. The body's resources are drained both energetically and physically, leaving the individual exhausted, stressed out and open to receive all manner of stress-related disorders. Here we see that the root of some stress-related and psychosomatic complaints can originate in the very early stages of our development. If you have not considered your connection to the earth and issues around inner security, dependence, or fear, then a journey through the chakras makes available a whole new means of exploring your innermost Self and any stress-related disorders you may be prone to.

Staying with the root chakra as an example, we will see how the related body parts – legs, spine and feet – are affected by fear and insecurity. This is best described using everyday metaphors:

'I just can't stand up for myself'

'I have no real backbone'

'He is spineless'

'I was shaking at the knees'

'I can never put a foot right'

Imbalance in any chakra will affect the mind, which in turn affects the body. This is the message given in the above sayings; they all relate to our emotional anatomy. Thus the connection between chakras and the body/mind emerges.

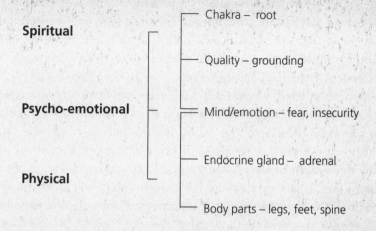

Spiritual

Psycho-emotional

Physical

Chakra – root

Quality – grounding

Mind/emotion – fear, insecurity

Endocrine gland – adrenal

Body parts – legs, feet, spine

Energy travels from the spiritual realm, affects the mind[4] and eventually crystallizes in the physical body.

The above example shows the connection between the physical and emotional aspects of the root chakra. Likewise, the remaining energy centres have equivalent correspondences. As energy flows through a chakra its quality is stimulated; when the quality functions, the mind and emotions function. When the mind and emotions function, the related endocrine gland functions and hence the body maintains health. This unity has been known for thousands of years.

Ancient Wisdom, Modern Science

Diverse cultures throughout the ages have understood that people exist not as solid matter but as vibrational beings in direct contact with the greater source of energy surrounding us. Spiritual practices, rituals, mythology, astrology, philosophy and magic the world over bear testament to this understanding. Science now confirms that what we perceive as our physical selves and the world around us is in fact energy.

> In modern physics, mass is no longer associated with a material substance, and hence particles are not seen as consisting of any basic 'stuff' but as bundles of energy.
>
> *Fritjof Capra*

Energy takes on many forms, from the subtlety of *prana* (vital energy) to the solidity of the physical body and our material universe. The Ancients were aware that energy moves from the subtle to the gross and from the gross back to the subtle. This takes place in our journey through life. Initially, from the spirit world we cause a twinkle in the eye of our parents. We then walk proudly upon the earth, before returning to the spirit world as Ancestors to distant relatives. Thus what we know as 'Self' is in fact a constantly changing flow of energy.

In the past, philosophy, magic, mythology, etc. were closely entwined in the life-styles of our Ancestors. This remains today in some parts of the world. The Ancients did not gain their knowledge from books; instead they observed nature and felt its pulse, they felt the vibration of the earth and stars, the rhythm of day and night. They did not view themselves as separate from their environment but as functional parts of a whole. They were able to learn about themselves in what they saw and felt. Through rituals based on nature, especially the seasons, animals and elements, people were able to enter into the spirit of what they saw. In this way they achieved inner knowledge.

Rituals were the scientific experiments of ancient people. By returning to the ways of the Ancients we can learn to live in harmony with ourselves and our environment. No separation was made between wo/man and God, between people and nature. Oneness was recognized in all things.

Pure Spirit

Energy has been established the world over as the unifying principle. Without energy there can be no mind or body. From energy the body/mind is created. The entire universe is created from spirit and will return again to pure spirit. We are the passengers on this greatest of journeys. Spirit takes many forms, while in essence remaining the same, just as water is liquid as it flows downstream, steam as it heats and gently rises, and solid as a rock when frozen – its appearance changes but it remains water. The universe and the people in it can be viewed in a diversity of forms: young, old, man, short, tall, black, white, woman, graduate, labourer, animal, tree, the good, the convicted, holy, ignorant – the list goes on. Applying names to thought and form helps us grasp the vastness of creation, but it can also limit our perceptions of reality. I am a woman, therefore I am not a man or a plant or the sun. Yet this concept of who I am, a woman, teacher and therapist, masks my very nature. For within myself as woman I find man, tree and sun, and within each of these three I find myself. We are all the same pure spirit manifest in different forms. There is no separation between spirit and matter, matter is simply a continuation of spirit.

Core Energy

Chakras form the energetic core of the human organism. They are our **gift of divinity**. This core shapes the body, mind and spirit. As a result, the chakras directly link and influence:

> the growth of spiritual awareness
> psycho-emotional development
> physical health and well-being.

By returning to the chakras, the very core of our being, the control box, we learn to understand natural and sacred laws which are governing ourselves and our environment. We see the movement from spirit to gross physical matter and the return from gross physical matter to pure spirit. As our universe takes this journey, we too have a personal voyage. This course from the infinite to the finite and back is the basis of all natural laws. Just as a beautiful flower germinates from a seed, grows up towards the sun and blossoms before dying and returning to seed, we also will grow, blossom and die. Pure spirit is woven into a physical body in the womb of the mother. On the first part of our journey the soul travels from spirit (ether), through to thought (air),[5] conception (fire),[6] gestation (water) and finally birth (earth). We move into our independent reality, creating a unique physical existence. The process of dying is not so clear, as it can be brought about in many different ways; we can assert, however, that death occurs when the soul no longer requires, and therefore leaves the physical body.

Between birth and death we have life. During this period of animation there are many choices and challenges. Opening to Spirit and understanding the chakra system offer help that can make life a lot easier. The chakras provide a complete system, enabling us to gain a greater understanding of all of life's experiences.

The Cosmic Ladder

The chakras are like a ladder on which we can climb up to the clouds – this is our expansion – or down to earth – our limitation. Each rung has a different lesson. We can get stuck in one place – up high, unable to see down, or down low, unable to see above us. We may have no knowledge of the ladder and the opportunity it affords. Some rungs may be wobbly and therefore a bit scary to climb. One side may be stronger, so we may avoid the weak side and step confidently only to the left (feminine) or right (masculine).

The chakras are no ordinary ladder because at each rung you can move in or out, as if a piece of wood had been laid on the rungs to deliver you inside, to yourself, or outside, to the world. From each rung the experience is different. Viewing in the appropriate direction from the relevant step can bring clarity to life's challenges and make decisions crystal-clear. There are seven rungs and four directions. The rungs are each of the chakras. The directions at each chakra are upwards (to the next chakra above), downwards (to the chakra below), in (towards the Self), and out (towards the world). We can develop the chakras individually, but the relationship of the whole must always be remembered. Although each chakra has dominant characteristics it also has within it the infinite possibilities of the other six chakras.

The reader is not expected to take for granted or believe what is written. Instead you are encouraged to work with energy and your chakras as the Ancients did. 'Ins-periment' for yourself. At this point I would like to share a favourite quote by Carl Rogers:

> Experience is, for me, the highest authority ... Neither the bible nor the prophets and neither Freud nor research – neither the revelations of God nor man – can take precedence over my own direct experience.
>
> *Carl Rogers*

If I speak to you about love-making, can you feel it and therefore have no need to experience it for yourself? You cannot feel it. If I were an expert at martial arts and told you everything I knew, would you then be an expert? Only with practice. Can I really explain the taste of honey to you? No, you must taste it for yourself. The same applies to the chakras – to feel, taste, know and truly embody the experience of the chakras you have to enter into the spirit of yourSELF. (Exercises for you to follow are in italics.)

HAND ENERGY-SENSING EXERCISE

Take some time to yourself in a silent space. It can be out in the open or in a quiet room. Sit comfortably, either cross-legged on the floor or, if that is difficult, upright in a chair with both feet flat on the floor.

Straighten your spine – this allows the chakras to sit one on top of the other in alignment. If you cannot straighten your back, do not worry, do the best you can. Support your back if necessary using cushions. Place your hands, palms facing upwards, on your knees. Close your eyes and take a few deep breaths. Begin to let your body relax. Remain upright and release any tightness. Feel the contact of your body with the floor and feel as though you are sinking into the ground more and more. Relax the shoulders and allow them to open. Feel the chest expand, lift your spine and take up more space in your body. Now bring your attention to the point just below your navel; feel the sensation of energy or visualize a healing colour. Draw energy up from below the navel through the abdomen and chest. Feel the energy move, and direct it around each of your shoulders and along your arms to your hands. Be still and feel the sensation of energy in your hands.

When you feel a sensation in your hands, lift them up from your knees and turn them to face each other. Begin to bring your hands very slowly together, sensing the energy. Explore the space between your hands. The more subtly and imperceptibly you move your hands, the more powerful is the feeling of energy. Draw your hands slowly together until they touch. Then very slowly return your hands to your knees. Take a few deep breaths and remain with your eyes closed for a moment.

———— • ————

Through this exercise you can feel the minor chakras of the hands and sense your aura. The sensation in your hands is caused by the minor chakras – it may be of heat, tingling, excitation. These minor chakras are used in healing. As you draw your hands together you may encounter a resistance, a sense of something solid between your hands. This is the electromagnetic field which permeates and embraces the body, known as the aura. If nothing is felt during the first few times you practise 'hand energy-sensing', don't give up. It may just be that your concentration needs to be a little more focused on feeling within. Possibly you moved your hands too far, too fast. Continue practising the exercise and try to develop your physical awareness of energy and the chakras.

Hopefully you now have an intellectual idea and a felt sense of what the chakras are. However, as Rosalyn Bruyere says and I quote at the beginning of this chapter, 'the chakra system ... is life itself.' Life, we know, is very complex, and since the chakras and the aura are the blueprint for all life-energy, they are also complex.

2

THE RAINBOW AURA

YOUR TRUE COLOURS

Carlotta was yellow. The young hopeful immigrant colour, the colour of balance,
the colour of autumn leaves, half the planet's flowers, the colour of endurance
and optimism. Green was his own colour, soothing green, the best colour for the
heart. And Zede – Zede's colour was peach or pink or coral. The womb colours, the
woman colours.

Alice Walker

THE AURA

AS THE CHAKRAS REVOLVE, THEY CREATE AN ELECTROMAGNETIC ENERGY
field[1] which penetrates and surrounds the physical body. This personal
energy field is known as the aura. Many people are able to sense the aura –
some through sight, known as clairvoyance, others through touch, or clairsentience.
I sense the aura most reliably through touch. Physical contact is perhaps the easiest
way to experience the aura because we are already familiar with touch. On a daily
basis we interact with both our own energy field and those of the people around us.
We are not generally conscious of this interaction.

In this chapter, I try to lift the veil of mystery that surrounds the aura. I explain how we already use it and how we can develop this use for the benefit of our health and well-being.

The Aura Every Day

Although very subtle, auric vibrations are phenomena we are all familiar with. We speak of liking and disliking a person's 'vibe', and we speak of positive vibrations. This is the felt sense of energy we get when meeting people. We literally step into their aura and feel the energy. The aura is also evident when we verbally communicate with people. We do not go right up to someone's face and begin talking into it, instead we leave a comfortable distance around the person. Some people we feel closer to than others. We step comfortably into their aura and feel safe. We hold an unconscious awareness that people extend beyond the physical body. Performing everyday actions such as relating with people is dependent on us sensing the aura around them.

Communication is approximately 10 per cent verbal, the rest is non-verbal. Part of non-verbal communication is sensing a person's aura, feeling the vibration and judging how then to relate. We may even say a person has a nice aura about them. Such expressions are not confined to esoteric use but are found in common language.

Colour and projection within the aura are different for each individual, and change constantly. We all try to sense the right moment to approach a loved one for a favour, and know when to stay away. They do not have to say anything; we sense the changes in their aura.

Events, people and environments can affect energy. All experiences leave lasting imprints on the aura. Trauma, for example, can create spaces or holes in the aura, and a subsequent loss of energy called 'leaking'. The body and energy fields contract in response to trauma in an attempt to prevent energy-leaking. Chronic contraction interrupts full expansion and disturbs the natural rhythm we need in order to maintain health. Pleasure and love have an expansive effect on the aura, which can help to repair some of the damage caused by trauma.

Everything we do has a consequence on the aura. Diet, lifestyle and the company we keep all cause vibrations throughout our energy fields. Thoughts have a very powerful impact on our energy. 'Energy follows thought' is one of the basic laws of nature. Through our thoughts we are capable of changing our lives. Therefore, we must be vigilant and think with awareness. A negative belief can manifest just as easily as an affirmative thought. The universe supports 'My life will never change,' just as easily as 'Things are going to improve for me.' The choice is yours. You are gifted with a high level of consciousness, so you can make choices. When you truly Open to Spirit, help is available to you. As director of your life story, you have the ability to rewrite the script and make changes; this is your 'respons-ability'.

People we spend time with affect our auras. Some people leave us feeling tired and drained, while others help us to feel uplifted and joyful. This positive effect is utilized in healing. A healer's vibration (vibes) will affect the vibration of the client. This is explained using the principles of resonance, as found in the study of physics and harmonics. For example, imagine two tuning forks of the same natural frequency. If you tap one of them to set it vibrating, and then hold the other fork in close proximity, in a short time the second fork will begin to vibrate in harmony with the first. The forks are then said to be in resonance. As humans we share the same natural frequency, although we can become out of tune at times. It follows that a client will be uplifted in the presence of a healer who is vibrating positively and fully. The responsibility is with healers to be aware of their own well-being in order to be of help to others.

We each know of situations when someone has entered our space feeling down and giving off negative vibrations. If we are not careful, we also begin to feel the same negativity. On the spiritual path it is sometimes necessary to make new friends and let go of people who do not support your growth.

We can feel our energy lowered in certain places where the energetic frequency is low. Likewise, our energy can be lifted in specific environments. We often experience a sense of expansion when we get out of the city and into the countryside. This is why people enjoy spending time by the sea, or up in the mountains. People take pleasure from being outside in open spaces because their aura is allowed to expand. This is also the reason for needing to get outside after being in a building all day, or for going to the country after being in the city for a while. The aura actually requires more space.

Auric energy is very subtle, but by improving your awareness it is possible to interact more consciously with auras in everyday life.

Aura Awareness

This is not exactly an exercise, but rather an invitation to develop your conscious awareness of the aura. For the next few days, be attentive to your own vibrations and the auras of those around you. Fully use your senses: feel, look and tune in to vibrations. Watch how you respond to certain people, and they to you.

Observe:

- *your family at different times of the day*
- *people in your workplace*
- *how people interact on public transport*
- *children, lovers, colleagues. Notice how they move in and out of each other's auric space.*
- *what it is about people that attracts you and draws you close?*
- *what makes you pull away from people?*
- *a calm aura*
- *an agitated aura.*

Try to see people's auras: their colour, shape and density.

Make some notes in your journal (please refer to Chapter 5, Journal-keeping) *and see if any recurrent patterns become apparent.*

When I do this I seldom see colours. Instead I notice the size and energetic quality of the aura. Some people's aura is so dense that it is hard for them to hold the attention of even one person. Another character can hold the attention of many individuals around them because people feel embraced by their aura. For example, the pure energy of babies and small children has an amazing ability to attract people. Adults often look to babies and children for the peace and serenity that is lacking in their own energy fields. It is possible for children to become drained from this attention, especially if they are not allowed space to regenerate. They need time when nothing is being expected of them.

VEHICLES OF THE SOUL

Egypt and India share a similar understanding of energy bodies and esoteric anatomy. Age-old wisdom from Egypt and India provides the foundation of my perception of the rainbow-coloured aura. The ancient Egyptians identified nine vehicles of the soul. Each vehicle differed in density, with *khat* – the physical body – being the densest. Energy was seen to travel down from the universal *Ba* (Divine Soul), animate all parts of the spirit and maintain the *khat* until death. When the physical body is released, depending on the individual's spiritual development, the individual *ba* either unites with the universal *Ba* and attains permanence (the ultimate goal of yoga), or reincarnates in another *khat*.

Nine Ancient Egyptian Vehicles of the Soul

VEHICLE	FUNCTION
Ba	The Divine Soul. A spark of this Divine soul resides within each one of us.
Khat	The gross physical body.
Khabit	The shadow. Lower nature that is dominated by the senses.
Shekem	The realm of Divine power and vital energy.
Ab	The heart. This vehicle was seen as the home of the conscience.
Khu	Divine intelligence, which organizes all things in time and space.
Ka	Divine Self, the animating spirit which lives on after the khat dies.
Ren	The name. African names usually reflect the life purpose and the gifts and blessings carried to the earth realm at birth. The sonic vibrations bring harmony. The names of our Ancestors can be called after their death, to ensure that harmony prevails.
Sahu	The glorious spiritual body. This vehicle is used to transport the Eternal Spirit – ka – to the heavens after death. Appears to relate to the astral sheath.

THE RAINBOW-COLOURED AURA

Comparative research and personal experience indicate that the aura is made up of seven three-dimensional energy bodies, which connect us with the universe. Each energy body differs in vibration and projection, creating a series of layers which extend beyond the physical body. Each layer corresponds to an element and to a colour:

Auric layer	Element	Colour
Core energy – the chakras	Earth	Red
The gross physical body	Water	Orange
Physical heat layer	Fire	Yellow
Pranic sheath	Air	Green
Etheric sheath	Ether	Blue
Astral sheath	Light	Indigo
Causal sheath	Spirit	Violet-Gold

As seen on the first colour plate, the various vibrations of the aura cause different colour frequencies and relate to the various elements, as do the chakras.

THE AURA THROUGHOUT THE AGES

The aura, and its function in connecting us to the universe, has been known throughout the ages. Different civilizations and people have seen, felt and understood the energetic field that surrounds each one of us. In divergent cultures, ritual, trance, meditation, breathing exercises, music, therapy and numerous physical disciplines and arts continue to be used to gain knowledge and heal the aura. We see from paintings, mythology and surviving oral tradition that an understanding of the energy field was evident in antiquity. Ancestor reverence as practised in Africa and Asia demonstrates an awareness of the etheric field. Einstein said 'energy never dies; it only changes.' This confirms that, although physically dead, the energy of our Ancestors remains. Their wisdom and knowledge live on in the ether.[2] This phenomenon is known as *dafa*[3] in Nigeria, *akashic record* in India, and *the collective unconscious* in Jungian psychology.

It is possible to tune in to the etheric sphere and gain knowledge that can be of help physically and emotionally in daily life. You may have a difficult decision to make, about which you feel pressured and alone. By asking the Ancestors for guidance we realize we are not alone and a burden is lifted. Through meditation or divination, space is created for communication and insight to occur. Ancestor reverence not only aligns the living with the etheric knowledge of the dead, but it recognizes that we learn much from those who went before us, and provides us with the opportunity to offer due respect.

Rainbow colours play an important role in the complex cosmology of the Dogon people of Mali. The first Ancestor, a blacksmith, holds knowledge of both the celestial realms and the earth. He therefore helps the community remain connected with the universe. He originally descends to earth along the rainbow. The rainbow with all its colours connects heaven and earth, as the aura joins the body to heaven. To the Dogon, rainbow colours form an integral relationship between the universe, the Ancestors, the soul and the physical body. These colours are used in divination and diagnosis, much like the colours of the aura can be read to give an indication of imbalance in the physical body. The colours of the rainbow are said to be reflected in the organs and joints. This shows that the Dogon have knowledge of the auric field and its effect on the physical body.

Shamans, temple priests/priestesses, clairvoyants, healers and some scientists study the aura. In parts of Africa, Original[4] Australia and Original America, shamans study animals, trees and all aspects of nature. This is achieved through focusing on the spirit of the animal or tree. The shaman leaves the lower physical realms (where science bases its studies) and journeys to the astral plane. In this way the shaman unites with the animal or tree spirit and learns from its sacred wisdom.

We have always considered all life-forms on our Mother Planet to be our relatives and our equals. For centuries, we have sought to learn the language of every life-form in order to know how to live life on Earth with gratitude for all the lessons each teacher in nature brings.

Jamie Sams

In yoga, many postures are named after animals; you can roll up into the cobra pose, roar like a lion, stand like a crow or lie down like a crocodile. There are also tree and mountain poses – again revealing a desire to understand and harmonize with the spirit of nature.

There is so much intelligence around us, yet man has come to see himself as superior to the natural world. This is one of the biggest mistakes modern man has made. We have so much to learn, and perhaps the first lesson is humility. When we see the sacred in all, then we can truly begin to see the sacred in ourselves. Once we are able to focus our attention on the aura and higher aspects of trees and the animal kingdom, then nature itself becomes a trusted friend.

The Power of Dreams and Music

Dreams and music are perhaps two of the most well-recognized means of transporting us into another reality. Dreaming is believed to be a method of tuning in to the etheric field. Dreams have long been associated with prophecy. Some people are

OPENING TO SPIRIT

able to tell the future by them. Dream chambers were used in Egypt, Greece and by the Celts in Britain.[5] After cleansing, fasting and ritual preparations, an individual would enter the chamber for a night, hoping to receive a vision that would shine light on a difficult question. Temple priests or priestesses would be on hand to help interpret any hidden message. Most of us are aware that particular dreams hold significance for us, and we too can use our dreams to help us on our spiritual journey.

Musical vibrations have always played an important role in healing because of their ability to resonate across each level of the auric field. It has been suggested that what is known as sympathetic resonance in music also occurs in the energy field of humans.

> At the same moment a string is vibrating, the sonic energy causes corresponding vibrations to occur in that same key but in other octaves. In other words, striking a low 'C' note on a piano will result in a resonant stimulation of the higher 'C' notes as well ... energy vibrates in the octave of physical matter but strikes a resonant note in the higher etheric octave as well.
>
> *Richard Gerber MD*

When a particular note is sounded, the harmonics register with each layer of the aura. The energy field may then retune the out-of-balance physical body, much like any other instrument is tuned.

The harmonic effect of music on the aura makes clear why music has been so widely used. *Listen to your favourite piece of music and really be aware of how it is affecting you. What physical changes do you experience? How is your breathing, your mind?* As I write, I listen to music that helps clear my mind and lifts my spirit. My concentration improves and I feel more in contact with the spirit that moves through me.

During the early 20th century a number of Europeans took an interest in the mysteries of Egypt and India. The Theosophists, led by Madame Blavatsky, Annie Besant and Charles Leadbeater, published writings on Egyptian spirituality, hermetism, yoga and traditions of the East. Jung also wrote on eastern philosophy, and was known to use mandalas in his work. Their teachings, which owe much to ancient spiritual traditions, are still recognized today. The Reverend Leadbeater was clairvoyant, and he recorded his personal visions of the aura and chakras.

Kirlian photography, developed by Semyon and Valentina Kirlian in 1940s Russia, has enabled many people to see the aura. It is now possible to make photographic images of the electromagnetic field. People have been able to see pictures of the aura around their hands. In some cases the images are being used for diagnostic purposes, although this particular skill is still in its infancy.

Beautiful colours and spark patterns are observed in the electrographic image in what has been described as the 'Kirlian Aura'.

Richard Gerber MD

Perhaps the most important result of Kirlian work is the 'phantom leaf effect', whereby a corner of a leaf is severed and the damaged leaf photographed. Although the entire leaf is not present, its energy field is unchanged. The severed part of the leaf remains in the Kirlian image. This provides an explanation for the pain that exists in a limb long after it has been amputated, known as a 'phantom limb'. This also proves scientifically the continued existence of the intact energy field even when gross physical matter is no longer present. The Ancients have always known this. Much ancient wisdom has been misunderstood and seen as primitive. This is largely due to the limited perception of anthropologists.

During the 1970s, healer Rosalyn Bruyere and scientist Dr Valerie Hunt conducted an eight-year research project on the human electromagnetic field.[6] They were able to verify the colours of the chakras and the aura. Rosalyn Bruyere was able to see the colours which Dr Hunt measured with electrical instruments. Emissions of the energy field and how they changed in relation to emotions were also recorded in this study. This objective work validates years of subjective knowledge, for those who require science to justify subjective reality.

THE FUNCTION OF THE AURA

First Layer[7]/Core Energy Body – The Chakras

The innermost layer of the aura is made up of the chakras themselves. The chakras are the core energy body. They are three-dimensional and extend well into the body. Spinning around a central column they form a spiral-like pattern which creates the aura. Wheels within wheels are seen by those with extended vision. The chakras should not be thought of as tiny inner discs but as large wheels which spiral out. The hub of the wheel (*Shushumna*) is the neutral, non-changing aspect of the chakras relating to the Divine. As they rotate, the spokes generate an energy field that is the aura.

Each chakra gives rise to a different frequency of the aura, and consequently to different sounds and colours. This energy formation is clearly depicted in the illustration of Dr Babbitt's atom (*see illustration on page 23*). We can see how vibrations at the centre of Babbitt's atom create the outer rings. Likewise, spinning of the chakras creates the aura. Because this innermost layer resonates at different frequencies, it is a focus for spiritual development and healing. Working directly on the chakras has a simultaneous effect on each layer of the aura.

This first layer is responsible for bringing about our physical reality and maintaining our connection to the earth plane. It is this layer that grounds us, while also connecting us to the whole of the universe.

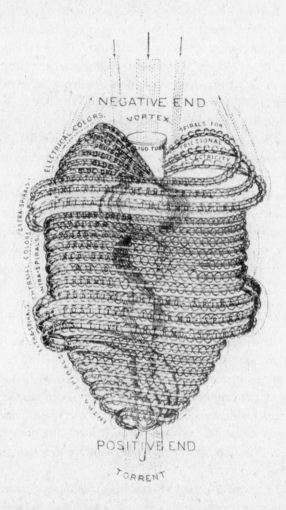

Babbitt's atom shows how energy is generated from a central core and radiates out in electromagnetic frequencies corresponding to the colours red, orange, yellow, green, blue, indigo and violet. This pattern is also seen in the human body, where the cosmic forces create the chakras, and the chakras generate energy that spins out and forms the rainbow-coloured aura.

Second Layer/Gross Physical Body

The second aspect of the aura is the one we are most acquainted with: the physical body. It is important to remember that, although the body appears solid, it is energy and therefore continually changing. Even from a materialistic perspective the body is not viewed as solid, because it is at least 70 per cent water. Fluid and space surround every cell in the body. Cells expand and contract in order to breathe. Every organ has its own sound and rhythm. Applying touch and subtle energy healing to this layer conducts messages through the water, directing vibrational change on electrical and cellular levels. DNA can be reprogrammed to replace dis-eased cells with healthy ones. As you read, parts of your body are dying and being replaced with new cells. Even the bones are being broken down and rebuilt as they exchange minerals. At this physical level, change is the only constant.

You might like to try this simple exercise. *Picture in your mind's eye the constant fluid movement of your body, go deep inside yourself – for a few moments stay with the feeling of fluidity.*

Despite its fluidity, the physical body is still the most crystallized layer of the aura. It provides us with a vehicle in which we can experience a limited physical reality and, through spiritual practice, perceive our universal existence. Through the body we can know the polarities of pleasure and pain. Using this same body as a temple we also have the ability to transcend polarity and know true peace.

Third Layer/Physical Heat Layer

The physical heat layer permeates the two lower layers and extends about 1 or 2 centimetres from the body. It duplicates all aspects of the physical body. The density of this level determines the constitution,[8] which is set from birth. You can still effect change in this layer, but your constitution will construct certain limits. Emotions, spiritual practice and healing can all create change in this layer. This layer is used in healing when it is not possible to actually touch a specific body part because of contra-indications. The dominant colour is yellow, which can be visualized to strengthen and heal.

The physical heat layer is a good place to begin feeling energy since, as its name suggests, this layer is characterized by heat and therefore reasonably easy to feel. *Try simply placing your hand over different parts of your body and hold for a while until you feel a connection of energy. Is the sensation of heat different on different body parts? Does any change in feeling correspond to your inner experience? For example, if you have an area that is painful, does it emit more or less heat?*

The physical heat layer is also known as the emotional body. Fluctuations in our emotions have a profound effect on this layer. If we are able to maintain emotional balance, which is one of the aims of spiritual practice, we reach a place where emotions are felt but they are not controlling us. When the emotions are relatively steady, energy is preserved at this level. This strengthens the entire system. When our emotions are not acknowledged they can flare up at any time, draining our energy and controlling us. This, of course, weakens the body.

The physical heat layer provides a protective envelope to the body. Fire can be used as a protective shield to safeguard those within its confines and keep away intruders. This third aspect of the aura provides a protective role for the physical body. On the surface of the skin's seven layers[9] we have what is known as the acid mantle, which is responsible for keeping bacteria and unwanted microbes out of the body. The acid mantle forms a base to the physical heat sheath, which then subtly extends out into the aura surrounding the body.

Transition Points

A main transition point occurs between the third and fourth layers of the aura. Transition points are gateways that occur between each of the chakras and the energetic fields they generate. When unrestricted they allow the successful flow of energy from one chakra and its energetic field to another. As subtle energy crystallizes into physical form it creates bands of connective tissue such as the body's three diaphragms: the pelvic floor, respiratory diaphragm, and the vocal diaphragm (also known as the thoracic inlet) at the base of the throat. These are transition points as they become manifest on the physical level.

In yogic terminology these transition points are referred to as *granthis*, which means knots. The term is suggestive of the obstacles that can occur on the spiritual path as we ascend the chakras. Brahma granthi is at the base of the root chakra; Vishnu granthi is between the third and fourth chakras; and Rudra granthi is at the third eye. Our spiritual journey may cease to progress rapidly if we are blocked by Brahma granthi and become overattached to the earth plane and its material pleasures. As we seek spirit, we will also advance slowly if we are blocked by Vishnu granthi and get attached to our spiritual practices and forget that they are merely the tools through which we will reach our spiritual goals. As we evolve spiritually, the tools become less important because we learn to connect more directly to spirit through the chakras and the aura. We must also learn to transcend Rudra granthi, which causes attachment to the five elements and all their manifestations. When all the transition points are transcended, we will be one with our creator.

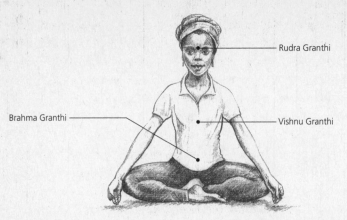

Granthis is the Sanskrit term referring to knots or obstacles in the body. Three granthis exist: **1. Brahma Granthi** (creation) – names and forms are the first obstacle, attachment to the material world. This granthi is positioned at the base of the root chakra. **2. Vishnu Granthi** (preservation) – spiritual names and forms are the second obstacle, attachment to institutions and spiritual orders. This granthi is positioned between the third and fourth chakras. **3. Rudra Granthi** (destruction) – when attachments to the five elements are transcended the aspirant becomes a true Yogi. This granthi is positioned at the third eye.

In Western bodywork it is recognized that restrictions occur in specific body areas, causing blocks in the flow of energy. Reich referred to these blocks or transition points as *segments*. Each segment is manipulated to release the build-up of tensions that occur throughout childhood and adult life. The segments correspond roughly with the areas of the seven chakras.

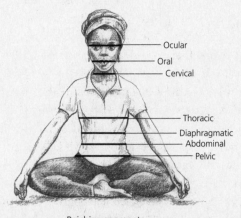

Reichian segments

The most important transition point is found between the third and fourth chakras. This transition point also resonates into the aura between the third and fourth layers. This is a major place where transformation occurs. It is the transition between the personal realms and the universal realms. Energetically this is the point of the Vishnu granthi. Physically it relates to the diaphragm segment, which is the connective tissue that creates the respiratory diaphragm. We know that breathing fully plays a large part in both releasing physical tension and enhancing spiritual experience. Transformation takes place when we release this transition point and open the gateway. This transition is experienced as a rebirth – the virgin birth, where the soul travels beyond the personal energy fields and is reborn into a light body. The first three parts of the aura (personal fields) are dependent on the physical body. The latter sheaths exist without a physical body. To quote Swami Sivananda:

Prana is the link between the astral and the physical bodies. When the slender thread-like prana is cut, the astral body separates from the physical body. Death takes place. The prana that was working in the physical body is withdrawn into the astral plane.

Let us now look at the four remaining subtle auric sheaths.

Fourth Layer/Pranic Sheath

Prana is related to mind; through mind to will; through will to the individual soul and through this to the Supreme Soul. If you know how to control the little waves of prana working through the mind, then the secret of subjugating the universal Prana will be known to you.

Swami Sivananda

The pranic sheath is seen to pervade and animate the whole of the physical body. The chakras, the organs, the nerves, the vessels, every tiny cell has its counterpart within this pranic body. The pranic body is responsible for maintaining our contact with the astral plane. Just as the first layer (core energy body) brings about a physical reality, the prana brings about a spiritual reality. The actions of mind have a strong influence at this level; in some descriptions of the aura it is actually known as the mental body.[10]

Our thoughts are powerful entities in their own right. They are not contained and therefore, like the wind, they are able to travel freely. When our thoughts are positive we can excite similar thoughts in others, likewise hatred in the mind of one has power to create hatred in another. In the same way that electricity and sound are transported, undetected by the eye, so too are our thoughts.

Our thoughts move within the prana; they are an aspect of the pranic sheath and can become crystallized into physical form. Put another way: our thoughts have a habit of coming true. To be reading this book, at some stage there must have been a desire within you to Open to Spirit. Some readers, of course, are already on a spiritual path, whilst others might consider themselves sceptics. Nevertheless this applies to all readers, sceptics included. You can only really be sceptical about something if what you sincerely desire is to know the truth.

Visualization techniques utilize the power of thought for healing. Some people living with HIV, cancer and less threatening illnesses have managed through positive thinking and visualization to slow or even halt their condition. By altering subtle energy on a pranic level these people have been able to bring about physical change.

Ancient traditions speak much about the use of this pranic aspect of our being. In Yorùbá tradition, people are often recognized for the attributes of their àṣẹ – pronounced 'ash-eh'. Àṣẹ is akin to pranic energy. Your unique gifts are an expression of your àṣẹ and can be used for the good of all. Your àṣẹ may allow you to manifest a natural way with children. Poetry or art may flow from you as a result of your àṣẹ. You may possess healing hands. Through spiritual practice àṣẹ can be enhanced. As we work with the chakras and develop a greater understanding of ourselves, we can begin to see how best we can express our àṣẹ.

Each one of us has a vital role to play in the overall scheme of things. For some of us this is already evident and we are taking the responsibility seriously. And for many of us, our true role remains a mystery. Chakra work helps us to reveal our energetic strengths and identify our innate gifts.

In order to have a better understanding of ourselves and to advance in spiritual practice, the pranic sheath needs to be purified. Cleansing on this level, through thought and action, paves the way for the spirit to communicate on higher planes. We can travel comparatively easily to the outer realms, but if the pranic sheath is not clear of disturbance then communication will be limited. Difficulty might exist in deciphering the information gained. Both a psychotic and a mystic are exposed to the same outer realms. The difference is that the mystic is swimming in familiar territory; s/he remembers being there before and knows how to gain knowledge. The psychotic meanwhile is sinking, unprepared for the influx of material and unable to discriminate. I am aware that I am using two extremes. This is, however, important to understand. Astral travel and other kinds of ESP are not goals in themselves; in fact they can prevent us realizing the truth. It is the knowledge gained from such pursuits that holds significance.

To enrich the possibility of receiving and interpreting truth, cleansing and preparation are essential. When shamans, healers or elders journeyed into the outer planes, they prepared for the journey through fasting, cleansing and ritual ceremony. I will try to illustrate this point with an analogy. Imagine a stream with water running from the foot of distant mountains. The water is pure as it leaves the source. Providing the water can flow in a reasonably unrestricted way, it will remain pure. However, if there is an obstruction somewhere downstream – a fallen tree or a muddy bank – the flow may be hindered, slowing the water's movement. As the water slows, more obstructions are able to gather, until eventually the water becomes contaminated. What began as pure water is no longer reliable.

The same can happen when the pranic sheath is not cleansed. Pure energy from the astral plane will have difficulty passing the pranic level. Negative energy that exists – as thought-patterns, addictions, misused power, low self-esteem, whatever we hang on to that holds us back – will contaminate our energy field, rendering any knowledge we gain unreliable. Preparation for working with the upper chakras and higher realms of the aura is detailed in Chapter 5.

Lessons are being learned very quickly at this point in time (the late 20th century on the Gregorian calendar), with many people tuning directly into the next auric layer, the etheric sheath, and gaining valuable insights which the planet and her people need immediately. The importance of preparing one's system for this work, through purification of the pranic level of the aura, cannot be over-emphasized. It is vitally important to prepare oneself for the ongoing process of spiritual unfoldment.

Pure water   Contaminated water

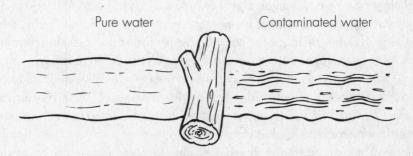

Obstruction to the waterways

Fifth Layer/Etheric Sheath

Ether is the level on which sound begins to shape physical form. Through speaking and singing, things are brought into being. Soon after I had the inspiration to write this book, I began to 'sing it into being' by telling people I was working on a book. Telling everyone was in fact the first work I did. Once enough people had heard, they began mentioning the book to me and I started to feel truly committed. Finally, I read in the Mind/Body/Spirit Festival brochure that I was writing this book. I knew then that the book had been brought into being. Use of sound in this way is an important aspect of the philosophy of the original people of Australia. They believe the Ancestors during Alchera (Dreamtime) sang everything that lives into creation. We are all accustomed to naming things; by naming something we give it a place in our reality.

As already mentioned, the etheric level is the home of Ancestors,[11] dreams and the collective unconscious. Residing in this level are all manner of entities which can be given shape. As the etheric plane is relatively close to the material world, negative energies can get held there; for example victims of sudden death who were not prepared to die and who wish to return to deal with unfinished business, may get stuck at this level. They may, in a vengeful manner, seize any opportunity. Experience of the etheric plane can be positive or negative. Ghosts, nightmares, hexes, bad trips and evil spirits are all negative phenomena of the etheric plane. People may open up their energy fields when they are not strong enough in energy or will to repel negative forces. Negative use of ether power accounts for some of the mind-programming that goes on in some cults. Discrimination is always necessary when working with energy, as is a strong sense of Self within the universal whole.

The etheric sheath, or template as it is known to some, creates a kind of blueprint for the physical body. Before we exist on the earth plane, we exist in the ether. This is not just us but all creation. Swami Brahmananda, speaking about ether, says, 'Akasha is the substratum of the entire material universe.'[12] This means that, in very much the same way as a negative precedes a photograph, so the etheric body precedes that of the physical body. Ether is the subtle vibratory level from which the other four elements (air, fire, water, earth) are derived. From the space that is ether comes forth what we experience as our world.

The existence of the etheric sheath is slowly becoming accepted as an organizing principle in medical circles and among allopathic practitioners. Science and medicine have not yet been able to explain the intelligence behind life itself; from where comes the ability to reproduce, for example, or to self-repair damaged parts, such as bones? Understanding the etheric energy field provides answers to these questions. Dr Richard Gerber has researched healing through the energy field.

He writes:

> This etheric body is a body that looks quite similar to the physical body over which
> it is superimposed. Within the etheric energetic map is carried information which
> guides the cellular growth of the physical structure of the body. It carries the spatial
> information of how the foetus is to develop in utero, and also the structural data
> for growth and repair of the adult organism should damage or disease occur. It is
> the template of the salamander limb which allows a new foot to grow if the
> present one is severed. This energetic structure works in concert with the cellular
> genetic mechanisms that molecular biology has elaborated upon over the last
> several decades of medical research. The physical body is so energetically connect-
> ed and dependent upon the etheric body for cellular guidance that the physical
> body cannot exist without the etheric body. If the etheric field becomes distorted,
> physical disease soon follows. Many illnesses begin first in the etheric body and are
> then later manifested in the physical body as organ pathology.

If, as Dr Gerber mentions, the etheric sheath becomes distorted and disease soon
follows, we can see why healing is often directed at the etheric level. Correcting the
frequency at which the etheric sheath vibrates has been known for millennia to have
a restorative outcome on the physical structure that it guides. Vibrational remedies –
such as homoeopathic medicine, essential oils, sound, flower and plant essences –
are all effective in bringing about healing. This is because they are holistic in nature
and work on all levels of our organism through the subtle energy field.

Sixth Layer/Astral Sheath

The astral plane is sometimes referred to as 'celestial', meaning 'resembling the
stars'. At least 5,000 years ago, some say as long ago as 12,000, the ancient Egyptians
believed we came from the stars and would one day return to the light from which
we came. Only through gaining knowledge and attaining sacred wisdom would this
be possible. With this understanding in mind, the ancient priests and pharaohs of
Kemit[13] studied natural laws and understood their relationship within the cosmos.
The Egyptian book *Coming Forth by Day*[14] contains writings which were used to
guide the spirit back to the astral plane.

An altered state of consciousness is required in order to communicate on the
astral level. This plane is one that can be reached through divination, trance and
meditation. Deities, Òrìshà[15] (natural forces and spiritual messengers in the Yorùbá
tradition) and Angels are all of this plane. When contacted, they act as our guides

and teachers, helping us to truly see the light. Through spiritual practice we can prepare ourselves to receive insights from the astral realms. It is to this aspect of ourselves that we attempt to attune in order to gain sacred wisdom.

Astral travel and near death experience (NDE) are both phenomena where the astral body is separated from the physical and returns to the astral sphere. This occurrence has been described by several individuals, who appear to have undergone a common experience. People, temporarily classified as clinically dead, have reported the experience of floating above the physical body and looking down on it. These same people have been able to detail accurately the actions of medical staff, and repeat things staff have said while they were working to save their lives. Many such people have described a beautiful, welcoming light at the end of a tunnel. Some say they hear voices telling them to go back. This direct knowledge of the astral plane has changed people's lives for ever.

These experiences may seem quite explainable – imagination is, as we know, very powerful. However, research on NDE done by Dr Karliss Osis suggests that some kind of energetic disturbance takes place, which seems to correlate with NDE and astral travel. One of Osis's subjects successfully viewed items in a box which could only be seen in a specific arrangement from above or within – any other viewpoint would have identified another arrangement.[16] Osis also measured changes in electrical activity in the room at the time the astral body was thought to have entered. Thus the ancient understanding of the astral body seems to be backed up by modern science.

The astral plane is the final sphere of duality; the remaining sphere is pure undifferentiated spirit.

Seventh Layer/Causal Sheath – Pure, Undifferentiated Spirit

This is the outermost aspect of the aura, known as *Ba* (the Divine Soul) in the Kemitic (ancient Egyptian) tradition. This layer enfolds the astral body and relates directly to the chakras, which at their very core are neutral. No duality exists on this plane. This is pure, undifferentiated spirit, from which the entire universe is born. This is the place of Being, a place of oneness where everything simply Is. Further explanation separates us from this oneness and would be regarded as moving away from the real nature of spirit and returning to duality. When we are truly in the spirit there is no more to be said. This sphere is known in yoga as *Anandamayakosha*, which means the bliss sheath.

OPENING TO SPIRIT

I have detailed seven levels of the aura. These are the seven that I work with, both personally and in my practice with individuals and groups. At our present evolutionary stage, we still have much to learn from working on these levels. In ancient yoga texts there are more levels, and some teachers and clairvoyants work with new levels. Our evolution is not static but ever-changing.

THE AURA: REAL OR IMAGINED?

Franklin Sills, in his book *The Polarity Process*, says:

> The causal and astral realms are not mystical places outside ourselves but are representations of an ongoing inner process of thought, emotion and form.

I believe that what we call the aura is within and around us. Due to the vastness of our personal realities, we need ways of organizing everything, both within and outside of ourselves. The chakras and the aura provide this organizing principle. We are organized via the chakras and the aura; when we begin to understand how they work we see how we are organized.

'As above, so below' is the well-known universal law from the Kemitic texts of the ancient Egyptians, who knew that in order to understand the vastness of ourselves, we need to study the ways of the universe and vice versa. I have searched for truth in many places, both outside of myself and within. I have spent time analysing whether certain esoteric beliefs are true or false. Do mystical places actually exist outside ourselves or not? I have reached the conclusion from 'in-perience' and experience that the answers to such questions are not really useful. Proving the truth is not as powerful as knowing the truth. If I can use esoteric knowledge to develop myself as a person in this life, then this is truth enough for me. To quote the physicist Fritjof Capra:

> Faced with a reality that lies beyond opposite concepts, physicists and mystics have to adopt a special way of thinking, where the mind is not fixed in a rigid framework of classical logic, but keeps moving and changing its viewpoint.

3

COSMOLOGY

THE CIRCLE OF LIFE

All matter is an expression of the crystallized light and energy of the creator, which is itself pure consciousness. Whether or not one accepts a creationist or evolutionist concept is irrelevant to this point. It is merely being suggested that the cosmic energy from which all matter is formed, whether originating from a big bang or from one great divine thought, is the energy of pure consciousness.

Richard Gerber MD

COSMOLOGY, WHICH IS THE STUDY OF THE UNIVERSE AS A WHOLE, HAS occupied people's thoughts from time immemorial. People have always tried to understand from whence we came. How did we come into being? What sustains us? What part do we play in the whole scheme of things? Why are we here? Where are we going? Myths, legends, religions, philosophies and scientific theories have grown up around our desire for knowledge of our creation.

Although we all ask the same questions, what constitutes the answer appears to differ among us. Traditional cosmologies shared by kin and society, like Alchera (Original Australians) or Ifá (Yorùbá), help individuals unite with their people and environment. Such knowledge creates an understanding of the Eternal Spirit and enhances respect for the Ancestors and all living beings. Scientists and scholars attempt to map evolution, and believe only what can be scientifically defined and measured. This objective approach can cause duality between the Self and the environment. A pagan may look back to ancient matriarchal societies and see all life coming from the womb of the Goddess, thus empowering women and respecting the planet. Others believe in the holy word, be it the Bible, Quaran or Bagavad Gita. Most religions believe that pious living is rewarded in heaven or another incarnation.

The diverse beliefs of African traditional healers, original Australians, pagans, Christians, Hindus and scientists may at first glance appear different, but when examined closely a common essence is revealed. They each share an essential understanding of interconnectedness. Each believes in an energy which creates and unites all matter. For some it is a force, for others it is the substance of matter itself. Definitions vary: to the Yorùbá, Olódùmàrè is viewed as the Supreme Being who makes all things possible. For a Christian it is God. To a Pagan, it is the Goddess and the Earth herself. To original Australians the Earth is seen as the sacred creatrix. Modern physics speaks of particles and waves as the ubiquitous stuff from which we and the universe are made. Many concepts and names abound, but each system, in its own way, defines the essence of unity and interconnectedness.

It is not my intention to examine all these concepts. My concern here is with the very essence of all philosophies and belief systems. This essence is the unifying energetic force which I refer to as **core energy**.

THE LAW OF EXPANSION AND CONTRACTION

The following cosmology has been inspired and informed by many spiritual traditions and philosophies. However, my work is mainly influenced by African traditions, yoga and body psychotherapy, as listed below:

1   The traditional culture and spiritual practice of my Ancestors and family, the Yorùbá of West Africa.[1] Oral tradition, language and literature indicate that the Yorùbá migrated from Egypt.[2]
2   The Kemitic (Hermetic)[3] tradition of the ancient Egyptians.
3   The Dravidian[4] people and Nagas[5] of the earliest civilizations of the Indus Kush[6] (India). These Ethiopians practised tantric yoga and nature religions.[7] Many aspects are still seen in Hinduism, Buddhism, Jainism and yogic practices and philosophies today.

4 Present-day psychotherapy and somatic therapies, in particular the work of Jung, Reich and Dr Stone. Jung was learned in alchemy,[8] a practice with its roots in Kemitic science and mysticism. His work was greatly influenced by his travels in Asia and Africa. Reich was also familiar with Indian philosophies. Dr Stone, the founder of Polarity Therapy[9] (Natural healing system), based his work on Ayurvedic (traditional Indian medicine) and Kemitic/Hermetic principles. The work of these men brings ancient traditions into present-day healing sciences.

From both ancient and modern scientific thinking on cosmology I have evolved a fundamental principle for understanding the chakras. Central to this principle is the law of expansion and contraction. The universe itself – with its stars and galaxies, planets and satellites – is observed, according to astronomy, to expand and contract slowly. This is known as the pulsating or oscillating model of the universe.[10] We too, like the universe, follow the same oscillating rhythm. Our likeness to the universe is expressed in the Kemitic saying 'As above, so below.' The chakras themselves, like mini-solar systems, spin around a central axis.

The solar system and spinning chakra

When we Open to Spirit we allow energy to flow from the periphery of our being to the core, and vice versa. Energy is free to expand from the body out to the universe, and return from the universe back into the body. Awareness is extended from the very centre of our being, the chakras, out to the universe and back again. We learn to maintain a rhythm and flow of energy that keeps us in tune with the laws of nature. Throughout nature, energy is seen to be in polarity – that is, it moves out so far and then returns. The spinning universe is maintained by a constant rhythm of expansion and contraction.

In Kemitic mythology the sky Goddess Nut is the mother of the sun God, Ra. She is seen to swallow Ra at night, embracing the sun in her body, creating 12 hours of darkness. Daily she gives him birth, delivering 12 hours of light.

Nut represents the polarity of day and night. Each day shines out until night closes in, light becomes dark and warmth gives way to coolness. The same polarity is witnessed in the plant world. A flower will grow up towards the sun, blossom and bloom before going to seed, which provides the potential for new life. Slowly the flower falls, returning to the earth, which receives the decaying flower as nourishment.

On a physical level we know the body shares this polar experience. As we breathe, inhalation of the breath is followed by exhalation. The blood continuously circulates, flowing out from the central position of the heart, through the arteries, to the body's periphery, feeding each cell on the way. When the blood can go no further it returns via the veins to the heart. Messages come into the sensory nerves from our environment; they inform the central nervous system, which responds with movement triggered by motor nerves. Once again, energy is seen to come into the core and then move out to the periphery. The natural law of expansion and contraction is obeyed. This law is repeated in the muscles and the endocrine system and other systems of the body.

Socially, we also have the means to expand out towards the world, engaging in life and with the people we meet. We then need to contract into our own world, renewing our resources for another day.

Spiritually we also follow the laws of nature. The individual *ba* (soul) contracts and journeys from the universal *Ba* to the earth plane. Through upholding the laws of nature during our lifetime and raising our spiritual awareness we can experience a rebirth which facilitates expansion of the individual *ba* and a return to the creator. As we descend from pure spirit into a physical body we pass through the higher planes:

- At the astral sphere we become known to our parents.
- With blessings from the creator they then weave us through unconscious thoughts, intuition and instincts into ether, the most subtle of elements.
- We then become conscious thought, which is air energy.
- Fire energy is responsible for our conception and growth.
- In water we reside for nine months before the sacred waters give way –
- to our manifestation on the earth plane. We have descended.

From this point on our task is to live life in a fulfilling way which will lead us back to our creator.

Embodiment

Following the basic laws of nature we are born, we live and we die. Birth is the ultimate contraction, and death the final expansion. During the period we know as life, it is my belief that we have the capacity to experience and know the polarities of liberation and limitation. In my understanding, spiritual liberation or transcendence is only a part of our spiritual journey. Accepting and celebrating our descent into a physical body and its subsequent limitation is also a valuable aspect of the spiritual voyage. Through the gross physical body we experience all aspects of life. The body is a temple of pleasure, pain and much learning. The flesh is worthy of love, honour and respect. It is the home of the spirit on earth and, if we are to fully experience spirit, as earth beings, we need to feel truly embodied; by this I mean at home in the body. We cannot enjoy a spiritual life without a physical body. Through the body we delight in the spirit. The body offers many limitations to embrace, and the spirit offers liberation. Knowledge of the chakra system provides the opportunity for both embodiment – feeling the spirit move in the body – and enlightenment – freeing the life of the body. These are two equally important aspects of spirituality which sustain the rhythmic pulse of contraction and expansion.

Ancient civilizations made use of this polarity. Healing in Africa and Asia still utilizes this knowledge today. Dancing and drumming are ways of awakening the spirit in the body. Bodily trance is a method used to reach higher levels of consciousness. Rituals and ceremonies involving movement, adorning the body, preparing food and feasting are widely-used ways of honouring spirit and celebrating rites of passage.

Today in the West the body does not enjoy a very high status. It is seen as inferior to the mind, with academic pursuits rewarded far more highly in society than physical activity. Generally the physical body is poorly respected: we are constantly fed a diet of violence and physical abuse in films and on television. Images of female bodies are abused in advertising and pornography, leaving many girls and women with a distorted view of physical beauty. Boys and men learn to disrespect women. From *Power Rangers* to *The Terminator*, children learn to fight and kill; yet apparently they are too young to learn about love, sensuality and sex. Thus when young we learn that to abuse the body is fine, but to touch and love the body is taboo.

Before enlightenment is possible, embodiment must be achieved. We are in a physical body and, through this vehicle, we can know enlightenment – not by abusing or disregarding the body, as is sometimes advocated. Through body aware-ness and communicating with spirit, enlightenment is achieved.

Early Reverence for Nature's Rhythms

The introduction and development of major patriarchal religions have masked early notions of cosmology which embraced the body and the earth. Christianity, Judaism, Islam and Hinduism[11] are built on the shoulders of matriarchal traditions whose practices followed the rhythms of nature. The elements of earth, air, water, wood, fire and metal were felt in the environment. They were identified as a range of energetic frequencies ranging from the solid matter of earth through fluid and gas to space which is characteristic of ether. The power of the elements was revered by the Ancients and their very essence praised as Gods and Goddesses. These elements have an immediate and visible effect on both the internal and external environment – this is discussed in detail later in this book.

The Ancients studied this relationship and built their religions, healing-medicine, mythology and moral culture around the rhythms observed. The effects of the sun and moon on plants at specific times of the year were recorded, and the healing qualities of plants were found to be greater at certain times than at others.

The organs of the body were seen to function under the energy of specific ele-ments: wind in the lungs, the fire of digestion, earth of the colon. Africa, Asia, China and Original America still have elaborate healing systems which make use of nature's rhythms in healing the sick body, mind and spirit.

In the West, religion and medicine pay little attention to nature and its rhythms. (Fortunately this is slowly changing.) Religion largely negates the body, and the earth is viewed as inferior to heaven. Orthodox medicine negates the role of the spirit in healing. The separation of healing and spirituality, nature and medicine, has contributed much to a sense of alienation experienced by many people today. Getting to know the spirit in the body through the chakra system helps us reconnect with the rhythms of life and the sacred laws governing both us and our universe.

PRIMORDIAL SYMBOLS

Symbols are an inherent part of the chakra system, as are numbers, colours and sounds. Since the beginning of civilization African people have used symbols and hieroglyphs to define ourselves and the universe. For us today, if we are to grasp the cosmology of the Ancients and understand the chakras we need to interpret the meaning of some primordial symbols used in the chakra system.

Consciousness can be divided into three main levels:

○ = **The Divine**   Olódùmárè – **level of higher consciousness**

The circle represents wholeness, that which is complete in itself. Circles have no beginning or end and are symbolic of infinity and creation. A circle, however, must have a central point around which the circumference radiates. In the body, the chakras are the central core energy, with the Divine as the circumference. Core energy and the Divine are both of the same pure essence. ○ = **Pure Spirit**

✡ = **Soul consciousness**   Òrìshà – **level of the subconscious mind**

The dynamic play of opposites is portrayed in the interlaced triangles – the meeting of heaven and earth, male and female, soul and psyche. ▽ The downward-pointing feminine triangle represents movement from the universe to earth, and △ the upward-pointing masculine triangle represents movement from the earth towards the universe. The six-pointed star shows the play of opposites in equilibrium. ✡ = **Polarity**

□ = **Gross physical body**   Ara – **level of the conscious mind**

The quality seen in the square is one of solidity and inertia. Matter is symbolized, rather than the pure spirit of the circle. Matter is temporal, forever changing, destroyed in order to create again anew. □ = **Material**

In yogic philosophy consciousness is also divided into three principles: Sattva, Rajas and Tamas. These correspond to the forces of creation, maintenance and destruction respectively. As seen in the chart that follows, many versions of this creation triad can be found the world over. It is in refining our multi-dimensional soul consciousness (central column of the creation triads chart) through disciplined spiritual practice that we are able to integrate the gross physical body with the Divine Pure Spirit. This union is the ultimate goal of yoga. The physical level with which we are most familiar always finds ways to gravitate towards Divine Spirit, its very essence and creator.

Creation Triads

Tradition	○	✡	☐
	Pure Spirit Neutral	Soul consciousness Positive	Gross Physical Body Negative
Kemitic	Universal Ba	ba – Soul Ka – Spirit	Khat
Kemitic	Neter Neteru, God of Gods	Neters (Deities) Stabilizing forces	Nun Primordial waters
Yorùbá	Olódùmárè Creator	Òrìshà Natural forces	Ara Humans
Dogon	Amma	Nummo water spirit	First 8 Ancestors Humans
Dravidian	Shiva	Vishnu	Shakti
Yoga	Sattva	Rajas	Tamas
Polarity Therapy	Sattva	Rajas	Tamas
Jung	Higher Conscious	Subconscious Unconscious Collective Unconscious	Conscious
Physics	Energy	Waves and particles	Atoms
Reich	Core	Segments Muscle Armour	Persona

Chakras are the core energy of the gross physical body. Core energy is at the centre of all living things, rather like DNA is central to cells. Core energy is also the universal force-field that surrounds, supports and animates life. Just as DNA has the programme which allows a cell to grow and become differentiated, core energy holds the programme for the individual. We can take this analogy further by observing DNA. The double helix structure of DNA is very similar to that of the *caduceus*. The caduceus is an image of two spiralling serpents which cross over at stages along a central staff. The crossover points symbolize the seven main chakras. Symbols depicting the chakras date back as far as 6,000 years and possibly further. Certainly the entwined snakes on the caduceus predate the electron microscope, which made the DNA spiral visible in 1953. The ancient Egyptians and Indians have depicted the double helix as a symbol for the programming of energetic activity for thousands of years.

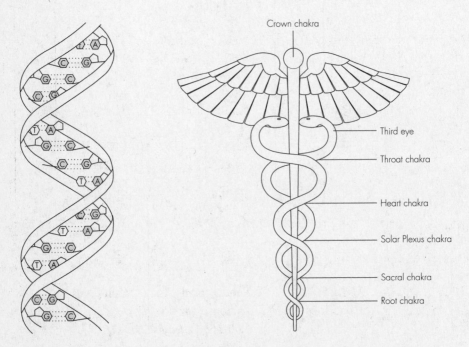

The microscopic double helix of a DNA molecule as seen under an electron microscope. DNA is the molecular structure responsible for programming all cellular activity.

The double helix shape of the ancient caduceus symbol as depicted by the ancient Egyptians. This image symbolizes the core energy and the programming of all energetic activity.

DNA directs the individual cells so they know what to do and how to orientate themselves in the body. Cells are also programmed to reproduce and repair themselves. Likewise, the chakras provide knowledge from the higher consciousness, so that, as individuals, we can know our purpose in life, become individuated and orientate ourselves in the cosmos. We too have the ability to reproduce ourselves and Self-heal. Spiritual information is passed from source to the individual, and we can utilize this knowledge as and when we are ready.

Soul Consciousness

Soul consciousness has many aspects. Although each unique soul is energetically connected to the Divine, we appear separate. The vision we often hold of each person as separate is an illusion. We remain linked to each other by the air we breathe, the ground we stand on and our invisible connection to the universal *Ba*. Like a child to its mother we are ever-connected to our creator.

The energetic force-field created by our soul consciousness contains the following subtle energy bodies:

Physical heat layer	Fire	(emotional body)
Pranic layer	Air	(mental body)
Etheric layer	Ether	
Astral layer	Light	

The layers get more subtle as they step up from the physical heat layer to the astral plane, the physical heat layer being densest and easiest to feel. This layer, about 1 – 2 centimetres away from the surface of the skin, is useful for healing.

The astral body connects us directly to the Divine – it is like an umbilical cord linking us to our creator. The astral sheath is responsible for receiving thoughts, emotions and intuition from the higher consciousness.

As the subtle energies of soul consciousness step down from the astral body they become more and more crystallized, until eventually the gross physical body is made manifest. This we see in water: as temperatures fall water becomes crystallized, resulting in ice. Throughout creation it appears that as the frequency of energy slows down it becomes more solid, tangible and visible, having the qualities of matter. Soul consciousness is the part of ourselves we need to discover and allow to unfold.

THE CIRCLE OF LIFE

Energy flows from the Divine through the soul to the physical body. It also returns from the body to the universe. This constant rhythm follows the law of contraction and expansion governing the cosmos.

As this cosmology takes shape we see that everything is pure consciousness, created into different vibrations and densities. The force responsible for creation has acquired many names – God and energy to name but two. Although a diversity of names and myths exists, the basic essential principle of unity and connectedness remains. Life is a cycle, there is a source from which life comes and we are each connected to this source. At the heart of this source is the law of expansion and contraction. Like flowers, we are born in spring, blossom in summer, decay in autumn and, after the winter of our lives, we are destined to return to the earth. We descend from pure spirit into a physical vehicle and then ascend from our physical state back to pure spirit. This is the journey of creation, the cosmic journey of the soul. The soul travels from embodiment to enlightenment.

Through the Eternal Spirit we are each connected to an unbroken circle of life that goes back to the very beginning of time. We can choose to tap into the wisdom of times past, of our past lives, our ancestors' lives, the lives of enlightened beings, and the ancients. We exist as part of an infinite pool of wisdom. From this infinite source of wisdom and knowledge we can develop our soul consciousness and the sacred essence we hold within. It is through the chakras that we connect to this source.

Chakras are the centre of all life. Through the chakras, the individual soul is ever-connected to the universe.

Opening to Spirit is to tune to the ever-present subtle energies that facilitate the soul's voyage. Developing body awareness and knowledge of the first three chakras helps us to fully embrace the soul's birth in a physical body, and to live harmoniously as part of the earth. This is the contractive journey of embodiment. The expansive journey to enlightenment is achieved through rebirth into a light body (the higher chakras and aura) and through honouring spirit on all subtle levels of our being. Heightened spiritual awareness can lead to earthly abundance and the fulfilment of our highest aspirations. It is a misunderstanding to see these two as mutually exclusive.

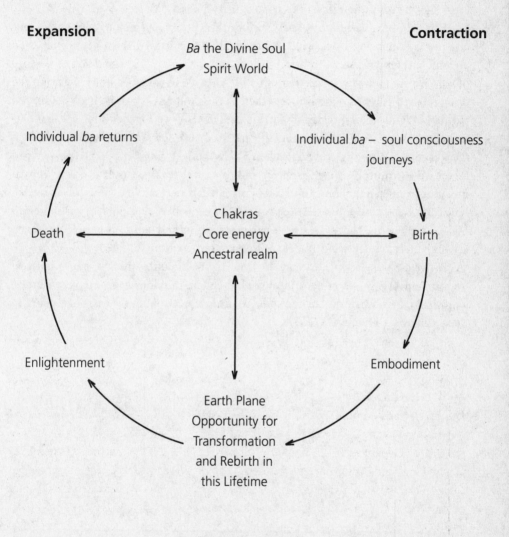

Expansion

Contraction

Ba the Divine Soul
Spirit World

Individual *ba* returns

Individual *ba* – soul consciousness
journeys

Death

Chakras
Core energy
Ancestral realm

Birth

Enlightenment

Embodiment

Earth Plane
Opportunity for
Transformation
and Rebirth in
this Lifetime

Spiralling Journey of the Soul

From a place of stillness and bliss we agree to return to earth in an effort to complete karmic responsibilities created in previous life cycles. We leave the Divine realm fully conscious of our karmic mission and purpose for reincarnation. We carry gifts, helpers and blessings from the Divine as our soul consciousness begins its descent to the physical realm. It is believed in Yorùbá tradition that the shock of birth and the resulting fear causes us to suffer amnesia. We forget our true purpose.

Life will be a continuous trial, with the Ancestors and guides waiting for our attention, wondering if we will ever remember to ask for help. Often it takes an extremely traumatic event to bring us back to our senses and regain some memory of who we are and why we are here this time. As we re-member – that is, bring the dismembered parts of our spirit together, as the Goddess Isis did with her spiritual partner Osiris – an appreciation for life returns and we journey towards embodiment and knowledge of the creative capacity of the lower chakras. Isis fashioned from earth a phallus, the missing part of Osiris' body. Using her creative powers and secret words from Thoth (the etheric and Ancestral realm), Isis gave Osiris eternal life, and from their union Horus was created. Isis became known as 'the giver of life'. The opportunity for transformation and rebirth is ever-present on the earth plane. Once we are back on track we can use our gifts and blessings to help us ascend the higher chakras, moving gracefully towards our creator.

As we embrace and transform our lives we are lifted towards our soul's spiritual destination. We can experience enlightenment in this life; it is our very nature. Eventually the flesh abandons the soul, granting it freedom to return, once again, to the realm of the Divine.

4

HONOURING THE ANCIENTS

RE-MEMBERING OUR FIRST ANCESTORS

There a people now forgotten discovered while others were yet Barbarians, the elements of the Arts and Sciences. A race of men now rejected for their black skin and woolly hair, founded on the laws of nature, those civil and religious systems which still govern the universe ... This race of blacks ... is the very one to which we owe our arts, our sciences, and even the use of the spoken word.

Count Volney (French academic), 1789[1]

OUR AFRICAN ANCESTORS

THERE IS ONE ETERNAL SPIRIT, ONE TRUTH, ONE COSMOLOGY AND, IN essence, only one religion. Truth existed before the human race took its first breath in Africa two million years ago. This truth gave rise to the spiritual and religious systems we see in the world today. The natural laws and sacred teachings of our first Ancestors have travelled around the globe. Numerous religions, spiritual traditions, mythology and healing arts are founded on this original knowledge. Through this knowledge we see the unity of all people.

Since the beginning of time Mother Africa has been in service to the Divine. She birthed our planet's first people and blessed them with an everlasting love of the Eternal Spirit. Mother Africa taught her children to respect the earth and all that dwell on her. She taught them the laws of nature and helped them understand the cosmic rhythms. The celestial realms and elements were known to her people, who created rituals to communicate with these forces, which they then deified and praised. Her rich oral traditions form the foundation of world mythology and religion.

Africa is a large continent with many different people and languages, yet in the ancient spiritual systems we can find unity. Belief in the Eternal Spirit and respect for our Ancestors is probably the world's oldest spiritual practice. Ancient Africans believed in the continuation of Spirit. For this reason they returned the dead to the womb of the earth, ensuring a long lineage and unbroken cycle of life.

To the Dogon of Mali, conception and death are closely related. The bed in which conception takes place is symbolic of a grave in the earth where the seeds of new life are sown. Amma, the creator, transforms the spirit of the dead into a child who will continue the lineage and care for the land. The spirits of all those who went before us, ancient and recent, do not die. We carry their genes, we embody their life-force, they imbue our children, our environment and the air we breathe. We still appreciate the temples and sacred sites of the Ancients. We continue to live in the buildings our not-so-distant Ancestors lovingly built, we read the books they painstakingly wrote and we listen to music they created. We hold their memories and we live their dreams. We exist today because of our Ancestors; they gave us life. Their love continues to nurture us, yet often we deny their very existence. In allowing our First Ancestors to be forgotten we dismiss the Eternal Spirit and abandon the powerful forces of the circle of life. The relationship between the Ancestors and modern people is in desperate need of healing. We must learn again to acknowledge our Ancestors, for they walk with us and can light our path.

In this chapter I highlight the influence of ancient Africans on spirituality and religion. I summarize the history that is relevant to spirituality as a whole, and to the chakras in particular. The importance of the chakras in ancient times, the number seven, the third eye and the serpent are each explored. I acknowledge the relationship between Egypt and India. They both had powerful spiritual systems. Through ancient mythology we can see how Egypt influenced Christianity.

Ancient Africans lived closely with nature and they realized that internal energies are also governed by the elements. Knowledge of the elements forms the basis of religio-spiritual practice in many parts of the world. This inner science is still of relevance today. With all our so-called sophistication and scientific advancement, perhaps more than ever we need the love and inner wisdom of our ancient Ancestors.

OUT OF AFRICA

Magic and spiritual practices appear to go back as far as the human race itself. DNA[2] tests indicate that all humans alive today are descended from a single female Ancestor who lived in Africa 140,000 – 280,000 years ago. She is known as the first Eve. According to the work of Dr Albert Churchward, physician, anthropologist and archaeologist, writing in 1921, people originated in the Great Lakes region of Tanzania. From here they spread over the continent of Africa and eventually migrated in waves all over the globe.[3] Two-million-year-old tools, building sites and bones found in 1959–60 by Louis and Mary Leakey in the Olduvai valley in northern Tanzania support the theory that humans originated in Africa around the lakes and mountains of Tanzania, Uganda and Kenya.

The ancient Egyptians always gave priority to their birthplace in the south; in the Hunefer Papyrus it is said:

> We come from the beginning of the Nile where the God Hapi dwells, at the foothills of the moon.[4]

Kilimanjaro, Africa's highest mountain, and the Ruwenzari mountain range seem to be the Mountains of the Moon and the source of the Nile remembered by the ancient Egyptians as their place of origin. Close to Kilimanjaro among the lakes and mountains we find Mount Meru. Interestingly, Mount Meru is a sacred place in Indian mythology. This mountain is not merely mythological, as is often assumed, but is an existing mountain in Tanzania, the birthplace of humanity. Mount Meru is referred to as the dwelling place of the Gods by Egyptians and Indians. It seems the ancient Indians also identified Mount Meru/Tanzania as their place of origin. As the cradle of humanity, this sacred mountain has remained in Indian Spirituality until today. To the ancient Egyptians, Meru means 'all things surrounding love'. In Sanskrit it means 'the centre of the universe'. This sacred mountain is love, the Divine love of our creator. I opened this book with a quote that begins, 'In your body is Mount Meru'. Meru is the heart of all things, including the radiant centre of love within. To ancient Indians, Mount Meru also relates to the spine – known as 'Merudanda' – and the chakras. The base of the mountain represents the root chakra, and its peak, the crown. Through the breath, chromatic sensation and intense meditation, tantra yogis are able to experience embodiment – full awareness of being in an earthly body. They can also reduce earthly consciousness and travel to other levels of reality. These planes of reality are inaccessible to ordinary consciousness. This spiritual practice is known as 'moving consciousness as far as Mount Meru'.[5] Mount Meru is of the earth but reaches high up to the stars and communes with the Gods.[6]

Identifying Mount Meru as an actual mountain in Africa and detailing its relationship to the chakras is one of the most important connections I make in this book between Africa, India and the chakras. The existence of Mount Meru and the mythology and sacred practices surrounding it suggest that knowledge of the chakras dates back to the beginning of the human race in east Africa.

MIGRATION

Migration out of Africa is said to have taken place in two stages. First the movement of shorter people, known as the Twa (Pygmies), and secondly the passage of the Nilotic Blacks (Nile) who spread across the earth. To quote John G. Jackson:

As these early Africans wandered over the world, they differentiated into the various human subspecies that now inhabit our planet. The men who remained in the tropical and equatorial regions retained their dark complexions, whereas those that settled in the temperate zones lost a portion of their dusky pigmentation and developed a fairer skin.

Godfrey Higgins wrote the following in 1836 (at this time racism was an inevitable part of academic work):

Now I suppose, that man was originally a Negro, and that he improved as years advanced and he travelled westwards, gradually changing from the jet black of India, through the shades of Syria, Italy, France, to the fair white and red maid of Holland and Britain. On the burning sands and under the scorching sun of Africa, he would probably stand still, if not retrograde. But the latter is most likely to have happened; and accordingly we find him an unimproved Negro, mean in understanding, black in colour.

Higgins tells us of the migration of Africans around the globe. He tells of the change in skin colour. This is due to climatic shifts such as the Ice Ages. These changes have produced two additional races, thus the three major races are the Ethiopian,[7] the Mongolian and the Caucasian.

Unfortunately some people maintain the negative views that have been passed down through the years by racist historians and anthropologists. Far from standing still, early Africans created the foundations for many civilizations both in and out of Africa. The religio-spiritual themes, symbols and practices of ancient African, Indian and Mexican civilizations appear to be influenced by the same race of people. Ethiopians migrated from East Africa and populated Egypt, Canaan, Sumer and Babylon (later known as Mesopotamia) before inhabiting the rest of the globe. They took with them knowledge of the sacred earth, fertility rites, the rhythms of nature and rituals for the burial of the dead and resurrection of the spirit. This explains similarities between spiritual traditions worldwide. Much of the value and importance afforded the Ancestors and the sacred have been lost in modern societies. This loss has cost us heavily. As the wheel of life continues to turn, the increased feelings of alienation, discontent and longing for more purpose in life are directing us towards the ways of the Ancients.

EARLY HISTORY OF YOGA

Yoga, which helps many people deal with the problems of modern living, is one of the oldest systems of spiritual development. The roots of yoga can be traced back thousands of years in India. During my study of yoga I recognized almost immediately a discrepancy in the teachings I received. Vedanta yoga, and one of my main teachers, Swami Vishnudevananda, advocated celibacy as a means to enhance spiritual progress. I also received teachings from the tantric texts – which, as many people know, view sexuality as Divine and sacred. Why should the art of unity and creation be negated in some schools and honoured in others? An obvious contradiction existed between the Tantric and Vedic schools of yoga.

Tantric yoga dates back to pre-Aryan India (3000 – 2500 BC). The words 'tanoti' – to expand, and 'trayati' – to liberate – gave rise to the term Tantra, which means *'to extend knowledge and to liberate'*.[8] Tantra includes among its teachings the chakras, astronomy and astrology, Kundalini,[9] hatha yoga, and the worship of Goddesses (Shakti and Durga) and Gods (Shiva and Vishnu). Tantric yoga was one of many spiritual paths practised by the Dravidians and other early people of India.[10] Dravidians are descended from Ethiopia.[11] There are similarities among pre-dynastic Egyptian spiritual practices[12] and tantra of ancient India. Dravidians founded the Indus valley civilizations.[13] They built the large cities of Mohenjo Dara, Chanhu Dara and Harrappa, which flourished between 3000 – 2500 BC.[14] Their descendants still live in the middle and south of India. Ancient Dravidian teachings are practised today by Sadhus, who are the wandering holy men of India.

Vedanta philosophy, on the other hand, was written down in the Upanishads – around 800 BC. The word Vedanta means *'the end of the Vedas'* and is a combination of 'anta' meaning 'end' and 'Veda', the name of four sacred texts from around 1500 BC.[15] The Upanishads are the conclusion of the Vedas. These sacred texts are studied by Hindus, seers and philosophers. Vedantic philosophy has adopted some Dravidian teachings. Tantric practices are included, such as hatha yoga, meditation, chanting and the worship of deities. Vedanta, however, also has a strong Aryan influence and is a part of Hinduism. According to Radhakrishnan Sarvepalli, Vedanta has a strong influence on Hindu religion:

> Of all the Hindu systems of thought, the Vedantic philosophy is the most closely connected to Indian religion, and in one way or another form, it influences the world view of every Hindu thinker of the present time.

Since Vedanta includes Dravidian practices and also underpins mainstream Hinduism, we can get an idea of how the early Ethiopians in India influenced India's main religion. The religion of Aryan invaders to India was superimposed on Dravidian and other original spiritual practices. Following numerous battles and the destruction of the Indus Valley civilization (approximately 1700 BC), matriarchy fell to patriarchy and many traditional Goddesses and Gods were misrepresented as demons. Eventually some of the original Gods were accepted into the Hindu pantheon, adding to its richness. Shiva and Vishnu were promoted to the highest roles in the Hindu trinity alongside Brahma – the Aryan supreme God.[16]

Not only Gods but a rigid caste system was imposed on the Indian people. Of India's current 950 million inhabitants, 70 per cent are black, and 40 per cent of these blacks are Dravidian,[17] the people who gave us the tantric spiritual tradition. As we study the chakra system today it is important to acknowledge this history.

> India's black population is much more than the entire population of Europe. It is also the world's largest black population living outside of Africa.
>
> *V T Rajshekar*[18]

Still today Aryans/Brahmans enjoy the highest three positions in Indian society, with the Sudras and Dalits[19] creating the country's undercaste. These Blacks provide a physical and spiritual foundation from which much has grown, including yoga.

Wayne Chandler writes:

Given the fact that the black race is by far the oldest, the presence of black culture at the dawn of Indian history should not be surprising.

Quoting from the Bharatiya Vidya Bhavan (Institute of Indian Culture), Chandler goes on to write:

We have to begin with the Negroid or Negrito people of prehistoric India who were its first inhabitants. Originally they would appear to have come from Africa through Arabia and the coastlands of Iran and Baluchistan.

Consequently, when we look far enough back into yoga and Indian spirituality, we meet our African Ancestors.

ANCIENT FOUNDERS OF RELIGION

The Greeks, often credited with the birth of civilization, were greatly influenced by the ancient Egyptians. They refer to Egypt as a parent. The ancient Egyptians had colonies in Greece around 1500 BC, and greatly influenced Greek culture.[20] Many of the Greek Gods, and the planets that share their names, derive from Egyptian deities. Early Egyptian civilization is African. The oldest Egyptian Gods and Goddesses are African, as are many of the Pharaohs. Cheikh Anta Diop states:

...the typically negroid features of the pharaohs (Narmer, 1st Dynasty, the actual founder of the pharaonic line; Zoser, 3rd Dynasty, by whose time all the technological elements of the Egyptian civilization were already in evidence; Cheops, the builder of the great pyramid, a Cameroon type; Menthuhotep, founder of the 11th dynasty, very black; Sesostris I; Queen Ahmosis Nefatari; and Amenhophis I) show that all classes of Egyptian society belong to the same black race.

Bernal, in *Black Athena* states:

...Egyptian Civilization was fundamentally African and the African element was stronger in the Old and Middle kingdoms, before the Hyksos invasion, than it later became. Furthermore I am convinced that many of the most powerful Egyptian

Dynasties, which were based in Upper Egypt – 1st, 11th, 12th and 18th – were made up of Pharaohs whom one can usefully call black.

Throughout this book I draw on the wisdom of the ancient Egyptians. These Africans[21] are responsible for creating a rich civilization and spiritual tradition that relates to the chakras. Egyptian spirituality, with its broad array of deities, provides a gateway into understanding the chakras.

Egyptian spirituality has also influenced Christianity. Anyone knowing the myth of Isis, Osiris and their son Horus[22] will immediately recognize this trinity. Mary's Immaculate Conception was not the first. Isis also immaculately delivered a boy child around the winter solstice (December 21st). She is of course the original Black Madonna. Both Horus and Jesus received initiation at the age of 30. Gerald Massey, the English scholar, suggested (in 1907) that the entire Christian Bible, Old and New Testaments, is traceable to the religious records of ancient Egypt.

Egyptian themes in Christianity were familiar to other Africans. Enslaved Nigerians taken to the Americas and forced to convert to Christianity maintained their Yorùbá religion by disguising it with Christianity. Africans survived because they quickly related the Christian God and his angels to the Supreme God Olódùmárè and the Òrìshà. Communication with the Òrìshà was carried on 'under the skirts of Mary', as Yorùbá Priestess Lusiah Teish puts it.[23] The Yorùbá religion was maintained and synchronized with Catholicism. This is known as Santeria.[24] Ifá, the original Yorùbá religion, is one of the fastest growing religions in America and Latin America today. In later chapters I relate the Yorùbá deities to the chakras.

Numerous well-known deities of the Hindu pantheon, such as Hanuman, Kali and Krishna, originated in India's black civilizations, which explains why they are often depicted as black. The unbearable plight of Sudras and Dalits caused many to convert to Buddhism, which is a religion free of caste. Jainism, with its central precept of 'ahimsa' (non-violence), also arose in black India as a reaction to injustice. Bodhidarma, who is said to have been Dravidian,[25] travelled from India to China, where he introduced a new approach to Buddhism. His approach was primarily meditative, devoid of ritual and intellectual analysis. It was not immediately popular, but it later in all its simplicity became known as Zen Buddhism, which is widely practised today.

People have always made statues and sculptures in their own image. We see from early images of the Buddha that he has African features, complete with a broad nose, full lips and tightly curled hair. African features can also be seen on one of the oldest stone carvings of a meditating yogi.

Five-thousand-year-old meditating yogi. This stone carving has a broad nose and full lips.

These images of the Buddha show characteristically African features such as full lips and tightly curled hair. This way of styling the hair and piercing the ears is typically African.

Mystic traditions associated with, and in some cases predating, the main religions (Hinduism, Buddhism, Christianity, Judaism and Islam) also appear to share characteristics that suggest a common ancestry. The Judaic Kaballah, for example, depicts the tree of life with seven levels of evolving consciousness. They are situated along three vertical pillars. Tantra cites seven chakras and three vertical main nadis.[26] An early wall carving resembling the Kabalistic tree of life can still be seen at the temple of Komombo in Egypt.

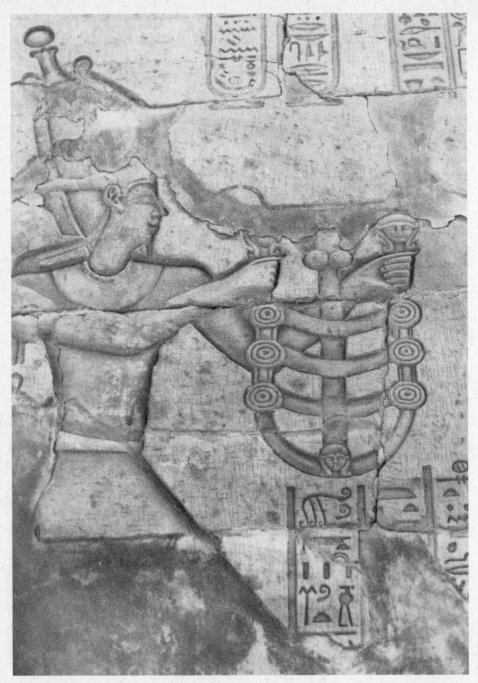

An early wall-carving resembling the 'Kabalistic Tree of Life' as seen on the Temple of Komombo, Egypt.

Inner knowledge of the Kaballah works on the chakras and takes the aspirant on a journey of Self-discovery leading from Earth to Heaven. Initiations, gateways and journeying into the underworld all suggest spiritual and psychological development that lead a person to enlightenment.

The Essenes were a religio-spiritual community existing in Palestine between the 2nd century BC and 2nd century AD. They observed similar ascetic practices to those of the early Indians and the Sadhus of modern-day India.

Sufism, the esoteric tradition associated with Islam, also appears to have been influenced by the ancient Africans. Doctor of religion Muata Ashby says:

> Historical evidence and Sufi mystic literature clearly show that Sufi followers had relationships (cultural, ethnic and social ties) with Egypt, the Essenes (Jewish tribe of Jesus) and the Hindus and Buddhists of the Far East. Thus it is not surprising that the energy centre system (chakras) of Sufism is closely related to the Tantric systems of Egypt and India concentrated on four energy centres instead of seven.[27]

Today's major religions and mystical traditions are built on spiritual foundations laid by ancient Africans, particularly the Egyptians. Chakras, found in most spiritual traditions, connect us with our first Ancestors.

THE IMPORTANCE OF SPIRITUALITY AND THE CHAKRAS IN ANCIENT TIMES

When exploring the chakra system it is easy to see the unity of diverse cultures. We begin to see the importance of the number seven in creation, nature, religion and spiritual development. It is also possible to see the connections between the ancient lands of Egypt and India. Ashby lists 55 such connections in his book *Egyptian Yoga*. Professor Albert Smith in *The Ancient Egyptians*[28] lists at least 20 similarities between the Egyptian and Indian philosophies. Much harmony exists between these two ancient spiritual systems. I list 12 themes (*see pages 58–9*) that are common to Egypt and India and which are relevant to the understanding of the chakras and the cultures from which this spiritual wisdom grew.

The acclaimed Greek historian Herodotus travelled to ancient Egypt:

And on his return to Greece they gathered around and asked 'tell us about the great land of the Blacks called Ethiopia.' And Herodotus said, *'There are two Great Ethiopian nations, one in Sind (India) and the other in Egypt.'*

Godfrey Higgins[29]

CORRESPONDENCES BETWEEN ANCIENT EGYPTIAN AND INDIAN SPIRITUAL PHILOSOPHIES

	Egypt	*India*
1 Sacred River	Nile	Ganges
2 Sacred Mountain	Mount Meru (centre of 7 continents)[30]	Mount Meru (centre of 7 continents)
3 Mother Goddess	Isis, Hathor	Amma, Durga
4 Divine Couple	Osiris & Isis	Shiva & Shakti
5 Ithyphallic God	Amoun, Ra	Shiva, Vishnu
Sun God	Ra	Rama[31]
6 Divine Animals	Cow/Hathor	Cow/Nandi
	Bull/Apis	
	Monkey/Thoth	Monkey/Hanuman
	Snake – Uraeus	Snake – Kundalini
7 Caduceus	Staff of Tehuti (Thoth/Hermes/Mercury)	Caduceus Ida and Pingala
8 Levels of Consciousness	Scale of Maat	7 Chakras
	9 parts of the Spirit	Aura
	Esoteric gateways	Transition points
9 Symbols of the Chakras	The lotus	The lotus
	Third eye – Udjat	Third eye – Ajna chakra
	Eye of Horus/Maat	Eye of Krishna/Buddha Shiva
10 Symbol of Life and Transcendence	Ankh ☥	Aum ॐ
11 Spiritual Practice and Rituals	Gods/Goddesses of the elements air, fire, water & earth	Gods/Goddesses of the elements air, fire, water & earth
	Meditation	Meditation
	Hekau (words of power)	Mantra (words of power)

	Hathor: union of sun & moon	Hatha: union of sun & moon[32]
	Martial Arts	Hatha Yoga
	Dance/movement	Dance/movement
	Trance	Trance
	Divination/oracle	Divination/oracle
	Sacred sexual act	Sacred sexual act
	Crowns – head covering	Head wraps – turbans
	Burning oils and incense	Burning oils and incense
	Pouring libations	Pouring libations
12 *Sacred Writings*	*Coming Forth by Day*	Tantras
	Temple art	Temple art
	Pyramid texts	Vedas
	Coffin texts	Upanishads

The above 12 correspondences show the commonality of two ancient spiritual traditions. This legacy is between 6,000 and 12,000 years old. They have influenced many diverse paths of personal and spiritual development all over the world, including Ifá (Yorùbá religion), Original American Shamanism, and Jungian psychology.

We will draw on this great legacy in Part Two, when we work with the chakras. Meanwhile let us explore the widespread use of the number seven, snake symbolism and the elements, all of which relate directly to the chakras.

THE UNIVERSAL AND SPIRITUAL
IMPORTANCE OF THE NUMBER SEVEN

SEVEN PLANETS
The seven planets known to the Ancients were seen to revolve around the earth, guiding people through their earthly existence and then on into the afterlife.

SEVEN DAYS OF THE WEEK
These are still named after the planets:

Sunday	Day of the Sun
Monday	Day of the Moon
Tuesday	Day of Mars
Wednesday	Day of Mercury
Thursday	Day of Jupiter
Friday	Day of Venus[33]
Saturday	Day of Saturn

PLEIADES/THE SEVEN STARS
In Egypt these stars were called the **'Seven Hathors'**, Judges of men. They were also known as 'the Seven Priestesses who guarded the seven gates of Thebes.' The dead had to be judged and were expected to utter the names of the Pleiades/seven Goddesses in order to pass from this world into the next.

(The seven Goddesses may symbolize the energies of the seven chakras. Knowledge of the chakras/Goddesses brings eternal life.)

'Seven mothers or midwives of the world' is the Indian term for the Pleiades; they are also called Krittikas, which means cutters. The Greek word 'Krittos' means both judge and critically wound by cutting.

The archaic mysteries of the seven sisters have permeated numerous cultures. They are or were known to the Dogon of Mali, Original Australians, Greeks, Jews, Olmecs, Aztecs and Mexicans.

SEVEN COLOURS OF THE RAINBOW
Red, orange, yellow, green, blue, indigo, violet are the dominant colours of the chakras. According to Dogon cosmology, people make their descent from heaven to earth along the rainbow.

THE SEVENTH ANCESTOR

Numerology is highly developed in the Dogon spiritual system. The people are descended from eight Ancestors; the seventh Ancestor is 'the master of speech'. To the Dogon, words are capable of creation.

SEVEN AFRICAN POWERS (ÒRÌSHÀ)

Òrìshà are natural forces of the Yorùbá traditional religion. Each of the Òrìshà has specific characteristics and is consulted before all actions if one is desirous of peace, harmony and success. Although hundreds of Òrìshà exist, seven are prominent. These relate to the different levels of consciousness which can be experienced at each chakra.

SEVEN GATEWAYS

Many Egyptian temples have seven gateways leading towards the sacred altar. Entering the temple encourages consciousness to travel from the outside world of distractions, towards the sacred stillness of the innermost sanctuary, which is situated furthest from the entrance. This is akin to a meditative journey through the chakras. Gateways also refer to journeys into the underworld, where Shamans guide initiates on a descent through the gateways of consciousness.

MUSICAL SCALE

Seven notes are found in both the European and Asian systems:

    Do-re-mi-fa-so-la-ti   Sa-re-ga-ma-pa-da-ni

    Each of these vibrational sounds relates to a particular chakra.

KWANZA

Kwanza is the African American holiday celebrated by Africans throughout the diaspora over seven days from the 26th December to 1st January. It advocates seven principles to be practised all year round:

1 Umoja — Unity
2 Kujichagulia — Self-determination
3 Ujima – Collective work and responsibility
4 Ujaama – Co-operative economics
5 Nia – Purpose
6 Kuumba – Creativity
7 Imani – Faith[34]

One candle is lit daily for each principle, until all seven are alight.

SEVEN DAYS OF CREATION
This is part of the Judeo-Christian creation myth, in which God takes six days to make the world and rests on the seventh. The world exists in duality – the first six chakras. The seventh day represents the crown chakra – oneness, timelessness and the state of perfect rest (peace).

SEVEN IN THE BIBLE
(Mainly found in the book of Revelations [or Visions].)

Mystery of the 7 stars
7 churches of Asia
7 angels of the 7 churches
7 spirits of God residing on the earth
7 seals (describes visions likely to be associated with the development of the chakras)
7 deadly sins (temptations and imbalances of the chakras in relation to the soul's descent from heaven to earth)
7 golden candlesticks

MENORAH
The Menorah is a seven-branched candlestick originally symbolizing the moon priestess (Menos) and her seven powers (chakras). The Menorah was decorated with lilies and almonds, which are well-known female symbols. It was eventually seen to relate to the Hebrew Archangels.

Revelations 1:12-20 tells how St John saw a bright aura and received wisdom from that light:

> His head and his hairs were white like wool, as white as snow; and his eyes were as a flame of red; and his feet like unto fine brass, as if they burned in a furnace; and his voice as the sound of many waters, and he had in his right hand seven stars ... write the things which thou hast seen, and things which are, and the things which shall be hereafter; the mystery of the seven stars which thou sawest in my right hand, and the seven golden candlesticks.

CHRISTMAS LIGHTS
Christmas tree lights traditionally had seven lights, each one higher than the last. Today the spiritual significance and the fact that these lights symbolized the seven chakras is all but forgotten.[35]

SEVEN AGES OF HUMAN DEVELOPMENT

The chronological maturation pattern of people appears to mature in cycles of seven years. Each cycle ascends a chakra, beginning at the root chakra (0 years) and rising to the crown chakra (at 42 years). The maturation process involves spiritual, psychological and physical development. I feel that in order to honour and encourage this progress, major initiations could be celebrated in seven-year cycles. To some degree this already happens, with birth celebrations, puberty (becoming a teenager), 21st birthday festivities, marriage, etc. Significance could also be attached to other turning points in life. (*See 'Rite of pass-age' in Chapter 6 and the individual chapters on each chakra.*)

The number seven exists in nature and is used by various cultures as an organizing principle. Many of these sevens relate directly to the chakras; others relate indirectly. The seven chakras have acted as a focus of initiation for thousands of years. Seven is found in many spiritual traditions. This number relates to levels of consciousness, as do the chakras.

THE MYSTERIOUS POWER OF SNAKES

Serpents are another common mythological and spiritual symbol. The snake is used to signify both good and evil. It is also seen to depict the balance of these two opposites. Snakes are symbolic of fertility and creation. Ouorborous, the encircled snake carrying its tail in its mouth, is seen to resemble the female yoni, while the outstretched snake represents the penis. The ability of snakes to shed their entire skin and develop a new one highlights their creative and regenerative qualities. This cycle of renewal resembles that of the female menstrual cycle – in early traditions, snakes symbolized the Goddess. These qualities together have earned the snake a lifelong place in healing traditions. To this very day, two snakes can be seen entwined around a staff as a symbol of the orthodox medical and pharmaceutical professions. This symbol is known as the caduceus and has a history going back over 5,000 years.

The caduceus is of direct relevance to our study of the chakras. It is the symbol used to interpret many aspects of development relating to spiritual growth and the ascent and descent of soul consciousness through the chakras and along the Shushumna (*see page 66*). We will look at the caduceus in more detail, but prior to this let us continue exploring what the snake represents in mythology. This will aid our understanding of the chakras and how we can best work with them.

In Egyptian mythology, the God Horus wears the serpent Goddess Uatchet on his head. She is the all-seeing eye. Osiris, the father of Horus, was killed by his brother Set. As Horus grew up he determined to avenge the death of his father. During the battles that followed Horus eventually killed his father's brother Set. Wounded in battle, Horus was left blind in one eye. His lost eye was given as an offering to his dead father Osiris, while Horus himself took to wearing a serpent on his head as a second eye. The Gods honoured Horus and made him King of Egypt. Thereafter rulers of Egypt wore a serpent on their crowns as a symbol of second sight and royal wisdom.

In the Mayan myths of Central America, the moon Goddess Ixchel wears a snake as a crown on her head. Her close companion and colleague is the sky serpent. Ixchel is capable of causing complete havoc on earth by whipping up the winds and sending destructive storms. Despite her fiery temper she is also the cosmic midwife and looks over women during pregnancy and childbirth. We see here her use of serpent power in both its destructive and creative aspects.

The creative powers of the serpent are recognized in many parts of Africa. The Fon people from Dahomey view the creator as both Mawu – female – and Lisa – male. Mawu-Lisa is dependent on Da, the cosmic serpent, who is responsible for manifesting the desires of Mawu-Lisa. Without Da there would be no creation; the united twins Mawu-Lisa would exist alone.[36] Here the serpent, symbolizing the creative energy of the spine and the chakras, brings forth all creation.

In the spiritual traditions of Original Australians (Ngukurr people), Wawalu is the rainbow serpent. The rainbow serpent is the carrier of the life force, who connects heaven to earth. Wawalu relates to the seven chakras and their rainbow colours.

Understanding the nature of the snake and honouring the snake can bestow great gifts. This is the message of a Nigerian folk tale which I would like to share with you:

Jaliya was a young girl who lived by the river. One day Jaliya was out collecting water with friends. They began to tease her and she accidentally fell into the river and disappeared. Jaliya felt herself being pulled deeper and deeper into the belly of the river. She allowed herself to fall and landed on the soft river bed. In front of her stood a magnificent palace. She entered the palace and found a crowned serpent sitting majestically upon a throne. The serpent asked her to sit and sing to him. Jaliya knew many songs from her village and joyfully sang for several hours. Meanwhile, sailing along the river was the King of Gongola. He hushed his entourage and listened carefully to the beautiful voice he could hear coming up from the river bed. Immediately he ordered his followers to divert the flow of the water and create a shallow path on which he could approach the singing. As he approached the voice, a serpent's head arose from the shallow waters. The serpent hissed into the sky and caused rain to fall. The serpent then flapped two giant wings and flew off to a deeper part of the river. The singing continued, and soon the face of a beautiful woman became clear in front of the king. The woman sat on a throne wearing a golden crown. Jaliya – for it was she – announced to the king that the serpent had made her queen of the river and had bestowed upon her gifts of great beauty. The wise serpent knew that Jaliya and the king would fall in love. For this reason he had told Jaliya that, for her to remain crowned queen of the waters and to live an earthly life, she would need to honour the serpent by making an annual sacrifice.

This tale indicates the descent into the underworld, the deep watery unconscious. Jaliya allows herself to fall deeply into the abyss; in so doing she gains the power and wisdom of the snake. As long as she continues to honour serpent energy, she will remain blessed with the knowledge of both heavenly (crowned) and earthly bliss. She now has the ability to unite opposites.

It is written in the Bible, *'Be ye wise as serpents and harmless as doves.'*[37] The snake appears several times in the Bible and is associated with feminine energy, personified by Eve, as well as being associated with wisdom and the tree of knowledge. In the Garden of Eden the snake again portrays the dual aspect of good and evil.

On a physical level, the human spine resembles a serpent. Therefore it should come as no surprise to find that the mysterious power of the snake is considered to reside, coiled up three and a half times, in the sacral region of the spine. The sacrum houses the body's physical centre of gravity and is a spiritual power centre. The sacrum is literally a 'sacred' centre waiting to be awakened. In yoga this serpent power is known as the Goddess Kundalini. Kundalini is our potential energy source, waiting to be released and actualized.

From this exploration we see the significant role of the snake in mythology and spirituality. Snakes are symbolic of numerous aspects of duality: creation-destruction, female-male, underworld-sky, etc. Various levels of experience are expressed through the wisdom of the snake. This multiplicity and the relationship between snakes and chakras is summarized in the caduceus symbol, which is widely used to signify the chakras.

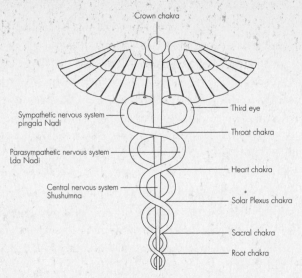

Crown chakra

Sympathetic nervous system
pingala Nadi

Third eye

Throat chakra

Parasympathetic nervous system
Ida Nadi

Heart chakra

Central nervous system
Shushumna

Solar Plexus chakra

Sacral chakra

Root chakra

The Egyptian caduceus symbolizes the three main nadis – Ida, Pingala and Shushumna. It also symbolizes three aspects of the nervous system – the central nervous system, and two antagonistic divisions of the autonomic nervous system: the sympathetic division, which relates to Pingala nadi, and the parasympathetic division, which relates to Ida nadi.

CADUCEUS AND THE CHAKRAS

The caduceus shows one or two snakes wound around a central staff. The snakes represent the polarity of opposing forces, and the wings illustrate transformation and freedom. Snakes live on the ground, while wings transport birds high above the earth. For me the caduceus symbolizes limitation and liberation. Our physical existence has many limitations, yet as we develop spiritually we can be reborn into a light body and experience liberation. The caduceus encapsulates the soul's journey along the chakras. The symbol, first depicted in ancient Egypt, is associated with Tehuti[38] (Thoth) the God-scribe. With Maat, he measures the hearts/souls of the dead and passes judgement. Good deeds in this life maketh the heart light and the soul free to enter the after-life. The caduceus features again in Greek myths, attributed to Hermes, the Greek version of Tehuti. The Greek God of healing, Asclepius, also carries a caduceus. Mercury, the Roman equivalent of Hermes, embodies another aspect of Tehuti and the caduceus, which is communication.

The twin snakes Ida and Pingala found in yogic philosophy are often depicted using the symbol of the caduceus. Ida and Pingala wind around a central column known as the Shushumna. The point where the snakes cross corresponds to the chakras. Ida, Pingala and Shushumna are three main *nadis*.[39] Nadi means stream or energy pathway; it is the channel through which energy travels. According to yoga and Ayurveda,[40] there are 72,000 nadis in the human body. Chakras arise where many nadis meet. This is mirrored in the nervous system: a plexus is a place where many nerves meet. The main nerve plexuses in the body are situated at the same locations as the seven major chakras. There are 14 principal nadis, of which the aforementioned three are the most important. Ida represents negative energy, Pingala positive energy, and Shushumna neutral energy. Ten primary nadis correspond to the ten gates of the body:

1   Anterior fontanel, which is the soft spot on a baby's head
2,3   right and left nostrils
4,5   right and left eye
6,7   right and left ear
8   the mouth
9   genitals
10   anus.

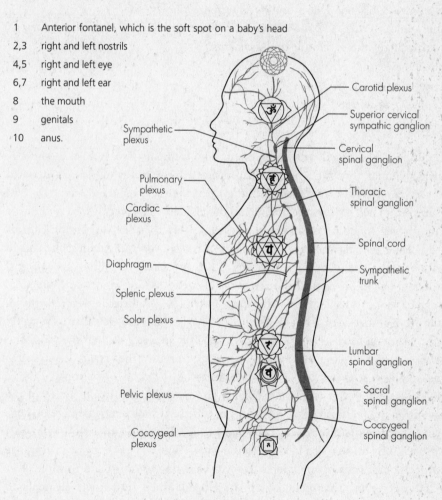

Chakras and corresponding nerve plexi

The two snakes spiral along the Shushumna, transporting us through the chakras on an ascending and descending journey of psycho-spiritual development. This is explored in the chapters on the individual chakras.

Physically, the caduceus relates to the autonomic nervous system (ANS), which has two main branches (represented by the snakes). The sympathetic branch activates the body (causing stress if overworked). The parasympathetic branch has a cleansing and calming effect. Working on the chakras helps balance the ANS. Energy flows alternately through positive poles (sympathetic – Pingala) and negative poles (parasympathetic – Ida). In order to maintain health and reach a higher level of consciousness, we can direct energy up the central column (Staff of Tehuti, or Shushumna). This ends duality and we experience wholeness.

Jung tells us that *'The snake's role is as a mediator between Heaven and Earth.'*[41] Not surprisingly, this is the role of the chakras.

THE ELEMENTS

Each chakra is associated with an element. The elements have always profoundly influenced human thought. Ancient Africans lived at the mercy of the elements and were very familiar with the overwhelming force they had on their existence. Our early Ancestors had to learn to understand the elements in order to survive. Energy has the power to both construct and destruct; this they saw in nature. Storms destroy, while the sun creates. This duality was also observed in animals, and in human nature. The elemental rhythms of nature bring creation, growth and destruction. For this reason, Africans saw the elements as Gods and Goddesses. The earth, sun, wind, water and even the space in which we all reside were worthy of honour to our Ancestors. They devised ways of appeasing the elements to ward off disaster, maintain food supplies and support healthy living. They felt the Gods and Goddesses respond to their rituals and sacrifices; in return they created more ceremonies to give thanks for the blessings they received.

A close relationship with the elements and nature made people aware of the forces within the body as well as the forces outside it. Winds remove water and have a drying effect; they scatter seeds, playing a part in all creation; they shift with great speed; an illusive nature also belongs to the winds. The Ancients began to liken the mind to the character of the wind – forever changing, creative and illusive. Over thousands of years, a complex system developed which relates the elements to human experience. Part of this legacy remains in commonplace metaphors.

Referring to someone as 'full of hot air', a 'bit wet' or 'too fiery' are expressions we all understand today which have their origin in humans' early relationships with the forces of nature.

What is often considered primitive is in fact ancient physics. The Ancients understood good and evil spirits and the spirits of animals and trees. They acknowledged that energy unites all things and affects us in positive and negative ways. The 20th-century scientific world is just beginning to accept that all things are connected. Einstein's famous equation $E = MC^2$ informs us that what we think of as matter, is actually energy in a constant state of change and motion. Studies, such as wave and particle theories in physics, demonstrate that all things are connected. The Ancients appear to have known this. Additionally they realized that, because of their own energetic nature shared with all creation, they could affect people and the environment. Rain could be made to fall and people could be healed, if the Gods willed it to be so. As we study the chakra system we will gain a deeper knowledge of our essence and begin to recognize ourselves as microcosms within the macrocosm.

THE LEGACY OF OUR ANCESTORS

The spiralling nature of evolution is returning us to the ways of our Ancestors. Inner science is taking on increasing importance in modern societies. As we search for ways to rescue ourselves and our planet from destruction, we begin to see, as our Ancestors did before us, that the forces of nature are overwhelming. If we are to survive, then we also need to appease and give thanks to the Gods, Goddesses and our Ancestors. They are ready to help us as soon as we recognize our earthly limitation, humble ourselves and seek guidance. Many say that the Ancestors are unhappy because they are not honoured in the modern world. It is on the fruits of their labour that we live today. If they had not learned to survive physically, emotionally and spiritually, we would not be here today. And we would not carry the genetic survival mechanisms that we now carry. The chakras are our spiritual survival mechanism. The first Africans are Ancestors to us all. If peace and unity are to preside, both within each one of us and on the planet we inhabit, then we need to remember our Ancestors and honour the circle of eternal life through prayer, celebration, meditation and ritual.

James George Frazer wrote in *The Golden Bough* that human evolution has passed through three stages. He called them *the age of magic, the age of religion and the age of science.*[42] It seems to me that we are moving towards a fourth stage, the age of unity, where it is essential that we bring together the wisdom of old with that of the new. Synergy will be created when all three ages are respected. Science, religion and magic need to sit side by side as the new trinity.

The place of the Africans in ancient spirituality is clearly evident. Since the beginning of time Africans have worshipped Gods, they have used touch to heal, they have studied the elements and collected healing plants. This rich legacy has been greatly developed by many cultures in numerous places around the globe. Diverse yet common mythological and religio-spiritual themes can be found the world over. These themes have also found their way into modern science in the works of people like Carl Jung.

There is an argument that these coincidences, similarities and identical beliefs grew up independently in far corners of the globe. Several thousand years from now, people may think that Buddhism grew up independently in different parts of Asia, Europe and wherever it may be practised by then. At present, we know that 2,600 years ago, Buddhism had its beginnings in India and spread from a 'specific origin'. It is my understanding that thousands of years ago, Africa was a 'specific origin' and from her people came the common spiritual themes and rituals that underpin many religious and spiritual traditions of today. These practices have grown and been developed by different cultures the world over.

I also think that recognition should be given where it is due and that our First Ancestors and all the Ancients should be honoured with love and respect. In this way we keep alight the flame of Eternal Spirit. As the Ancestors rest, harmony will prevail, individually and globally.

The Black role in Asia, as elsewhere in the world, has been submerged and distorted for centuries. But it has not been totally eclipsed and it rises now like a star which was hidden by a cloud but never faded into oblivion of the night.

Ivan Van Sertima

CLEANSING

PREPARATIONS FOR CHAKRA WORK

O people of the Earth, men born and made of the elements, but with the essence of divine within you, rise from your sleep, rise from your ignorance. Be ye thoughtful and understanding. Know that your home is not the earth but the light ... prepare yourself to climb through the seven rings (chakras) and blend with the eternal light.

Divine Pymander of Hermes Trimegestus

THROUGHOUT TIME IT HAS BEEN RECOGNIZED THAT, TO OBTAIN MORE FROM the universe, people must be ready to receive more. Living in light is your birthright, abundance your legacy. A grand capacity for moving energy and communicating directly with spirit is yours. A prepared vessel and willingness to expand ordinary reality is all that is required to fully claim this legacy. Opening to Spirit means increasing your awareness of the spiritual dimensions that are constantly within and around you. It is the inclination to reach out and touch people in a way that is truly meaningful. Opening to Spirit acknowledges the individual journey of your soul. As we descend from spirit into earthly bodies, we experience a longing that causes us to seek unification with spirit.

The physical body is the vehicle for the soul's journey. The chakras, aura and subtle bodies are keepers of the soul's knowledge. Recorded in the subtle bodies is the information of all you have experienced before, either in this or another life. The template for all that you will become is also held in these fine, invisible sheaths. Opening to Spirit means communicating with the energy deep inside and the forces around you. This way you gain a better understanding of both the universe and your part in the whole scheme of things. As you get acquainted with the spirit world, questions are answered and truth slowly unfolds. Many things fit together and begin to make sense. Suffering and pain hold deeper meaning, everything becomes a learning experience in what Dr Stone[1] called the 'kindergarten of life'. Our emotions, ills and traumas can be seen as the lessons they really are. What was once seen as coincidence, or a mistake, gains meaning. On the spiritual path there are no accidents, only opportunities.

As you begin Opening to Spirit and increasing the flow of energy in and out of your body, your vehicle will need fine-tuning. Sudden, intense chakra work, without preparing the system, can be very unpleasant. Increased activity will cause the body to eliminate accumulated toxins. Emotions that have lain dormant for years will rise to the surface, causing quite a shock, particularly if you thought they were already dealt with. Experiences from this lifetime, and possibly previous ones, are held in the body. Blocked energy in the chakras maintains these experiences. Conscious chakra work liberates energy in the body, changing the way energy is held. The increased flow of energy in and around the body makes one more susceptible to psychic influences. This is generally positive, the very reason for working with the chakras. But if the system is not cleansed, the changes may cause discomfort. Toxic overload results in muscular aches, often in the back or legs. Headaches and nausea are also quite common. Emotional overload is another problem: when so many feelings surface at once, things can become quite frightening. Depression and despair may occur. Without supportive people around you this can be quite difficult. Psychic experiences can flood you, and feel as if they are taking you over. It is important to know how to ground yourself if this happens. With correct preparation these unpleasant experiences can be avoided.

Any life change requires preparation, and spiritual work is no exception. I have seen people suffer because they did not have the skills to deal with the fragmenting experience of personal and spiritual development. The fire God Shiva is the force of destruction in the Indian trinity. Shiva represents that which has to be destroyed in order to create anew. After embarking on a conscious spiritual journey, things change. A new dawn will break. To accommodate the increase of energy as you Open to Spirit, there are various techniques that can be used:

- cleansing the whole system through fasting and dietary changes
- creating sacred space through cleansing and creating an altar
- mindful exercise
- breath work and concentration techniques
- meditation
- keeping a journal
- increasing awareness and Self-knowledge.

These are all ways we can prepare for chakra work. Each one is looked at in detail. Take time preparing your physical vehicle for chakra work. The spiritual, psycho-emotional and physical benefits will be multiplied and you will avoid unnecessary discomfort.

FASTING

To fast is to abstain from food, either entirely or partially, for a given period of time. We do this in a small way every night and we break-fast each morning. Extending the length of time we fast is good for the spirit. The whole system benefits from being cleansed and strengthened. This is seen in all major religions, where aspirants enter a period of fasting prior to intense spiritual work.

Fasting helps cleanse the physical body of impurities accumulated from poor dietary habits. It also reduces stimulation to the digestive organs and liberates energy. A feeling of lightness affects the mind; this improves concentration and aids meditation. We each know that when we have eaten a heavy meal it becomes harder to concentrate. You may feel sleepy and a bit lethargic. So it figures that when we fast, the opposite is true. The body feels light and is better able to focus. Along with the physical and mental benefits, fasting has another function, which is to begin clearing the nadis. Through these pathways energy either flows, or is restricted. There are many reasons why restrictions occur: smoking, abuse of alcohol, eating dead food (synthetic), eating dead animals, eating too much or too little, synthetic chemicals in food and prolonged exposure to air pollution are some examples. A period of fasting facilitates the body in throwing off toxins, and frees up energy. As a result the body is far less likely to suffer toxic overload when intense chakra work begins. Fasting can be followed by a healthier diet that will continue to strengthen the whole system.

Fasting requires three stages:

1 preparation
2 period of fasting
3 breaking the fast.

Preparation

When fasting for the first time I suggest you try one day only, or begin on a Friday evening and continue over the weekend. Make sure you will have plenty of time to yourself and will not have family and friends making constant demands on you. Try to arrange for the children to stay with a family member or friend. Let people you normally cook for prepare their own food, or better still invite them to join you on the fast. If possible get away for a few days into the country, where you can commune with nature. If this is totally impossible, don't worry, you can still fast. Call on the Goddess to help strengthen your will.

During the fast you will need to refrain from drinking tea, coffee, soft drinks and alcohol. Chocolate and smoking are also to be avoided. Because these are all addictive substances, it is advisable to reduce your intake a few days before the fast. This helps reduce any side-effects. Some symptoms such as headaches, bad breath and slightly aching muscles and joints can occur, as toxins are flushed out of your body. Don't let this put you off. It is much more likely that you will feel a sense of well-being and achievement during a fast, and certainly afterwards. This makes the fast worth while.

Gather together everything you intend to consume during your fast. For example: plenty of spring water, fruits to juice, or organic fruit juice. Have time and materials (skin brushes, oils, etc.) available for the practices that enhance the fast. You may like to use an affirmation to help prepare yourself mentally. Use the following affirmation or create your own:

AFFIRMATION FOR FASTING
Of my own free will I choose to cleanse my body, mind and strengthen my spirit.
I choose to fast for ? day/s.
I know I am fully worthy and will be supported by the spirit world.
I am capable of this task.

Period of Fasting

There are many methods of fasting, which I divide into two categories.

1. WATER ONLY

This greatly affects the subtle bodies and is used mostly for spiritual development.

One-day Fast

The evening before your fast, eat a light nutritious meal, low in sugars (sugar tends to create food cravings). On the day of your fast, drink at least 4 litres of pure spring water that has been kept at room temperature. If you can drink more, that is fine. The idea is to completely flush out the alimentary canal, the liver and the kidneys. Pure water, unlike other liquids, moves straight through the body, flushing out toxins as it proceeds. Eventually your urine will be clear and you will feel light. When I fast for a day, providing I am mentally prepared, I do not feel hungry. This fast is good to do one day a month.

Weekend Fast

Make sure you are well prepared.

Begin the fasting period on Friday evening. At around 6 o'clock eat a light meal of 3 – 5 different steamed vegetables and one type of grain, such as brown rice. Follow with one type of alkaline fruit, such as grapes. No more food is eaten on Friday night.

From Saturday through to 6 o'clock Sunday evening eat nothing and drink only pure spring water. Drink at least 4 litres a day, kept at room temperature.

Sunday evening: eat a small amount of fresh grapes.

(*See: Breaking the Fast, page 76.*)

2. LIQUIDS ONLY

This method is used for its balancing and regulating effect on the body and mind.

Freshly squeezed juices are used instead of or as well as spring water.

Particular vegetables and fruits are used for their healing qualities.

Some of the important ones are: grapes, apples, watermelon, carrots and cabbage.

The above juices are highly recommended by naturopaths. All of them are extremely good cleansers. They purify the blood, cleanse the liver and kidneys, remove congestion in the bowels and stimulate immune function.

The method is the same as for the water-only fast, except 4 litres of fruit juice is substituted for water. To achieve the best results drink only one type of juice during the fast. This keeps digestive activity to a minimum. I have found that mixing half juice and half water works well, as some juices alone can be very sweet. This fast can be practised for one day or up to ten days.

Break the fast by eating a small quantity of the fruit or vegetable you have been drinking.

A juice fast has some advantages over water alone. Hunger is definitely kept at bay. The bowels work better, so it would seem the physical cleansing effects are increased. It is also a little bit easier to contemplate for some people. Consuming copious amounts of fresh fruit juice has a luxurious quality about it, rather than the frugality which might be associated with water-only fasting.

Breaking the Fast

This final stage is as important as the fast itself and may be just as difficult. I remember deciding to fast one New Year. I began a water-only fast on January 1st, for ten days. This I did with little difficulty. I was very well both during and immediately after the fast. My meditations had improved and I felt uplifted spiritually. My experience was a good one, until it came to breaking the fast. I was not prepared. My stomach had shrunk and even drinking juice was an effort. I had to literally eat my drink, which we are, in fact, supposed to be doing all the time. Making use of the mouth to 'eat drinks' and 'drink food' should be commonplace. Fasting had retuned my system and it was asking me to use my digestive apparatus properly. Fasting was fine, but having food ready to eat and finding that I could only eat a very small portion of it was difficult. I recommend you prepare yourself for this, particularly if you fast for two or more days. You will not immediately return to eating as you did prior to fasting. Breaking fast is an ideal opportunity to begin that healthy diet you have been promising yourself.[2]

After a one-day fast, breaking the fast with fruit, steamed vegetables and other light foods is adequate.

For fasts lasting two or more days, breaking the fast should continue for half the duration of the actual fast (that is, if you have been fasting for ten days, break it using the foods listed below for the next five days).

On the eve of the last full day of fasting, begin breaking the fast with a few grapes, or a piece of whichever fruit you have been drinking.

The following day:

Breakfast	Fresh juice (still the same) and a piece of fruit
Lunch	Fresh vegetable salad, lightly dressed with olive oil[3]
Dinner	Steamed vegetables

The second day:

Breakfast:	Fresh juice and a piece of fruit with a little yoghurt
Lunch	Fresh vegetable soup and a slice of wholemeal bread
Dinner	Steamed vegetables on rice with a tahini dressing

Continue for the following days on a light diet of fresh fruit and vegetables. Avoid anything that is likely to clog up and adversely affect your newly cleansed system.

Fasting is perfectly safe for most people, but it is recommended that you check with a doctor or natural health practitioner if you suffer from any diagnosed illness, or take prescribed medication. Supervision may be necessary. Support is always helpful. If you can encourage a friend to join you, the fast is likely to be easier and more fun. If you experience extreme discomfort during a fast (this is very unlikely) stop immediately and see your doctor.

Enhancers while Fasting

There are several aids to de-toxifying the system.

DRY SKIN BRUSHING

Dry skin brushing is particularly useful. It stimulates the circulation and immune system, helping to drain lymph and speed up the removal of wastes. The colon is activated, helping the elimination of any impacted faecal matter. A dry natural bristle brush is used to rub the dry body first thing in the morning. This is done before bathing. Gentle strokes are made towards the heart. Each stroke moves from the periphery to the centre. First the arms are done: start at the fingers and use long strokes towards the armpits, brushing the entire arm. Repeat on the feet and legs. Do your back, towards the heart, down from the shoulders and up from the bottom. Brush towards the centre of your chest. Finally, make clockwise strokes around your belly, following the digestive tract, and draining the lymph. The whole procedure should take about 5 minutes.

SAUNAS

Saunas encourage elimination, so are good when doing a short fast or near the beginning of a longer fast. It is important not to stay in the heat longer than suggested (follow instructions given by the sauna room attendant). Relaxation after your sauna is as valuable as the heat. The body does much of its cleansing during rest.

MASSAGE

Massage provides a way of treating yourself and increasing the cleansing process. Massage provides time and space to connect with your body. As you focus on your body you can find yourself transported to the innermost part of yourself. Bodywork is an excellent way to relax. It also increases the healing benefits of fasting and prepares you for chakra work.

MEDITATION

Meditation becomes easier after fasting. The mind is more relaxed. The physical body and subtle bodies are cleansed, facilitating energy flow. Try one of the meditations detailed later in this chapter or in subsequent chapters.

When you have completed fasting, or any other task, remember to give thanks to the spirit world for helping you. This you can do during your meditations.

SACRED SPACE

When working with energy, it is useful to clear the space of any negative vibrations. Unseen and unwelcome energies can accumulate in our homes. Like dust they gather in the corners. Cleansing the space enhances any work that is done. When the room is clear you can prepare an altar that will raise energy and make the space sacred.

There are various methods of cleansing space. I have listed the cleansing tools needed according to the elements.

Earth	Crystals can be pointed into the corners of rooms; they absorb energy. *Amber* purifies and reduces negative energy. *Amethyst* raises vibrations.
Water	Two or three drops of *Frankincense* in a water spray can be sprayed into room corners and up to the ceiling. A fine mist of water will cleanse the room.
Fire & Air	A *sage smudge stick* that has been set alight and left softly smoking (with any flames put out) can be wafted around the room, especially into corners where negative energy accumulates. Alternatively, incense can be used.
Ether	Sound is a great transformer of energy: *hands* can be clapped, *bells* rung, *chimes* tinkled, *drums* sounded or *Tibetan singing bowls* played. All will help to clear energy.

To cleanse yourself of negative energy, run any of the above tools through your aura. Work up the front of your body and down the back, finishing at your feet.

Preparing an Altar

You will find an altar helps you focus energy. Giving thanks at an altar is tangible and grounding. Altars are sacred spaces where the physical and spiritual worlds communicate. They are used in religious and spiritual work to magnify energy. A carefully created altar has a powerful magnetic field around it and can be used to charge and uplift items, people, and yourself. There is usually a sense of peacefulness where an altar is, or has been. I have a space in my home that I use for spiritual practice. People often comment on the room's peaceful energy. This is partly because of how the room is used, but also because I keep several altars in this healing space. The altars and plants in the room generate peaceful energy.

How then do we create altars? Start by looking around your home and identifying the places where altars already exist. Do you have natural things standing together that decorate the place, such as stones, shells, crystals, bits of driftwood, plants, flowers or candles? These things serve the function of raising energy in your home. You may be surprised by how many such items you have. The task now is to arrange them consciously. Your altar can be as small or large, as you have space for. If you have a spare room, use it. Build an altar in the space and reserve the room for your spiritual practice. Otherwise a corner of a used room is fine. A small table top or shelf will work well. I keep a flat in London and have an altar running up either side of my stairs. An altar is central to your practice and communication with spirit. It therefore needs to feel special to you. Start with a neutral-coloured cloth, like brown, representing earth, or white, symbolizing light.

Choose something from each of the elements: earth, water, fire and air. I use crystals for earth. For water, a bowl of living water from a well, spring or rain is ideal. I have a sealed container of Ganges River water from India that I use. Candles provide fire. Air I symbolize with incense. If space is limited, a floating candle can be used for the water, fire and air elements. Place an element in each direction – North, South, East, West. Some traditions have fire in the East, water in the South, etc. I find a lot of different information on directions, and therefore I will leave it to you to decide where each element feels right. Consider the local climate: if winds blow from the east, then air would be east. If it is hotter in the south, place fire in the south, and so on. Tune in to the elements and directions for guidance. This forms the basis of your altar.

Now you can begin to personalize it. Photographs of spiritual guides, Ancestors and deities can be placed around. Be creative and try to avoid synthetic materials. Look to nature's garden for most of what you need. Choose flowers, sand and earth of different colours. See what stones, wood and shells you can find that are sculpted by Mother Nature. The more energy you put in, the more your altar will come alive.

When working with individual chakras your altar can be arranged to harness particular energies. This is dealt with in the appropriate chapters. Initially it is good to put together a neutral altar, attune to the energies of it and begin creating a working relationship with spirit. Keep your altar well looked after, honouring your Ancestors and guides in the spirit world. Attend to it each day and you will find it serves you well.

MINDFUL EXERCISE

We all know exercise has numerous benefits. Through exercise we are helped to gain and maintain health. Swami Vishnudevananda claims that such benefits achieved through yoga are merely side-effects. The real benefits are of a spiritual nature, such as cleaning the subtle bodies and opening up the psychic centres. Starting classes in tai-chi, chi-kung, yoga or kum-nye is an introduction to energy work for many people. Seeking mindful exercise is, itself, a sign of Opening to Spirit. Subtle energy exercises are discussed for use with each chakra. Here I introduce some basic principles for exercise and simple movements that can be used to assist you in Opening to Spirit.

The aim of mindful exercise is threefold. One, to **awaken** energy in the body. Two, to **ground** energy and maintain a connection to the earth. Three, to draw energy from above and below, and **centre** that energy in your subtle body. Basically, we need skills to awaken, ground and centre energy.

The root and sacral chakras are responsible respectively for grounding and centring. These subjects are dealt with in detail in the relevant chapters. The exercises below are primarily to prepare the vehicle for Opening to Spirit.

Unwind and Awaken: Exercise to Awaken Energy

Unwind and awaken

Stand upright with your feet hip-width apart, toes slightly turned in, heels out, the outside edge of the feet straight. Tune to the earth beneath your feet and connect with her. Breathing deeply, be aware of any sensations through and around your body. As slowly as you can, begin to let your spine fold down. Start at the head, allowing your neck to fall forward, followed by your shoulders. Relax your arms, feel them dangling down. Have your knees slightly bent. Continue slowly unwinding the spine until you are fully bent forward. In this position take a couple of deep breaths. Slowly lift your body, raising your head and arms last. Feel the vertebra releasing one at a time as you go forward, and see them stacking one on top of the other as you return to a standing position. Visualize the spine moving with the fluidity of a serpent. Once upright, be aware of your breath and sense the flow of energy as it is awakened in your body.

The gentle movement of this exercise works with the flow of energy between heaven and earth (head and feet). Tension along the spine is released, awakening and balancing energy currents through each of the chakras.

CAUTION

This exercise is not suitable for people with high blood pressure. Simply stand in the same position, raise your arms up towards the sky and stretch the full length of your spine.

Bouncing on the Earth: Exercise to Ground Energy

Stand with your feet hip-width apart, toes slightly turned in, heels out, the outside edge of the feet straight. Bend your knees and keep your spine upright. Shoulders are held open and there is space across the chest. Let your energy move down into your legs and feet. Connect with the earth energy beneath you, breathing deeply, aware of any sensations through and around your body. Keeping your knees bent, gently bounce your body up and down, keeping your feet in full contact with the floor. Exhale audibly through your mouth with each movement of your body. Let yourself be floppy. Feel energy flow into the lower half of your body. Stop, and be still. From a place of stillness feel the sensation of energy as it streams through your legs. Repeat between three and seven times. Do not allow your legs to get exhausted. You may feel an ache in the thighs, demonstrating a reduction in energy flow, or they may tremble, which indicates a charge and release of blocked energy.

Energy is often overbound – too rigid; or underbound – unreliable, in the legs. This exercise helps to gain awareness of how energy flows in your legs. It is also useful for balancing blockages in the root chakra and enhancing grounding.

Centring Ritual: Exercise to Centre Energy

Stand with your feet hip-width apart, toes slightly turned in, heels out, the outside edge of the feet straight. Tune to the earth beneath your feet. Breathing deeply, be aware of any sensations through and around your body.

Raise your arms up – touch the heavens symbolically with the palms of your hands. Circle both hands three times above the crown of your head. Then squat down towards the floor – touch the earth symbolically with flat palms. Return to standing and place both hands over your sacral chakra (lower abdomen), drawing the energy of heaven and earth into your centre. Observe the movement of energy while you breathe. All the movements are done slowly with awareness.

This ritual is used to draw dissipated energy back into the centre. Energy is focused and strengthened in the body's central core. It is good preparation for events that really need concentration, like exams, interviews and other potential stress-inducers. This ritual can help restore and cleanse your energy fields after a situation that has taken a lot out of you and left you feeling depleted.

BREATH WORK (PRANAYAMA)

To breathe is to be alive. When we leave our mother's womb we must take our first inspiration. This breath signals life. At the end of our earthly days breath will leave us, signalling expiration of the physical body. The root word for inspire, expire and respiration is the Latin word 'spiritus'. Thus we see that the breath and spirit are linked. In the yogic system, breathing exercises are called pranayama; *prana* means vital energy, *yama* means control. Therefore, in yoga, to breathe is to control the vital energy. The relationship between the flow of energy and breath is recognized the world over. It is of particular importance to healers, shamans and those of us who wish to develop our connection with spirit.

The subtle body can be influenced and entirely transformed using specific breathing techniques. Through the breath, vital energy enters the chakras, nadis and the aura. This flow of energy animates the physical body. Breathing therefore plays a significant role in Opening to Spirit. The exercises below will help you to develop breath awareness.

Three-part Yogic Breath

Begin by lying on your back, on the floor, in the relaxation posture: legs out-stretched, feet about 18 inches (45 cm) apart and falling out to the sides, hands about 6 inches (15 cm) away from the body with palms facing upwards. Your chin is down slightly towards your chest in order to lengthen the back of your neck. Your eyes should be gently closed, your mouth gently open. Take up space on the floor, letting go of any tightness or tension. Release and relax the whole body. Bring attention to your breath.

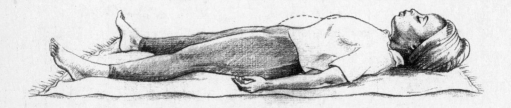

1st part	Breathe in fully through your nose, raising your abdomen. Open your chest and completely fill your lungs.
2nd part	Hold the breath comfortably, keeping your body totally still for a count of 4 (this count can be increased with practice).

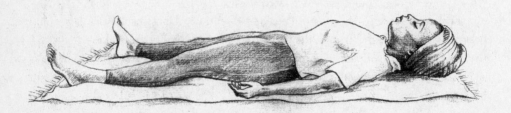

Three-part yogic breath

| 3rd part | Exhale slowly through your nose, empty your lungs completely. Feel your abdomen pulling down towards the floor. |

Repeat this three-part breath three to seven times.

This exercise allows full and correct use of the breathing apparatus. It restores movement to the respiratory diaphragm and intercostal muscles. Five times more oxygen is taken into the lungs for transporting around the body's cells. This produces the cleansing effect of flushing out toxins. The nervous system becomes relaxed and concentration improves. The ability to control the breath is fundamental to spiritual development.

CAUTION

People with back problems: you may wish to lay down with your knees raised and your feet flat on the floor.

Anuloma Viloma (Alternate Nostril Breathing)

This powerful pranayama is essential to chakra work. If you only do one practice from this book, let this be it.

As the name suggests, alternate nostril breathing alternates the flow of breath/prana through one nostril and then the other. This is in fact a process that we can witness happening naturally. The breath will flow predominantly through the right nostril and then change to the left nostril. In a healthy individual, this alternation occurs approximately once every two hours. Yogis learn to manipulate this flow of energy in order to influence two main nadis – Ida and Pingala. Their qualities relate to yin and yang respectively. Ida works through the left nostril, being the feminine, receptive, cooling moon principle. Pingala works through the right, as the masculine, forceful, warming sun principle. Yogis realize that through intense practice it is possible to balance the negative and positive flow of Ida and Pingala. Neutral energy is created, awakening the Goddess Kundalini from her sleep at the base of the spine and sending her rising up the central column (Shushumna nadi) of the chakra system. This awakening of Kundalini bestows great spiritual gifts on the aspirant. If the serpent Goddess Kundalini rises as far as the crown chakra and remains there for just a few minutes, enlightenment is permanently attained.

Apart from this ultimate goal of enlightenment, Anuloma viloma has numerous other benefits:

- balancing the autonomic nervous system[4]
- balancing the left and right hemispheres of the brain[5]
- improving concentration on any particular object or subject
- stimulating Ajna (third eye) chakra
- increasing awareness of each of the chakras
- purifying each of the 72,000 nadis (it is not until all nadis are purified that progress can be made in raising Kundalini)
- aligning the individual force-field with the universal force-field.

THE PRACTICE OF ANULOMA VILOMA

Sit in a comfortable meditative position where you will not be disturbed. This practice is always done to a ratio of 1:4:2; if you inhale for a count of 2, then you hold for a count of 8 and exhale to a count of 4. This is a good count to begin with. Gradually the count is increased. An advanced count may be: inhale 8, hold for 32 and exhale for 16.

Using your right hand, place your middle finger and index finger into your right palm, creating the Vishnu Mudra (a specific hand gesture that directs energy). Your thumb is then used to block the right side and the remaining fingers are used for blocking the left side.

Anuloma Viloma: alternate nostril breathing

There are six stages to each complete round of alternate nostril breathing. Choose an appropriate count and proceed with it through the stages.

1 block right nostril – inhale through the left
2 hold the breath – block both nostrils
3 block left nostril – exhale through the right
4 inhale through the right – left is blocked
5 hold the breath – block both nostrils
6 block right nostril – exhale through the left.

As you hold your breath during this practice close your eyes and focus on drawing energy from the muladhara chakra (root) to ajna chakra (third eye). Sense the energy travelling along the shushumna nadi (central canal within the spine) and stimulating ajan chakra. Feel a gentle pulsation in the third eye region. Awakening ajna is important preparation for chakra work as it helps establish a foundation of wisdom and insight that will prove valuable when working on other chakras.

Repeat between three and seven times. Increase the count as your practice and concentration improve.

MEDITATION

Imagine throwing a stone into a pond. As the stone hits the water it creates a series of ripples. The ripples gently dance on the surface of the pond, making it impossible to see the bottom. Eventually the movement ceases. As the water becomes still your image will appear on its surface.

The mind is like a pond, constantly bombarded with thoughts that create ripples of sound and movement. Meditation is a tool that allows us to still the waters of the mind long enough to see our true reflection and meet the Self that resides within.

There are multitudes of meditation techniques. They all share the goal of moving us closer to liberation, closer to knowledge of oneness, closer to unity with our creator.

Meditation is possibly the most difficult thing you can be asked to do. Initially it is hard to give up constant mind activity – it is, after all, what the mind knows best. Changing this pattern takes commitment and discipline. With practice you will find meditation requires less effort. Follow the guidelines below and your mind will become attuned to the practice of meditation. We all get attuned to eating, anticipating food because we have come to know our meal times. Likewise the mind will auto-matically prepare for stillness once meditation is practised on a regular basis.

Guidelines for Meditation[6]

1. ENVIRONMENT
Practise in the sacred space where you have your altar. Be sure the room has enough air and is warm. Create a calming atmosphere by lighting candles and burning incense or essential oils. Using the same place and time each day will attune your personal energy and lift the vibrations in the space, thus aiding spiritual practice considerably.

2. BODY POSITION
It is preferable to sit for meditation. When lying down, you run the risk of falling asleep. Sit either in the Egyptian meditative posture (*see illustration*) – upright in a chair with the feet flat on the floor, or in the Indian meditation pose – cross-legged on the floor. If sitting cross-legged, the hips need to be higher than the knees. For comfort, place a cushion on top of a folded blanket. Sit with your hips on the cushion and your knees and feet down on the blanket.

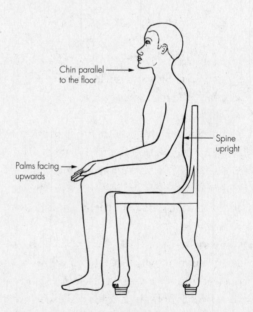

Chin parallel to the floor

Spine upright

Palms facing upwards

Egyptian meditative posture

Bring your hands into the centre, gently resting your right hand in your left. Let your thumbs touch. Support yourself against a wall if necessary. The main thing is to keep your spine and head erect. This ensures that the chakras are in alignment, one on top of the other. This meditative position directs energy into the core of the being, reducing dissipation. Concentration is improved and energy is encouraged to travel from the root chakra to the crown chakra.

3. MENTAL PREPARATION
Inform your mind of the duration of meditation; ask your mind to be silent throughout.

4. BREATHING
Consciously regulate your breath. Use your nose, not your mouth. Take several deep abdominal breaths. The stomach is pushed out on your in-breath and returns towards the spine on the out-breath. Your shoulders should not rise and each breath should be slow and rhythmic.

5. ATTITUDE
Do not force your mind to be still. Meditation is like taming a wild bird: at first it will fly around a lot, not wanting to be still. Eventually it will tire and look for a place to rest. Your technique or focal point will become the perch on which your mind rests.

6. TECHNIQUE
As mentioned earlier, there are numerous types of meditation, each offering a taste of enlightenment. They are all useful practices. Any one of the methods below can be used:

- concentration on the movement of your breath
- focusing on the point between the eyes (Ajna chakra)
- repeating the mantra *Aum* with each breath
- tratak: concentrating on the light of a candle
- dharana: concentrating on the chakra symbols
- chakra meditation
- techniques you already use.

Chakra Meditation
This chakra meditation is particularly useful for becoming familiar with the location of the chakras in your body and their different sensations (*see first colour plate*).

Focus your attention on each chakra in turn. Be aware of your breath and maintain contact with these centres for as long as feels right. Begin with the root, working up through each chakra. Then, from the crown, return to the root.

This practice takes between 15 and 45 minutes.

Guided Chakra Meditation

Bring your awareness to the root chakra – this is a vibrant wheel of energy, between the anus and genitals. Feel the sensations. Visualize the radiant colour red, positioned at the root chakra. Breathe into the area. Feel the pulsation at this point. Let the vibration and colour radiate out into your aura. Maintain each chakra contact for 1 to 5 minutes…

Now bring your focus to the sacral chakra, situated about 2 inches (5 cm) below your navel. Feel the sensation and visualize a bright, shining, orange light. Let the light shine into your aura…

Move to the solar plexus – this is at the base of the sternum[7] (breast bone). Tune to the vibration and visualize the luminous yellow globe of the sun, shining out into your aura…

Move on to the heart centre, located at the physical heart region. Be aware of its sensation. Visualize a clear green, or rose pink, wheel of vibrating energy. Feel it cascading out into your bright, shimmering aura…

The throat chakra is centred in the throat area. Take your attention there and tune to the energy. Visualize a brilliant sky blue. Hold the colour, then let it flow out into your aura…

Next is the third eye chakra, sitting in the middle of, and slightly above, the eyebrows. Look into this place and observe the sensation. The colour is indigo, the deep bluey black of night, when this centre is most active. Absorb the colour deep into your soul, then send it out, to surround your whole body…

Finally the crown, the golden, thousand-petalled lotus at the top of your head. Feel the golden light vibrate. Wrap gold around the rainbow aura of your entire being. Resonate with the highest energy of the Goddess, feel her in you, know you are Divine.

From here begin descending the chakras, stopping to focus and tune to each one. Notice any changes as you return to the root chakra.

7. STILLNESS

Remain peacefully for the chosen time of your meditation.

Meditation leads to spiritual wisdom. It is an essential practice that develops awareness and provides the foundation needed for working on the individual chakras. The practice of stillness and meditation is found in many ancient cultures. Each one of us holds the capacity to quieten the mind, enter the silence, and know.

JOURNAL-KEEPING

My own spiritual journey has taught me the value of keeping a journal. When studying yoga in India I was encouraged to keep a 'yoga diary'. This consisted of a detailed daily account of my spiritual practice. In my journal I noted any improvement in postures, the number of rounds of pranayama completed, time spent in meditation, obstacles, weaknesses, progress and spiritual experiences. I could then see at a glance how I was, or was not, developing. I found this useful, although occasionally a bit of a chore. I began to enjoy using my journal later, when I became more creative. Life had become emotionally tough for me and I was in personal therapy. I felt overwhelmed at times and my journal proved to be a real refuge. When I found myself alone with my feelings, sure no one would understand, I would lie in my bed and write. I asked questions and found answers, I scribbled and other times I drew. Poems appeared and dreams found a resting place. My journals are now trusted friends and guides.

In my workshops I introduce participants to journal-keeping. Most of us have at some time kept a diary – for many it was around those difficult teenage years. Unconsciously we found safety and release through sharing our most private selves with a paper friend. A parent may have read your diary and consequently you decided never to commit feeling to paper again. Or maybe, like me, you just grew out of it.

I would like to invite you to keep a personal journal, a journal that will record your journey through the chakras.

On the first page may I suggest you write the following statement:

This Journal is to be my companion and guide on a unique journey through the terrain I know to be myself – body, mind and spirit.

On my journey I have known love, joy and success; I have experienced fear, pain and challenge. This journal records my feelings, meditations, thoughts, reflections and dreams. With this journal, my *companion*, I share images, words, raw emotion and silent thoughts. From this journal, my *guide*, I receive insights, clarity, a newfound wisdom and creativity.

This journal is the story of my journey through life.

The subsequent pages are to fill, as you want. One idea is to divide the journal into seven sections, one for each chakra. As you move through the chakras you can work in the appropriate journal section. You may prefer to make entries as and where you feel. Either way is fine. Each chapter on the chakras has specific journal work. You can also create your own. Use your journal to record your practice; write or draw your feelings in it. Use it as a tool to work through conflicts. It can reflect back to you what you most need to know. When writing let the words flow, do not be concerned about grammar or spelling. If you are not sure where to begin, then write exactly that. Allow 'not knowing' to be your starting place and away you will go. Use coloured pencils, paints – be creative again. Even the youngest of children knows what to do with a pen and paper. When did we forget? Experiment with using your non-dominant hand for writing and drawing. This often taps directly into the unconscious. Try not to stand in judgement of yourself: remember there are no right and wrong ways to keep a personal journal. Everything reveals a valuable part of your journey.

Where I Am Now

This exercise will help you get started with your journal.

Contemplate your life at this moment.

Note the date, record your thoughts, feelings and motivation. Bear in mind that where you are today is not where you were yesterday and that tomorrow will be different again.

Here are some key questions. What does each mean to you at this very moment?

◉ Where are you now in your **body**?

Draw an outline of your body and fill in parts that are tense, painful, beautiful, loved, parts that are less loved. Do the pains coincide with the less loved body parts? Does anything need to change?

◉ Where are you now in your **mind and emotions**?

What stimulates your mind at the moment?

Who is emotionally close to you? What are your needs? Are they being met?

Do you respect your own thoughts and feelings?

Does anything need to change?

◉ Where are you **spiritually**?

Do you have a spiritual or religious orientation?

What is emerging in your life now that is calling you to address your spirituality?

What is changing? What do you need to do?

Keeping a journal brings light to hidden parts of yourself. You can discover lost parts of your soul. Your journal becomes a mirror reflecting your innermost Self. As illumination shines into the dark corners of your soul, you will begin to know better who you really are. Inner gifts, beauty, strength, power and wisdom are revealed as your friends and mentors. Journal-keeping gives form to the subtlest aspects of your being. Write daily or at times when you need a friend. I carry a notebook with me everywhere so I can write my thoughts and feelings whenever I choose. A journal by the bed allows you to wake up and immediately record dreams. Thoughts, feelings and images can be captured before they escape your mind. Your journal is for you only; write freely and openly in it. You need only share it if you wish to.

INCREASING AWARENESS AND SELF-KNOWLEDGE

All the above techniques increase awareness and Self-knowledge. What remains important is to maintain consciousness of internal changes as they take place. Whether it's through stillness in meditation or hunger from fasting or tension released during exercise, energy is flowing and speaking to you. In order to really Open to Spirit, you must hear the inner voice as it speaks. You must register subtle changes as they take place in your energy field. Everything is changing, including each one of us, the whole time. How do you want to change?

This is a good time to ask yourself the questions:

What do I want from my life?
What is my vision for myself, family, community and my environment?

It is paramount to develop a visual image of what you wish to create. Let the fine detail become clearer each day. **Perceive, believe, achieve.** As you journey consciously through the chakras you create what is seen within. A whole and beautiful inner vision gives rise to a rich reality, to wealth in body, mind and spirit. The external and the internal realms become aligned through spiritual practice. Heaven and Earth become one within your own unique being. Real knowledge is awareness of what is taking place energetically at any given time. All ancient traditions tell us this. If we are to increase our awareness and develop knowledge, then we must strive to be conscious in all we think, do and say. As you increase your own personal power, let your light shine out to brighten the path of all those you meet. Everything you do in the name of spirit will be of benefit to all life that shares our universe.

This chapter provides a broad foundation for spiritual development. Following these guidelines will prepare your vehicle for a safe ascent through the chakras. It also sets in place the tools and personal discipline required for Opening to Spirit. From here you can journey safely and successfully into the multidimensional spheres of your being and explore the extensive world of infinite spirit.

——— • ———

OPENING TO SPIRIT

—~— · —~—

THE CHAKRA
WORKBOOK

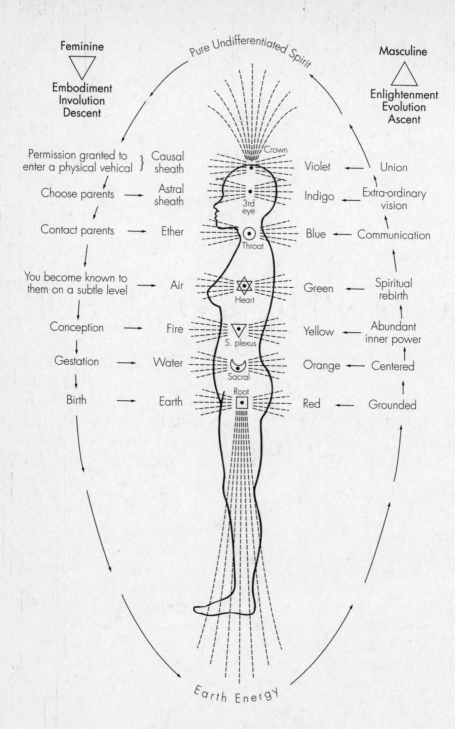

Embodiment to Enlightenment

THE SPIRITUAL JOURNEY

WE ARE EACH ON A UNIQUE JOURNEY THROUGH THE CHAKRAS, CALLED life. This journey is a cosmic dance, which begins and ends with the 'Eternal Spirit'. The main destinations are 'Embodiment' and 'Enlightenment'. From the realm of pure undifferentiated spirit we are granted permission to enter a physical vehicle – a chance to learn more lessons on the wheel of life and work through our karmic responsibilities. For this journey we require teachers who are already on the physical realm. Before birth, we in the astral realm look around and choose teachers who will help us work through our karma quickly – these teachers we make our parents. Once our choice is made we begin to make waves in the etheric field of our chosen parents. At this time they may be aware of our energetic presence or completely unconscious of our intentions. As we continue to journey our parents become more and more conscious of us; we are in their thoughts. They could be requesting a child from the realm of spirit or they could be trying to deny their desire to bring us down from spirit; either way we continue our descent and, through fire energy and, hopefully, love and passion, we are conceived. We grow in water for approximately nine months, before we are birthed and independently enter the physical realm. On arrival we are immediately ready and fully equipped to dance yet another earth dance. We are prepared to embody the life of the spirit.

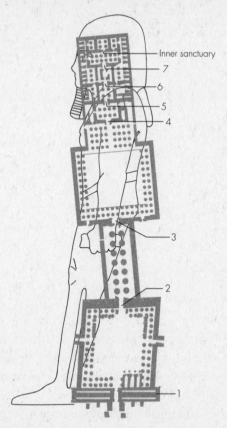

The sacred temple at Luxor superimposed over the sacred body of Osiris. The ancient Egyptians built their temples according to sacred geometry and ratios found in the physical body. The temple, like the body, was seen as the sacred home of the spirit (Ka).

To be fully embodied is to dance. The body is in constant motion. Every cell, tissue, organ and system keeps time with the cosmic rhythm. Energy pulses through and around each atom. Each tiny particle vibrates and dances. True embodiment is to know the unique cosmic dance of your body at all times, and move in ecstasy. All ancient cultures had sacred rituals involving movement and dance. All generations would join together to create ceremonies affirming their physical existence and celebrating the essential spiritual nature of their being. Spirit, which resides in the physical body, was awakened and raised to great heights. Body, mind and spirit were realigned and harmoniously experienced as one whole.

In contemporary societies, the felt experience of wholeness has all but paled into insignificance. We need to re-establish the cosmic, devotional experience of being in the body. This I refer to as true embodiment – being here, now, rejoicing in a physical body. Ecstasy is not an out-of-body experience, but a heightened sense of existing in the body. It is a felt sense that puts us in touch with our connection to the universe in all its glory. We are each tiny droplets of divinity and hold within us all the creative abilities of the Divine. Listening to the body and moving with both its gentle and its dynamic rhythms, helps develop a deep connection to the Self. As we retune our physical vehicle and come to know embodiment, we automatically move towards enlightenment.

As we become conscious of the spiritual significance of this precious journey we can reclaim our spiritual power, inner wisdom and truth. The journey, from body awareness to awareness of the soul, requires a transformation of consciousness. Spirit is to be received and expressed, as it manifests itself to you. Once spirit is embodied we must allow its voice to speak through us. The body is the sacred home of Spirit, a crystallized temple of vibrating energetic sound. The body is to be listened to and worked *with*.

Continuing on immediately from our descent into the physical realm is our journey back towards our source. On some level we all long to be permanently reunited with our creator. It is this longing that causes us grief and pain. We know what it is to exist in perfection and we seek that peaceful sensation each moment of every waking day. Unfortunately we often search in the wrong places. We hope that material goods, sexual partners, authority, power and success will bring the lasting happiness we so desperately desire. Of course these things bring us pleasure, but they also bring pain as we try hopelessly to hold on to them, as they begin to slip from our grasp. According to the Ancients, as long as we insist on seeking only external pleasures, lasting joy and bliss will continue to escape us.

As we involve ourselves in life we will learn many lessons. One of the greatest lessons we can learn is that life on the physical plane is limited and that, within these limitations, pain and constant change, there is a light that shines. This light shines from the Eternal Spirit. When we see this light and feel its inner warmth we are ready to recognize ourselves as Divine beings and make our ascent towards our creator.

The journey of evolution moves us through many vibrational shifts. At each of the chakras a lesson is learned and a different level of soul consciousness experienced. These lessons help us advance through life and allow us to Open to Spirit and experience consciousness as it manifests through the different chakras.

At the root chakra we learn the lesson of '*discipline*'. We have the ability to connect with our mother the earth and become grounded.

From this place of strength we begin our ascent to the sacral chakra, where we look into the waters of our soul and see our true reflection. From here we come to know the Divine Self with a capital S. We learn to *expand awareness* and locate a centre deep inside of calm intuition. When we fully open this chakra we can say we are truly centred and ready to move forward with wisdom.

As we ascend, we enter the solar plexus, the yellow centre of abundance. This is a place of challenge where we can learn to direct personal power into pursuits that will not only bring us satisfaction but also lift the vibrational energy around us. Fire energy can be positively used for the good of all beings that share our planet.

With the lesson of *responsibility to others* learned and the subsequent release of inner power we are ready to enter heart chakra consciousness. This is a place of spiritual rebirth. Here we have the opportunity to learn *devotion and compassion*.

The blue, throat chakra is the next level of soul consciousness. It is from here that we can communicate with all energies in and around us, incarnate and discarnate. We learn the lesson of *creation through sound*; the power of thought and word is known to us at this chakra.

As we continue our ascent we are moving closer to union with our creator. The third eye is a place of extended vision. Consciousness at this level brings awareness of life as it really is. The lesson we see is *unity in all things*.

As soul consciousness journeys from the third eye to the crown chakra it will become one with our creator. The journey is complete, but not finished.

It is my understanding that Spirit makes this circuit time and again during one lifetime. We continue to give birth to different aspects of ourselves. As we journey through life we move closer to spiritual understanding – no matter how wise or misguided we may be, life continues to move us closer to the Divine. I have worked with children, physically and mentally challenged people, the elderly, youths, prisoners, abused and abusers. I believe we are each continuously provided with the opportunity to glimpse enlightenment. Whatever path the soul takes, whatever position we hold in society, our inner potential is the same. Potential is always there, inviting us to evolve towards our creator.

The soul travels to earth and takes up residence in the physical body in order to experience pain, truth and ecstasy. It then returns again to pure spirit. I believe we repeat this cycle of involution and evolution until we reach a state of permanent enlightenment. Each new experience that moves us along our path needs to find embodiment. It needs to be totally absorbed into our being to be of use to us as we evolve.

Several clients I have worked with recently have been dealing with issues around grief and loss. Intellectually the continuum of Eternal Spirit was understood, yet the pain of their loss was physically excruciating and mentally tormenting. Learning to embody the knowledge of the Eternal Spirit takes time. Like all lessons, the new information and its energetic vibration needed to be absorbed into the whole system. It needed to step down through the healing space of ether (throat chakra) and become thought at the airy heart level, ready for conception at the fiery solar plexus. The energy then had to develop and be accepted by the watery emotions before a new understanding could be born and fully embodied at the root chakra. This embodiment leads to real change. After a slow involution, this new understanding could then evolve. As it becomes grounded at the root chakra, it can then be used to inform Self, creating changes in the sacral chakra. This knowledge becomes part of our abundant inner power, which fuels our spiritual evolution. Spiritual rebirth and enlightenment around this particular issue take place at the heart centre. As consciousness changes, communication on all levels opens up. At this point the despair is lifted and a vision of how things can be is clearly seen on the screen of the inner eye.

The journey is complete but not finished. Learning is ongoing. The spiritual journey is ongoing. Involution and evolution are ongoing. As we journey we see more, feel more and know more. Energy continues to move between embodiment and enlightenment until our karma is spent and we reside in Mahasamadhi. Meanwhile we will come to know more of our true Selves.

As we journey through life, energy can stagnate at any chakra. This may be during the phase of involution or evolution. We can experience difficulties as we try to ground ourselves or as we attempt to ground our individual lessons. Our difficulties will change at various times in our lives. Cleansing and working through all the chakras helps us to recognize energy blocks, clear the blockages and fully open the chakras, allowing them to resonate fully with the evolving soul consciousness.

— ∙ —

Please do not underestimate the powerful effects of chakra work. If your energy is too open and you are becoming overwhelmed, you may be receiving too much from the ether. If you experience this, return to root chakra work, work more slowly or stop altogether – your intuition will tell you which. It may be that you need to cleanse your system more through yoga breathing exercises (pranayama – *see Chapter 5*).

If you want to close your energy down, visualize each of the chakras, or a specific centre, as a flower head that opens and closes. Begin at the crown and work down to the root. See each flower gently closing down, all the petals slowly return to the centre. Energy still passes in and out as the flower breathes, but the central core is completely protected. Know that with your help, the universe will always keep you safe.

Part Two of this book offers numerous ways of working with the energies at each individual chakra. It is important, however, to appreciate that no chakra works independently of the others, just as no element is totally free of the others. Like instruments in an orchestra the chakras work together, creating harmonious music. If one instrument is out of tune it will affect the sound of the others. Disharmony in the root chakra will affect the tone of the sacral chakra above. When identifying blockages it is necessary also to work on the centres above and below the blocked chakra. Health is dependent on free flowing energy through all the chakras.

Chapters 6 to 12 form your chakra workbook. Each of these chapters is organized into two parts, and each part is divided into seven sections. A brief description of these sections is found below.

1. Chakras and their Correspondences

Main Function
This details the specific role of the chakra in the individual journey of the soul. In this section I also discuss the qualities of each chakra – such as centring, grounding, etc.
Element
The entire universe is made from energy. This energy is manifest in different forces known as elements – ether, air, fire, water and earth. The elemental force of each chakra is explained.
Planet
'As above, so below' tells us that the solar system exists within the body. Seven planets resonate through the chakras. The movement of the planets affects us all. I explain this in relation to each chakra.
Deities
In all cultures, Gods and Goddesses are known to preside over nature and different aspects of personal life. Deities of the chakras are introduced. These deities are to be honoured. Requests can be made to them and thanks given for their guidance.
Mythology
Joseph Campbell tells us that *'Myths are used to initiate the individual into the realities of his own psyche.'* I use mythology as a way of expounding the subtleties of the chakra psychology and also to demonstrate the common themes found in different cultures.
Expression
This section details how healthy, flowing energy positively affects each chakra.

Disturbance

This section explains how restrictions to the flow of energy limit health in specific areas.

2. Ways of 'Opening to Spirit'

Altar Work

This section gives guidelines for preparing altars. The aim is to harness the energy of the individual chakra you are working with at any given time. Your altar is used as a focal point, around which all chakra work can take place.

Journal-keeping

Exercises are suggested that encourage you to work in your journal. The focus will be on particular chakras. You can use writing, drawing, collage or any other way you feel happy exploring yourself creatively on paper.

Yoga Path

There are numerous approaches to yoga. They each differ in style but share the goal of uniting the individual *ba* (soul) with the universal *Ba*. Each chakra has a lesson we must understand and a yoga path that will help us learn that lesson.

Mindful Exercise

I introduce various physical exercises and energy exercises; these movements are to be performed with consciousness. They can be used to balance the flow of energy through a particular chakra.

Meditation

Ancient symbols belong to each centre. The symbols resonate with the vibrational energy of the individual chakras. Using these symbols, I teach meditations for each chakra. The dynamic practices were revealed to me during my own meditations.

Vibrational work

Subtle energy in the form of colour, gems and crystals, and essential oils can be used to support chakra work. The vibrations resonate directly with the energetic fields of the particular chakras. They are able to recharge energy, raise awareness, and effect physical change through the chakras and the aura.

Ritual

Ritual usually involves a ceremony capable of charging energy. I believe we all need ritual, whether we are initiated into a specific spiritual tradition or simply seeking more meaning in our lives. The rituals in this book are for everyone. Through ritual, we can both create and acknowledge change. We can develop awe and reverence for that which is greater than us. Ritual can be used conscientiously to mark the growth and development of all levels of our being. We can all reclaim the sacred practice of creating ritual.

Repeated practice of these exercises will feed and nurture your body, mind and soul. Allow between 20 minutes and one hour each day to enjoy your spiritual food. As energy is absorbed you will grow and change. Begin feeding your root chakra and slowly ascend to the crown.

The practices for each centre can be done in any order. You may want to meditate in the morning, stretch during the day, and write in your journal before retiring to bed at night. Explore until you find a way that works well for you.

Spiritual nourishment will eventually form an essential part of your daily routine. Your body will develop the ability to recognize spiritual hunger. This new appetite will cause you to gravitate towards your spiritual practice. Regular practice will ensure the gentle unfolding of your higher Self and lift the veil that conceals your infinite Divine nature.

ROOT CHAKRA

FOUNDATION FOR LIFE

Mother of all beings ... it is out of her watery depths that all life emerges, and in her caves and crevices that all potential life resides. Hers is the teaming womb of life, able endlessly to absorb and reabsorb, to create and regenerate. A perpetual source of cosmic fertility ... Woman and tree alike embody this great earth mother, for both are visible manifestations of her fruitfulness.

Roger Cook

THE ROOT CHAKRA: CORRESPONDENCES

Sanskrit Name	Muladhara
Meaning	Root/Support/Foundation
Main Function	Embodiment
Quality	Grounding
Location	Perineum in men – between the genitals and anus
	Cervix in women – between the vagina and uterus

Spiritual Correspondences

Colour	Red
Element	Earth
Symbol	Square, Symbol of the Four Directions: North, South, East and West
Seed Sound	Lam
Petals	Four[1]
Planet	Earth ⊕, Saturn ♄
Esoteric Anatomy	Physical manifestation of Core Energy
Yoga Path	Hatha Yoga, practised as part of Raja Yoga
Guna Quality[2]	Tamas (darkness and inertia)

Deities

Africa	Auset (Isis), Geb, Sekmet, Odùduwà, Onílé, Asaka
India	Shakti, Kundalini, Ganesha
Europe	Gaia, Persephone
All Earth Goddesses	
Mythology	Creation Myths

Physical Correspondences

Gland	Adrenals
Nerve Plexus	Coccygeal Plexus
Body Parts	Feet, legs, bones, spine
Earth Energy Triad[3]	Neck, large intestine, knees
Expression	Embodiment
Disturbance	Overbound (rigid)

Psychological Correspondences

Statement	'I have' (a physical body)

EMOTIONS

BALANCED	UNBALANCED
Safe	Fearful
Secure	Rigid

Excitement	Restriction
Acceptance of physical realm and its limitations	Held back
Sensational, alive	Lethargy, weighed down
Moved	Unmoving
Chronology	Birth – 1 year
Rite of Passage	Birth, naming, blessed by the Earth
Developmental Stage	Wise, dependent; still very connected to the Spirit World

Ways of Working

Foods	Root vegetables, pulses, heavy foods
Herbs	Comfrey, liquorice
Oils	Patchouli, cypress, vetivert
Gems	Red jasper, garnet, smoky quartz, obsidian, ruby, black star sapphire, red jade

The Descent from Spirit to Earth

Uninhibited energy flows from the crown chakra to the root chakra; it then returns from the root to the crown. The root chakra is, therefore, both the first ascending chakra and the final descending chakra. As energy descends, crystallization occurs and pure spirit becomes the body on the physical plane. As the waters around you break and the thunderous contractions of the womb come to an end, you are guided along a narrow passage. At the end of the passage, darkness becomes light. Born from woman, the mother, you complete your journey from pure spirit into earthly existence. Just as individuals are born from the mother's womb, so all of nature is born from our mother, the earth. Mother Earth is waiting to hold and support you from the very moment you are born into a physical body.

Main Function: Embodiment

We are all born with a body, yet simply owning a body is not enough: we need to be present in it. Embodiment means 'to fully enter your physical vehicle and experience life through it'. To experience and enjoy life within a physical body is the gift you are offered. The root chakra, when healthy, brings full expression to your physical existence. When we are born, most of us live happily in the body. Breathing is exercised to its optimum – the lungs expand and contract rhythmically. When hungry we eat, once satisfied we cease to eat. Elimination causes us few problems and, when we need rest, we sleep. We love attention and tactile stimulation, exulting in stroking, rocking and holding. As eye contact becomes important, we reach out and touch that which we see. For babies and young children the body is truly a temple in which to rejoice. The body offers so much, yet as we grow we become estranged from its expression and limit the energy that flows into the root chakra.

As we get older we easily become out of tune with the body's unique rhythm. We learn new patterns from our environment that do not always allow body/mind harmony. We may over-eat because other people are starving. Can you remember ever being told to 'finish up what's on your plate because other children are starving'? We may under-eat because it is not dinner time. Despite feeling hunger we tell ourselves it is not time to eat. Sleep can become distorted, either sleeping too much or not enough. We can drink an excess of tea, coffee and alcohol, and insufficient water. Breathing needs to be expansive (at least one breath out of five should be deep) yet we allow our breathing to be constantly shallow. Much of the time we do not realize our breathing is shallow because this has become the norm. The physical temple seems to be closed, with no caretaker.

Can I invite you into your wondrous temple right now? Take a breath, a deep one. Push your belly out as you inhale, breathe through your nose. Relax your jaw; release your shoulders and pelvis, let them both open. Uncross your knees, feet, arms and let them breathe. Let each finger breathe. Let each toe breathe. Take up some space – fill out your body. It is all yours and the only one you are going to have today, so enjoy it! Yield to the energy as it moves through you. Expand your muscles as you breathe. Gently close your eyes and for 5 minutes just listen to your body.

You may like to draw or write your sensations and thoughts in your journal, under the heading 'root chakra'.

Before the soul makes its ascent from matter back to spirit – from earth to heaven – we need to have arrived in the physical body. Our journey begins at the root chakra, working towards full embodiment. Being comfortable in the physical body means embracing the earth. Our bodies are moulded from the rich earth. We come in all shades, shapes and sizes, just as the Goddess does. Each one of us is unique and worthy of love. We are all here to recognize our individual gifts and celebrate them. You are meant to be here, dancing on the lap of the Goddess. You do not need to hang your head low, or be afraid of eye contact. You do not have to hold in your belly or hunch up your shoulders. There is plenty of space just for you – take as much as you need. Practise filling your temple, spreading out a little bit, and taking up more space in your body. Try wearing less restrictive clothing. Choose natural fibres when possible, so that your body can breathe.

As you own your space, life changes. Your posture will improve and your internal organs will be able to function to their optimum. Energy in babies or small children is free to flood the body and excite it. Adults can also feel alive and vibrant, when the life of the spirit is truly embraced by the body.

As your energy opens, people will respond to you differently. Your vibration has the power to bring out a positive vibration in those around you. Some people, however, may be afraid. People who hold their own energy back feel challenged by those who let energy flow, even attempting at times to restrict them. Children are often restricted in this way.

Let's say we all have the potential to shine like a 100-watt bulb, but some of us only put out 40 watts. When we see someone shining to their full 100 watts, it seems so very bright that we reach for the dimmer switch. We want to turn them down because we are not used to that much brightness. Some of us would prefer everyone else to turn down their energy rather than brightening up ourselves.

Think back to a time when you were fully in your body and shining bright. It may have been very recently, or maybe it was in your childhood. Try to remember the environment you were in ... Are you alone, among friends or with strangers? How are you holding your body? Be aware of the sensations you experienced. How long did those feelings last? What changed?

As I do this exercise I remember a recent time when I sat by the great Ọ̀sun River in Nigeria. Alone in the silence, I tuned my energy to the Goddess Ọ̀sun, who resides in the water. My body was still, and perched on the raised root of a majestic tree, which was so alive in that sacred grove. I felt totally elated. The stillness and silence reassured me. In that moment I was one with everything. I felt my body pulsing with the forces of nature. I let spirit fill my entire being and rejoiced as I gave thanks for my existence. I felt my guides with me and I knew I would be assisted on my journey. As I walked back to the bustling town of Ọ̀sogbo, the silence faded. My sense of stillness also faded from consciousness, but the safety and reassurance remain. These brief moments made me aware of the wonder of embodiment and the necessity of grounding.

QUALITY: GROUNDING

As we extend our roots down into the belly of the earth, she gives us strength to grow tall. Secure in her love, we make our ascent. When observing children, we see that as a child grows away from its mother: it starts by crawling a little way, then returning to make contact with the mother. Reassured that the mother is still present, the child will venture further. This pattern continues as we develop. The first day at school we need to know that mummy will collect us when the day ends. When adolescence arrives we want a parent close to push against. Eventually we leave the family nest, but often require mother's approval to top up our sense of security. Each time she affirms her love we can go further away and develop ourselves.

Our mother, the earth, provides a similar function, known as grounding. Grounding is about drawing energy from the earth. Like tree roots, the root chakra acts as a pump that conveys energy. This energy circulates through the nadis into the feet, legs and the entire body. Connecting deeply with the earth brings reassurance. This is seen in common expressions such as:

Stand on your own two feet
Stand up for yourself
Stand up to...
Stand up for what you believe in

These expressions all refer to the root chakra and grounding. We talk of standing our ground, maintaining enough inner security to allow us to move from a place of connectedness. When firmly grounded we feel safe because we cannot fall, we are already on the earth. If we get too airy, or ethereal, losing touch with the ground, then we risk falling. We each stand on the earth and in this way she unites us. At the same time it is the crystallized energy of earth that creates the illusion of separateness.

The symbol representing the root chakra is a square, which symbolizes the four directions – North, South, East and West. When an individual is grounded he or she can choose to move in any direction. In a difficult situation, a well-grounded person acts mindful and doesn't simply 're-act'. There are two primary modes of action we can take when times are hard – **acceptance** or **change**. We either surrender or shift. Working on the root chakra helps us to feel grounded and therefore clear about which primary action to take.

The desire for spiritual development sometimes masks the importance of grounding. The Ancients knew the necessity of contact with the earth. For this reason, drumming and dancing were used in ritual. Through such ritual, the vibration and heartbeat of the earth can be felt, and grounding established.

Kundalini

The serpent Goddess Kundalini resides in the root chakra. The Goddess lies coiled up three and a half times. This harnesses her power. When uncoiled, she rises up the Shushumna, conferring psychic gifts at each chakra until finally she reaches the crown. It is from awakening this reserve of energy in the root chakra and allowing her subsequent flight to the crown chakra that we achieve lasting enlightenment.

This book is not so much about raising Kundalini as it is about raising awareness. Working with Kundalini is best practised with the supervision of an experienced teacher. Intensive work on releasing Kundalini energy can raise unexpected psychological issues (roots = unconscious). With personal guidance and self-discipline the unleashing of Kundalini can be very powerful. Focusing on expanding awareness can be as beneficial and as beautiful as unlocking Kundalini, without the potential danger. Initially, we prepare our vehicle; then the whole system becomes familiar with the flow of energy from the root to the crown and vice versa. It is quite possible that, as you develop awareness and the chakras fully open, Kundalini will naturally find her place in the Shushumna and rise gracefully.

Element: Earth

Earth is the crystallization of spirit into form – the densest of all elements. The quality of earth is one of permanence and stability. As children of the earth, our wealthy mother provides us with ground on which to stand, food to eat and building materials for shelter. She is responsible and caring. Having thought of the problems we might face, she is well prepared. She organizes her plants in such a way that, if one upsets us, we will find another plant close by that will make us feel better again, like the stinging nettle and dock leaf. She has created a whole pharmacy of healing plants for us to discover. Like all good mothers, she is dependable and nurturing. Having supplied the basics, she shares with us a treasury of gold, precious stones and healing gems.

The earth element manifests within us as a desire to be rich like our mother. We seek structure, survival and the possession of wealth and wisdom. For people with strong earth energy, routine and a secure home life are of paramount importance. They will be great homemakers, providing regular meals with plenty of pudding! Managers, housekeepers and teachers – those responsible for organizing others – tend to have strong earth energy. We all know someone who is **down to earth** – no **airs** and **graces**. A person who is not afraid to get on with the basic things in life. That person is likely to be very practical and organized. They are seldom accused of being **airy** – all talk and no action. They are courageous people who can be relied upon to get things done. Earth energy creates form; it makes thoughts manifest. Without earth energy, 'no-thing' would exist.

Insufficient earth energy leaves you feeling lethargic, disorganized and not quite sure of your direction in life. Consequently, you will lack confidence, and fear will take hold. Completing projects, achieving goals and generally getting things done will be difficult when earth energy is not flowing. Oversleeping, overeating, addictive behaviour and lack of motivation are all signs of earth energy depletion.

When a person has an excessive amount of earth energy, they will be extremely rigid and possessive. He or she can be very controlling and persuasive. Work and money acquire the status of Gods for this person. He or she has the staying power of an elephant, which is the animal associated with the root chakra. Such a person is dominated by fear.

Either of these earth element distortions can manifest as complete inertia, a heaviness that leaves you feeling weighed down and held back – which is exactly what is happening physically. You will have a tendency to lower back pain, sciatica and depression. We all know the common syndrome of feeling stuck, 'I cannot change because ...' If any of this sounds familiar to you, start working on your root chakra straight away.

Planet: Saturn ♄

The ancient Egyptians called this planet Heru-Ka-Pet, the planet of Horus. It is believed in many spiritual traditions that, before birth, we make a pact in the spirit world. In Yorùbá, 'Orí' refers to both head and destiny. Prior to gestation we choose the sacred head, which holds our life path. We also agree on the lessons we are prepared to learn in this incarnation. Once we arrive on earth, although we may forget any such agreements, we still carry with us the tasks we chose to complete in this lifetime. Harmony between Saturn (external force) and the root chakra (internal force) helps us to achieve our individual destinies.

If spirit and liberation are the domain of the sun, then earth is the domain of Saturn. Saturn is the lord of karma[4] and bestower of gifts. He holds us to earth while we honour agreements made in the spirit world. He willingly shares with us earthly wisdom, and time in which to gather it. Discipline, responsibility and service are lessons taught by this great teacher.

Most of us have a desire to be of service to other human beings. When energy flows freely through the root chakra, it becomes open to the planetary energies of Saturn. The root chakra and the vibrations of Saturn bind us to the earth and help us manifest our destiny, by revealing the innate gifts we have to offer the world.

Deities

Earth Goddesses from all traditions relate to the root chakra. They personify numerous aspects of the earth's power. Knowing something of the different deities can help you understand the attributes of the root chakra. Root chakra deities can be thanked and praised for our very existence, for they are the great creators. Deities you feel an affinity with can be invoked for protection, healing and guidance.

An invocation might go like this: Call the name of the deity three times –

Oníle, Oníle, Oníle.
Then praise the deity –
Mother of the Earth
Blessed Mother of all beings
Owner of the secrets of the land.
Beautiful one, on which we all stand.
Be with me now.
Then ask for a blessing –
Sacred Mother, hold me in your loving hands
Fill me with your Divine power, teach me your ways.
Heal me. Make me whole again.
Peace* – Alafia – Hetep – Shanti
Practise invoking the loving energy of the deities in your own special way.
* Peace in Yorùbá, Ancient Egyptian and Sanskrit respectively.

AUSET[5] (ISIS)

Egyptian creatress, Divine mother and guardian of all beings. She is the giver of life and death. Healing, transformation, magic and wisdom are her secrets. Auset can be invoked to celebrate births and as an aid to all acts of creation and health maintenance.

GEB

Egyptian God of earth. Geb provides the physical foundation, while Auset provides emotional support. He represents the mountains and high places on the earth's surface. He is the father of Ausar (Osiris), Auset, Set and Nephys, with their mother the sky Goddess Nut.

SEKHMET

Her name means 'the powerful'. She is the mighty lion Goddess aspect of Hathor. She is the Sphinx, capable of destruction and annihilation. In ancient times, those with the ability to destroy were often, in addition, great healers. Sekhmet cured fractures and took care of bone ailments. Consequently, those who worked with bones were attached to her cult. Sekhmet can be invoked when seeking physical healing for Self or others.

ODÙDUWÀ

Odùduwà is the creator of earth in Yorùbá oral history. With only a few grains of earth and a chicken, the world was formed from the primordial waters. Odùduwà is sometimes referred to as female and the wife of Ọbàtálá, who is credited with creating people. Odùduwà is the first Ancestor of the Yorùbá people and therefore deified as an Òrìshà.

ONÍLÉ

Translates as 'owner of the earth'. This Yorùbá Goddess supports people during their lives and receives them into her belly at the time of death. For this reason, Onílé is also associated with the Ancestors. She is Goddess of the Ogboni cult, who preserve law and order.

ASAKA

Mama Earth Asaka sings these words to her children:

> ...Sit on Mama's lap
> And I will draw a map
> And whatever you need
> Mama will provide!
> I'll provide you...
> Moss!
> To soften the road.
> Rocks!
> To sit on.
> Trees!
> To sleep underneath.
> Sand!
> Fun for your toes.
> Plantain!
> To fill up your belly!
> Breeze!
> To fan your face.
> Grass!
> For making your bed
> ...whatever your need
> Mama will provide!
> > *Asaka Story Tellers*[6]

Benin Mother Goddess

SHAKTI

Dravidian Goddess and feminine principle of manifest energy. She is the life-force that animates her partner, Shiva. Together they bring about creation, preservation and destruction. Shakti's cosmic energy moves from the base chakra to the crown chakra, where she unites with Shiva. As she ascends through each chakra, she delivers her powerful force and changes her name and quality. (Look out for these changes in the following chapters.) Nothing has life without Shakti's consent.

KUNDALINI

Below is a description of the Goddess by Swami Sivananda:[7]

> Kundalini is glorified by all. She herself, when awakened by the Yogi, achieves illumination for him. It is She who bestows liberation and knowledge, for She is that herself. She is the source of all knowledge and bliss. She is pure consciousness itself. She is Brahman. She is Prana Shakti, the supreme force, the mother of Prana, fire, sound and the source of all things.

GANESHA

This elephant-headed God is the son of Shiva and Parvati. Ganesha is known as 'lord of hosts' and 'remover of obstacles'. It is no surprise to find him guarding the root chakra. His physical strength and spiritual wisdom can be called upon before any task is undertaken. If you want to move forward successfully, then Ganesha will make the way clear. He is a popular deity, honoured throughout India. In Egypt there also existed an elephant God and 'Lord of hosts'.[8] Elephantine was the name given to the sacred city where his worship was prevalent.

GAIA

Goddess of the earth in Greek mythology. Gaia is known as 'the deep-breasted one'. She has the same qualities as Earth mothers preceding her.

PERSEPHONE

The Goddess Persephone is queen of death and the underworld. She symbolizes energy when it passes below the root chakra into a place of deep depression and disillusionment. Jung called this 'the dark night of the soul' – the place we enter through endless pain and desperation. Eventually, a part of us dies and we lose our grip on things. It is this letting go, this surrender, which bestows on us great secrets. We learn of non-attachment to worldly pleasures and material gain. With this lesson understood, we are cleansed and spiritually reborn like Persephone, who after spending several months in the underworld, is born again in spring. The Goddess Persephone can help us confront grief and despair.

Mythology

YORÙBÁ CREATION MYTH

Olódùmárè, the Supreme Being, is pure energy. From his expression of energy, Olódùmárè created the universe. He created the sky where he lives and his companions, the Òrìshà, who live with him. Below the sky is the ocean, inhabited by its owner, the Òrìshà Olókun.

Ọbàtálá, ruler of the mind, is a thoughtful Òrìshà. One day, he considered that Olókun might be lonely and in need of company. He consulted Ọ̀rúnmìlà, God of divination, who, after reading the oracle, agreed that life should be created in Olókun's watery realm below the sky. Ọbàtálá was instructed by Olódùmárè to descend to the waters and create life. He descended along a chain and carried with him a huge globe, which he placed in the water. Immediately it broke into pieces and formed mountains and islands. Very soon 'agbon' grew, the palm tree from which Ọbàtálá made palm wine. He enjoyed plenty of wine, forgot his task and proceeded to fall asleep. Olódùmárè was not pleased and sent his daughter Odùduwà, Goddess of the earth, to put things right. Ajé, Goddess of money and wealth, accompanied her. Ajé took the form of a chicken and immediately got to work scratching up earth and sending it in all directions. The places where earth fell became expanses of land created and owned by Odùduwà. Odùduwà took seeds given her by her father and scattered them on the land. Plants, trees and flowers grew in abundance. Seeing that earth was at last created, Olódùmárè leaped down from the sky. The holy place where his feet landed became known as Ilè Ifè, 'the land of love'. This is the original home of the Yorùbá people, from where they migrated to all parts of Yorùbá land.

Obàtálá eventually woke and saw that Odùduwà had completed his work. Together they enjoyed the fruits of the land, until they became lonely and decided to create humankind. After they searched unsuccessfully for a suitable material, Ọbàtálá dug clay from the earth and started moulding people. Each creation was left to dry in the sun. Olódùmárè touched the figures with the breath of life and people came alive on Odùduwà's earth.

To this day Ọbàtálá and Odùduwà watch over all people. Odùduwà is honoured as the mother and first Ancestor of the Yorùbá people,[9] and Ọbàtálá is said to shape the unborn child in the womb of its mother.

Expression

When energy is permitted to flow freely through the root chakra, a person will feel:

down to earth and grounded

steadfast

stable

safe

practical

courageous

loving of life and nature

able to take risks

comfortable in a physical body

accepting of limitations

contained

separate

alone (as distinct from lonely)

non-attached

pain – emotional, spiritual, physical

able to let go

healthy in the feet, legs, bones, spine, knees, neck and large intestine

embodied

full of energy and life

structured and organized

generous

loyal.

Disturbance

Restricted energy flow in the root chakra can cause:

rigidity

fear of change

stubbornness

laziness

nervousness and a lack of confidence

a dislike of things natural such as getting wet, dirty, naked, flatulent, over-excited

a tendency to hoard

over-attachment

materialism

dissatisfaction

a dislike of your own body

Physically, insufficient energy in the root chakra can cause:

a tendency towards illness

haemorrhoids

constipation

sciatica

back pain

knee problems

obesity and weight problems

obsessional and addictive behaviour (drugs, alcohol, etc.)

phobia

lethargy

depression

tiredness and a shortage of energy

excessive demands on Self and others

greed

The root chakra offers a firm foundation. When energy flows, we feel safely anchored to our mother, the earth. Through her nurturing we receive the inner strength needed to project ourselves in any direction we choose. We know the body as a place of joy and we revel in it. If root chakra energy becomes damned up, then we are afraid to do anything. We cling tightly to what we know, fearing change. We stay in jobs that give us no satisfaction, and in relationships that seriously damage our health. We can literally strain muscles in the back, legs, knees and toes holding on and trying not to move forward. *Stand up for a moment and try to stop yourself going forward. Feel the tension that is created in your body.* This is what is known in emotional anatomy as 'overbound'. On the other hand, when energy is not rooted enough, we cannot hold on to a job or a relationship; we are simply too flighty. There is no staying power, no connection to the earth. Such a person may have a tendency to back pain and weakness in the joints of the lower body. Fear underlies both these scenarios. Root chakra-associated imbalance is one of the main challenges in modern society. Our reliance on material wealth has seriously distorted root chakra health.

SEVEN WAYS OF 'OPENING TO SPIRIT' AT THE ROOT CHAKRA

Altar Work

Prepare your altar to harness earth energy. It helps to take a walk in a garden, park or the countryside and tune to the element you are working with. To form the base of your altar, use an earth-coloured cloth. Remember that soil comes in many beautiful shades – brown, red, rust, fawn, yellow, black and white; any of these colours can be used. Cloth that is dyed using earth, such as mud cloth from Mali, is obviously a great conductor of earth energy.

If at all possible, build your altar on the floor; this will cause you to spend time close to the earth. You may even wish to make your earth altar outside, in your garden.

Once you have a base, place four red candles in the cardinal directions (north, south, east and west). Choose woody incense such as sandalwood, cypress or cedarwood. If you prefer, essential oils can be used in a burner. Smell is important for this altar, because, of the five senses, it is smell that relates to the root chakra. Place water on your altar. Crystals for the root chakra are red jasper and smoky quartz. However, earth energy is present in all crystals. Any stones you are fond of have a home on your earth altar. Use pictures of relevant deities such as Auset or other archetypal earth or mother Goddesses. Be creative – if something resonates with earth for you, find space for it.

Your altar is a focal point for spiritual work, so issues that you are working with should be represented. Health, the home and finances are all issues relating to earth. For physical healing, place your photo on the altar or that of the person who needs healing. To improve finances, offer money to the creator. Leave the money on your altar (it can be used later to buy spiritual items, such as your altar candles, etc.). Positioning these items on your altar creates the energy for change, and reminds you what you need to focus on. Whatever you offer will return to you tenfold.

Journal-keeping

DRAW A TREE

This is a creative drawing exercise. You will need a large sheet of plain paper and some coloured crayons or paints. Prepare your materials and find time for yourself. Allow yourself 5 minutes to draw a tree – be spontaneous, because instinctive creations will be most valuable. After 5 minutes, stop and look at your work. Ask yourself the following questions:

- What is my first impression?
- What is this tree saying to me?
- Is this tree beautiful, happy, strong, young, old, dull, colourful?
- How much space does this tree take up within the space available?
- Are there any roots? Do they touch the earth? Is this tree grounded?
- Is the tree alone or connected with other life?
- Are there any leaves, flowers, fruits, birds?

Record the answers in your journal; then ask the questions again, only this time relate them directly to yourself. What you see and feel about your tree will reflect some qualities of your personality. A colourful tree that takes up the full sheet of paper may have a colourful extroverted creator, while a tiny tree in a corner, looking a bit sad, may have a lonely creator with a poor sense of Self. It should not be difficult for you to gain some personal insights from your picture. Remember that the drawing reflects you at the time you drew it, and is not a rigid statement. On another day your tree may look quite different.

To take this exercise a step further, draw another tree. This is a tree you can aspire to. Choose your colours carefully and be clear about how much space you need and how close to other life you want to be. This is your ideal tree. When it is complete you can display the two tree drawings together. You will then easily see where you are now and where it is you are going.

Yoga Path

HATHA YOGA

When people in the West refer to yoga, they usually mean hatha yoga. Hatha yoga involves a series of stretches – many are based on animals relaxing or stretching after rest. It also focuses on breath awareness, concentration and relaxation. This physical discipline has won much popularity because of its numerous health benefits. The physical body can be rejuvenated through the practice of yoga. The muscular-skeletal system is toned and strengthened. Nerves are calmed. The immune and circulatory systems improve their cleansing effect on the body. Digestion and respiration increase their function of carrying nutrition to all cells. The endocrine system, which we know relates closely to the chakras, is re-balanced.

It is easy to see why hatha yoga is successful in alleviating numerous physical ailments such as back pain, headaches and digestive problems. The spiritual aim of hatha yoga is to draw together the polarities of *Ha* – solar energy – with *Tha* – lunar energy. This unification leads to enlightenment. However, hatha yoga by itself is not necessarily enough to reach *Samadhi*[10] (enlightenment). Hatha yoga – which consists of *asanas* (steady postures) – is traditionally practised as the third rung on an eight-step ladder towards unity. The first two steps concern attitude to spiritual development. As humans we have the gift of will and choice, as spiritual beings we have a response-ability to use our will with love and respect for Self and all creation. Adhering to the *yamas* and *niyamas* (*see below*) brings personal integrity, which is fundamental to spiritual growth. The remaining six steps are stages that lead to self-knowledge and wisdom. These eight steps are collectively known as Astanga yoga – the eight-fold path of the sage Patanjali. It is also called Raja yoga – the royal path of yoga.

THE EIGHT STEPS OF PATANJALI

1 Yamas (Social codes)
    non-violence
    truthfulness
    no stealing
    moderation in all things
    non-possessiveness
2 Niyamas (Personal codes)
    purity
    contentment
    austerity
    study of classical yogic texts and other scriptures
    constant awareness of the higher Self.
3 Asana: physical discipline
4 Pranayama: breathing practice
5 Pratyahara: withdrawal of the senses and stilling of the mind
6 Dharana: concentration
7 Dhyana: meditation
8 Samadhi: peaceful union with the universal Self

The traditional function of hatha yoga is to cleanse and strengthen the body. The vehicle is then prepared for the increase in energy that will flow as a result of further spiritual practice. Chapter 5 introduces some simple stretches and breathing techniques. The exercises below can be added to those in Chapter 5, creating a short, daily hatha yoga programme. The best results are attained when hatha yoga becomes a daily ritual. Each day, light your candles, say a prayer and begin your practice.

The main lesson hatha yoga teaches is discipline and steadfastness. These qualities form the basis of spiritual growth. In ancient Egyptian spirituality, the hieroglyphic for steadfastness is the Djed pillar. This symbol combines a tree with its branches cut off, and in their place is the severed sacrum of Osiris. This shows the stability of the tree fused with the sacred essence of God. The symbol relates to the root chakra and its potential for providing a strong foundation from which to grow towards the Divine.

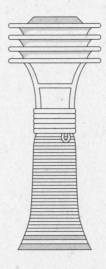

Djed pillar – symbol of steadfastness

CLASSIC YOGA SITTING POSTURE

Working with the chakras requires the aspirant to have a straight back whenever possible. This facilitates the flow of energy along the spine. Classic yoga sitting postures are used to develop the muscles of the back. When the posture is firm and steady you will be able to sit in meditation for a prolonged period, without discomfort. All the postures below have a strengthening effect on the root chakra. They each help energy to flow between the body and the earth, which develops grounding.

EGYPTIAN CHAIR POSE

Sit upright in a high-backed chair, keeping your spine lengthened. Gaze directly in front of you. Rest your hands, palms upwards, on your knees and gently close your eyes. Create a right angle at the knee and have both feet placed firmly on the floor. Maintain an upright and relaxed posture.

SUKHASANA (EASY POSE)

Sit on the floor on the edge of a cushion, with your back upright and your legs folded in front of you. No matter how stiff you are now, continued practice will bring results. When I first did this posture, my knees were around my ears. I could not sit at all without falling backwards. Eventually my knees went down and ceased to complain, even when I tied them into the lotus pose.

Sukhasana (Easy Pose)

THE BUTTERFLY

To warm up for the lotus pose, sit with the soles of your feet together, your knees falling out to the sides. Gently flap your knees up and down like butterfly wings. Keep your back upright; rest for a moment and then repeat. Continue for a few minutes.

The Butterfly

PADMASANA (LOTUS POSE)

Sit with your legs outstretched and separated by about 3 feet (1 metre). Keeping your spine erect, bend one knee and lift your foot onto the opposite thigh. Turn the sole of your foot towards the ceiling as much as you can. Now bring the second foot in and put it under the opposite thigh (to form the half-lotus) or over the thigh (for the full lotus).

Caution: this posture is difficult and it may be appropriate to attend classes or see a yoga instructor. Do not try to force your legs into this position. Allow yourself time and sufficient practice.

Padmasana (Lotus Pose)

TRIKONASANA (TRIANGLE)

Stand with your feet about 3 feet (1 metre) apart. Turn your right foot out, at a 90-degree angle and place your left foot in, at a 60-degree angle. Raise your left arm straight up alongside your head. Hold your right arm alongside your right leg. Now bend sideways to your right. Stretch your right arm downwards along your leg, stretching your left arm upwards all the time. Hold the posture for three deep breaths, then reverse position and repeat to your left. Repeat the posture on each side.

Trikonasana (Triangle)

Mindful Exercise

Some simple exercises can be used to tap into the earth's powerful energy. When done mindfully, these exercises resonate on a deep level of your inner being.

Nature speaks to us personally at all times, but we seldom listen. As you listen to the sound of nature you will hear messages that have the power to uplift and transform you.

WALKING SOFTLY ON THE EARTH

At some time in our lives we have all enjoyed walking barefoot in the sand or running swiftly through long grass. We have savoured the view from a hill or mountain-top after a leisurely climb. Some of us have scaled the peaks of Everest, while others wander in valleys of green. We have walked all over the body of the Goddess, stroking her with our feet. We have felt great peace and freedom in her embrace. Can you remember when last you walked softly on the earth?

I invite you to walk upon her body with awareness, feeling her flesh and her curves with your whole being. Let her energy flow into your feet and embrace you. Let sand run through your toes. Be aware of your breath as you walk. Listen carefully to her voice as she speaks to you. Walk in the garden, park, woods, countryside, city, wherever you can. Go out and enjoy communing with our mother, the earth. Dance with her sacred rhythm. If you have the freedom to dance naked under the moonlight, then so be it.

Wise people were once killed for loving her – the beloved Ancients of Africa, Asia, Australia, America and Europe. These people knew the pleasure of feeling the earth alive. Their ways have not died. We need no longer be afraid to love our mother and show our affection openly.

EMBRACING THE EARTH

I remember as a child how I loved being buried in the sand, immobilized by the sheer weight. The cold sand slowly became warm from the heat of my body, allowing me to relax. My head stuck out and I observed passers-by. Eventually my laughter would cause the sand to crack and I would lift myself out. Once I was out, digging began again and someone else would find themselves buried, this was such great fun. I didn't know then that this was very much like and ancient initiation ceremony.

Embracing the earth is, simply, to lay your belly, clothed or naked, to the belly of the earth. Put your ear to the ground and stretch your arms out – with your whole being embrace the earth, feel her vibration and listen to her message.

BODY AS A TREE

UPSIDE DOWN TREE

The spiritual body is often associated with trees. Just as energy travels up and down the trunk of a tree, the universal life-force passes up and down the spine, connecting us to heaven and earth. Our feet, like the roots of a tree, can connect us to our mother the earth. Our hair/spiritual antennae connect us to the heavenly creative force.

Headstand, the king of yoga postures, when mastered becomes a meditative position that stimulates energy in the crown chakra.

In yoga this is the 'imperishable tree'. We must climb this mystical tree with its roots/source in the heavens in order to obtain the truth.

HUGGING A TREE

Like humans, different trees have different energies. Some are old enough to know many secrets. Steadfastness is one of the secrets trees have mastered. Since this is the lesson of the root chakra, why not ask a tree for help? Go into a park or wood near your home and, as you wander around, choose a tree which has an energetic quality you like. Adopt your chosen tree.

I have adopted a beautiful old oak tree, which was severely damaged after powerful gales swept through England in 1987. This tree crashed and split into two. Only the stump remained of a tree that had stood proud for hundreds of years. Its beauty lay dying on the ground, separated from its roots. Slowly, from that stump, tiny buds began to appear, then leaves and branches. This tree retained its power to heal. Now a beautiful young oak grows from the stump, supported by its elder. I love this tree; it resonates and speaks to me of my own personal journey and the collective journey of Africans in the diaspora.

Make the tree your own. Bring gifts and lay them in its branches or bury them at its roots. Let the tree shade you and protect you. Hold its image in your body/mind at times of weakness. Decorate your home with its dried leaves. Draw courage and whatever you need from your tree by meditating beneath it or dancing around it. Hug your tree; place your back on it when you need to draw power and strength from it. Feel its energy fill your body. When giving thanks for its service to you, hold your belly to its trunk in a warm embrace. Always listen carefully to the sacred whisperings of your tree.

Meditation

> ...meditation involves far more than sitting with eyes closed in concentration ... it demands rigorous introspection and an overhauling of one's personality, life patterns and values.
>
> *Swami Vishnudevananda*[11]

As mentioned earlier, each chakra has it own specific symbol. When used in meditation these symbols resonate at various frequencies. The related chakra can be fully opened and energy permitted to enter the Shushumna, purely by meditating on these symbols. I introduce two methods of meditation:

⦿ The first is dharana, a yogic concentration technique.
⦿ The second is a dynamic meditation, using the chakra symbols.

Dharana is a technique where the mind is asked to focus on one point. Focusing is a means to meditation. Meditation is a state of consciousness; it is not concentration, or action, or focusing, visualizing or doing of any kind. Likewise the dynamic meditation is a tool that focuses on the symbol and the internal experience that is created. With experience both techniques lead to meditation. Meditation is simply to **Be**. (The word meditation is used here and in general to describe both the practice and the result. Traditionally it only referred to the result.)

DHARANA
The symbol for the root chakra is a square. It is red in colour and has at its centre the Black Dot.[12] This Dot is the Dark Seed of all creation. Prepare for meditation, following the guidelines in Chapter 5. With your eyes lightly closed, focus on the black screen in front of your eyes (*chidakash*). Slowly visualize the square – symbol of the root chakra – appearing on the screen; define it in your mind's eye, the four sides, the corners, its red colour and the Black Dot in the middle. Bring the symbol clearly into your vision. Now rest your focus on the Black Dot. Hold your mind still and maintain the image for your chosen time. I suggest you begin with a few minutes and increase the time with experience.

DYNAMIC MEDITATION
Begin your practice as above. Clearly define the square in your mind's eye. Now visualize this symbol as the base on which you sit. Feel the sensation as the symbol and your root chakra become one. Feel the square on the earth and your body on

the square. Become the Black Dot. Feel the square getting larger as you exhale; your body is shrinking as you inhale. Feel the pulsation of your body as your consciousness changes. You are the Black Dot in the centre. The square is the base of an inverted pyramid, with its apex buried deep in the belly of the earth. Feel your connection to the earth. Feel the vibration around you. Tune to the greater forces of the earth and draw energy through the pyramid and into your root chakra and your entire being ... As you near the end of your meditation, sense the pyramid and the square shrinking. Feel your body expand with pulsating energy. Sense the charge in your root chakra and gently deepen your breath. Follow the movement of energy as it flows through and around you. Be still and know that you are one with the earth.

Both of these meditations increase awareness of your root chakra. As energy flows uninterrupted through the root, you will feel yourself standing on a firm foundation. You may still know fear, but it will not prevent you from moving forward. The gift of steadfastness will go with you; your decisions will become actions. You will have the ability to gently create change in your life, when change is needed. Strength will be yours, allowing you to accept parts of yourself you have found difficult to own in the past. Innate personal gifts will be revealed to you. A new path will be opened and your direction in life will become visible. Nothing stays the same once you Open to Spirit. Through regular practice and a clear vision of your direction in life, the root chakra energy will make that vision manifest.

Vibrational Work

One of the simplest ways to begin effecting change in your energy field is through using vibrational support. With a few careful guidelines, remedies can be safely self-administered. Colour, crystals and essential oils can all be used. I have found them all useful in a number of ways. They each have the ability to penetrate the aura and create change on a subtle level.

COLOUR

Red is the colour associated with the root chakra. Firstly, examine your relationship to red. Do you have much red in your wardrobe, in your home, or in your food? Have you ever worn a lot of red? If so, what was happening in your life at that time? What emotion does the colour red raise in you? What does this mean to you? Decide whether there is a shortage or excess of red. To create balance, you can adjust the use of the colour generally in your life. Gradually add to or reduce your use of red, as it feels appropriate.

Red is often associated with fear and danger. Excessive use of red can act as a protective barrier, keeping the dangerous world at bay and holding people at a distance. It is a powerful colour, suggesting assertion and confidence. It is also a vital, passionate, stimulating colour with real warmth to it. Through root chakra work the positive quality of red can be integrated into your personality.

Seeing Red

This is a creative exercise that can be fun, either to do alone, or with children. Find as many shades of red as possible, and make a collage in your journal, or on a large sheet of paper. You can use red paper, paints, fabric, scraps – anything you can find. Give yourself permission to enjoy and express. The process of finding, gathering and making is more important than the end result.

Colour tinctures can be bought, such as the Aurosoma colour bottles, which contain half oil and half water, with the essence of colour, herbs and gems. The root chakra bottle is a beautiful deep magenta. The preparation can be rubbed onto the body, or a few drops can be poured into a bath or placed on your hands before meditation. The colour activates the frequency of your root chakra and aura. Likewise, visualization on the colour red will also raise the energetic vibration of the root chakra.

ESSENTIAL OILS

Capturing healing fragrances from flowers, trees, fruits, herbs and grasses is an ancient science. Essential oils are regarded as the life-force of plants, and therefore communicate directly with the human life-force. Aromatics were used by the Ancients for healing, removing evil spirits, raising spiritual awareness, purification, protection, ritual and pleasure. 'Evil Spirit' is a collective term that covers all manner of negative energies, such as lack of spiritual alignment, poisonous thoughts and physical disease. Many such energetic disturbances were treated with essential oils. The ancient Egyptians were renowned for their use of oils and knowledge of the spiritual properties they contain. Aromas were offered with prayer, in thanks and in praise to the Gods. As the smoke of incense rose towards heaven, it was seen to carry people's prayers with it. Deities were anointed each day and fed with fragrant waters. This secured the favour of Divine forces. Essential oils hold the power to bridge the gap between heaven and earth.

People who used essential oils, mainly royalty and the priesthood, were able to travel to different levels of consciousness and extend their spiritual awareness. The achievements of the ancient Egyptians are unparalleled to this day. I am not attributing all their greatness to essential oils, but scents certainly played an important role in Opening to Spirit for the ancient Egyptians. The Greeks and Romans carried on the tradition. In many orthodox churches frankincense and myrrh continue to be used to banish evil spirits.

Today we are still plagued by evil spirits. Having largely ignored the spiritual nature of our existence, we suffer from disorientation. Like our Ancestors, we need to placate the spirits. Having recognized a block in the root chakra, manifesting as fear, physical weakness, insecurity, etc., you can use essential oils to recreate balance.

Essential oils vary a lot in quality. For subtle energy healing, use only good-quality, pure essential oils with no synthetic substances added. Although small quantities of oil are generally used in aromatherapy, subtle energy work requires even finer dilutions. It is the vibrational effect of the oil that is important.

Essential Oils for Balancing the Root Chakra

Patchouli, cypress, cedarwood,[13] vetivert, sandalwood, myrrh.

Please note that essential oils should not be used during pregnancy unless under the supervision of a qualified aromatherapist.

Blending Essential Oils for Subtle Energy Work

Use seed oil as a carrier, such as grapeseed, pure almond or peach kernel. A good almond oil will have no odour; synthetic ones sometimes smell of almonds, so take care when you purchase oil. Seeds hold the potential for growth and therefore have a powerful energetic quality. Prepare small quantities at a time, as some essential oils quickly destabilize and go rancid.

In 20 ml of carrier oil, use 1% essential oils (that is, approximately 5 drops).

Your blend of essential oils can be used to massage your feet, hands and/or entire body. Place a few drops in your hands before meditation practice. Use a few drops to charge your energy before you go about your daily routines.

GEMS

Gems for the root chakra are dark in colour, ranging from red jasper and smoky quartz to black tourmaline. These gems have a grounding quality and are excellent for reducing stress and enhancing relaxation. Smoky quartz is probably the most popular choice because of its healing qualities. It dispels all kinds of negative energy, eases fear and develops courage. This gem is also used to lift the spirits and connect the root chakra to the crown chakra. All root chakra stones (see Correspondences, pages 105–6) can be used for protection.

Crystals are part of our mother the earth's body. When we use them we should be sure they have not been mined destructively. Rather than blowing the earth up with dynamite, many people mine by hand and pick the crystals like ripe fruit that is ready to be harvested. Try to find out where your stones have come from and how they were mined. This determines their energetic quality. Crystals and gems share some of the above colour qualities. They also act as channels for healing energies. Crystals amplify thought vibrations. They can amplify positive vibrations and create healing. In relation to the root chakra, we may wish to create grounding and reduce fear. Focus on this intention whenever you use your stones.

Cleansing and Charging Crystals

Once you have intuitively chosen your crystals, it is important to clean them. This removes any negative vibrations, recharges the crystals and makes them your own. This can be done in a number of different ways:

Earth	Bury your crystals in earth or sand for one or two days.
Water	Hold them under running spring water for a while, or leave them in sea salt water overnight.
Air	Smudging; use a smudge stick made from sage, cedar and lavender. Light it and, once it is smoking well, put out the flames and waft the cleansing smoke over your crystals.
Fire	Leave your crystals in the sunlight for several hours.

SIMPLE WAYS OF USING CRYSTALS AND GEMSTONES

◎ Choose the appropriate crystal for the chakra you are working with. For example: smoky quartz for grounding and strengthening the root chakra, turquoise for stimulating insight and perception at the third eye centre. After cleansing your stone, simply place it in a red pouch for the root chakra, or a blue/black one for the third eye, and carry it with you.

◎ I often hold a stone in my palms during my meditation practice. In the first part of my practice I hold the stone in my left/receptive hand, so as to clear my energy. I focus on cleansing, allowing everything that is going through my mind to slowly come to an end. Sometimes a revelation appears, but usually superfluous thoughts play themselves over and over again. I don't battle or associate with them, and eventually they slow down. During the second part of my meditation, I hold the stone in my right/active hand to charge my energy. I keep my mind as still as possible and resonate with the crystal I am holding, absorbing its energy and projecting the healing vibration into my aura. I extend my attention out into my energy field and feel energy pulsating around me. I always keep my journal close by to write down any messages I receive. Meditation practice is a powerful and stress-free way to do personal work. It is said that prayer is asking the universe for help, and meditation is listening to the advice given.

◎ Another method, which I use personally and with clients, is to place the appropriate gem over the relevant chakra. For a complete recharge I position gems over all seven major chakras. All that is needed after this is deep relaxation; the gems will balance the energy and do any other necessary work. Use:

- ◎ Smoky quartz for the root chakra
- ◎ Carnelian for the sacral chakra
- ◎ Citrine for the solar plexus chakra
- ◎ Rose quartz or green aventurine for the heart chakra
- ◎ Turquoise or lapis lazuli for the throat chakra
- ◇ Sodalite for the third eye chakra
- ◎ Amethyst for the crown chakra

To recharge the root chakra:

◎ Lie comfortably on the floor. Place two smoky quartz crystals at your feet, so that they are touching your heels. (If your crystal has a point, direct this end towards your body.) Smoky quartz stimulates the root chakra, encouraging grounding, and helps to dissipate fear. Above your head, place a clear quartz crystal. This helps open the energy field. Smoky quartz, which connects to the darkness of the earth, and clear quartz, which holds light, create a circuit that enhances both embodiment and enlightenment.

Ritual

Ritual is the art of performing spiritual acts and is a catalyst for awakening inner power. It is a creative way of communing with spirit and remembering our divinity. Through ritual, we raise energy and develop our auric connection to the universe. We tune to specific vibrations and create the order or freedom we need to make life changes. As we seek guidance we can offer thanks and praise. Ritual generally involves three stages: preparation, performance of rite, and celebration.

◎ **Preparation** starts by gathering materials for the ritual. Personal cleansing follows. This may be a fast or cleansing diet. Crystals, smudging and other tools described in this chapter and in Chapter 5 can be used. They are also used to create sacred space, which is the next task. After cleansing, prepare your altar and call the directions (*see below*).

- ◎ **Performance of Rite** is a blessing, rite of 'pass-age', request for guidance or other ritual that opens us to spirit and prepares us to move forward in life.
- ◎ **Celebration** is the third stage. Gather friends together to give thanks to the creator. Share refreshments, dance and celebrate.

CREATING PERSONAL RITES OF PASS-AGE

A rite of pass-age is a marker in time, a blessing from the gods which permits us to continue our spiritual growth and development. It is recognition of the grace and love of the creator that has brought us this far, and a celebration of our personal achievements. Rites of passage are used in many cultures to validate the experiences of groups and individuals. A personal rite of pass-age honours your movement from one developmental age to another. We can take ourselves back in time and honour the ages we have already passed, we can honour our children as they grow, and we can each continue to celebrate our bountiful life journeys as they emerge.

In many traditions, rites of pass-age are painful experiences where the opportunity is provided to overcome the seemingly impossible. Such rituals have the power to create major transformation of the soul. Without the guidance of learned elders we cannot emulate these ancient rituals. Instead we must seek the guidance of spirit and create our own contemporary rituals. Life itself provides us with copious amounts of painful experiences and I do not wish to advocate the creation of more. I feel we should lift our energies in celebration of our transitions from one age to another.

The guidelines and details on preparing and performing rituals, seen in this chapter, can be used to create personal rituals. Rites can be designed to honour different levels of development and the subsequent spiritual, psychological and physical changes each age brings. In the 'Psychological Correspondences' sections at the beginning of chapters 6–12 you will also find information that will help you.

The chart below details the developmental ages, the dominant element and the focuses for celebration that can be used when creating your personal rituals. The meaning you impose on the ritual greatly determines the results. Ritual needs to inspire awe; respect and reverence should be present. Remember your greatest guide will be your connection to spirit. Ritual can be a personal method of communing directly with spirit, therefore we are all entitled to reclaim this sacred art. Remain Open to Spirit as you prepare for your rituals; allow yourself to be creative, guided and ever-blessed.

Contemporary rituals based on ancient knowledge are offered for each chakra. Begin practising these rituals and, with experience, you will soon develop rituals and rites of pass-age of your own.

PERSONAL RITES OF PASS-AGE

Chakra	Dominant Element	Developmental Age	Focus of Celebration
Root	Earth	Birth	Birth and naming ceremony
Sacral	Water	Seven	Developing sense of Self
Solar plexus	Fire	Fourteen	Puberty – respons-ability Ability to create new life
Heart	Air	Twenty-one	Love and Adulthood
Throat	Ether	Twenty-eight	Creativity and life purpose Childbirth
Third eye	Light	Thirty-five	Knowledge and Spiritual Vision
Crown	Pure Spirit	Forty-two	Celebrating Wisdom

CALLING THE DIRECTIONS

Before performing your ritual, call on the guardians of the four directions (north, east, south and west). These gatekeepers open the way between the physical and spiritual realms. Stand in the centre of your sacred space and visualize a healing circle. From this centre turn to face the south, where you will begin. Earth is honoured first in the root chakra ritual, water in the sacral chakra ritual, and so on through the chakras. Water can be sprinkled in each direction before the invocation as a sign of peace. (To the Yorùbá, water symbolizes peace, as it is needed by all life and therefore has no enemies.)

Invocation to Open Sacred Space

Sprinkle water and say aloud – 'I call on the great guardian of the south, spirit-keeper of earth, mother of all creation. Be with me now.' Continue to call and sing praises to the mother. 'Beautiful one, who shares her beauty with us all, who blesses my body with health.' As you call, feel your connection with the ground on which you stand. Hear her rhythm.

Turn to your right, sprinkle water and say aloud – 'I call on the great guardian of the west, spirit-keeper of water. Be with me now. Owner of the oceans and rivers. Bestower of wealth and beauty. Friend to the moon and lovers.' As you call, feel your own waters and let your emotions be moved from deep within.

Turn to your right, sprinkle water and say aloud – 'I call on the great guardian of the north, spirit-keeper of air. Be with me now. She who goes everywhere and blows the great winds of change. Fill me with your life-giving breath. Temper my thoughts and fill me with inspiration.' Feel the movement of air whispering to you.

Turn to your right, sprinkle water and call – 'Guardian of the east, spirit-keeper of fire. Be with me now. Bright dancing flame of fire and passion, ignitor of spirit, provider of wisdom and light.' Allow yourself to fill with burning enthusiasm.

Face the centre and praise your Ancestors. 'I give thanks for your light which brightens my path. I ask that you will continue to protect and bless me. Fill me with your wisdom as I enter the realm of spirit.' Feel the powerful presence of your Ancestors.

Finish opening your sacred space by calling:
'Great Guardians of all directions
Spirit-keepers of all elements
Ancestors who passed this way before me.
Hear my praises and grant me your presence.'

Close Sacred Space

After completing the ritual, each guardian and spirit-keeper must be thanked and dismissed. Face each of the directions, beginning where you started. This time, turn successively to your left and give thanks to each of the directions. Closing the sacred space may not take as long as opening it, but it should be done with as much love.

Call:
'Great Guardians of all directions
Spirit-keepers of all elements
All those who walked before me
I thank you for your guidance and presence here today.
I carry your love within me as we part in peace.'

ROOT CHAKRA RITUAL

Connecting with our Foremothers

This ritual aims to connect you deeply with the earth and your ancestral foundation. In so doing, you thank those who went before you and receive the gifts they lay in front of you. Today, when we speak of healing and maintaining the planet, we do so for our children, our children's children, their children and all children to come. These children are not here yet, but we anticipate them and act accordingly. We will be their Ancestors; we have to look out for them. Likewise our Ancestors, generations ago, looked out for us. They did not forget us, and we should not forget them. Children should be raised to honour the Ancestors; in this way we too will not be forgotten.

Preparation
Gathering materials. You will need:

> Small stones from the garden or beach that have been cleansed with water.
> Drum or other instruments, your journal and a pen.

For this ritual, gather as much information about your foremothers as possible. You may be lucky enough to know your grandmothers and great grandmothers. Trace back as far as you can – try to find out the strengths and weaknesses of these women. What were their likes and dislikes? Create as clear a picture as you can. Then reflect on your mother and her character. Gathering this information is not always easy. Many people have lost contact with their family lineage, through slavery, migration, adoption or for other reasons. If this is your experience, this ritual is important because the energy of your Ancestors is still present. Through this ritual you can begin tuning to their energy, even without knowing your family details.

Personal Cleansing
An ideal way to prepare for the root chakra ritual is by honouring the body through massage. Use grounding essential oils such as cedarwood, vetivert or sandalwood, in an almond oil base. This blend gives a rich earthy aroma that is grounding and spiritually uplifting. Arrange for a therapist or trusted friend to massage you. Self-massage is another alternative. Surrender during the treatment and allow yourself to receive loving energy.

Massage cleanses the body, mind and spirit. Once your body and hair have been anointed with oils, stroked, rubbed and kneaded, you will feel relaxed and ready to 'Open to Spirit'. Your hair is your Spiritual Antennae and should be included in the massage, unless you keep it covered for spiritual reasons.

Creating Sacred Space
Be sure your altar is clean and well prepared. Create a large circle around you, using stones, or visualize yourself encircled in healing earth energy. Open sacred space by calling the directions, using the invocation described earlier. If this doesn't resonate with you, use whatever directions you know.

Ceremony

Pick up your drum (or other instrument), turn towards your altar and sit down. Play two beats a second, steady and even. As you sound the rhythm, allow yourself to connect deeply with the earth. Lose yourself in the rhythm. When you are ready (this could be after 5 or 50 minutes – you will know when to end) let the sound fade into silence. You will continue to hear the rhythm. This rhythm you know from your mother's womb, and she knows it from her mother's womb, and so it goes back to the first Eve and the great Mother Earth herself.

Sit or lay down in silence and fully relax. Breathe deeply once or twice; then bring your foremothers to mind. It may be that you do not wish to call all your foremothers, particularly those who met a traumatic death or any who were noted for evil acts. A separate prayer should be said for these foremothers, to aid in the transition of their souls. Your foremothers can be named or unnamed, known or unknown. Use all your senses: see them, hear them, feel them. They are with you now. Tune in to their powerful energy. Just as we exist in flesh now, they existed long ago. Flesh alone dies; energy does not die, it merely changes form. Take time to feel them with you. Give thanks to them for birthing. Thank them for the lasting foundation they have provided – you are here now, bearing witness to their power. Let them know they will not be forgotten again. Ask any questions you may have. Let them know you are ready to receive the gifts they offer. Ask for guidance to use your gifts wisely. Let them stay with you a while. Then, when you are ready, thank them for their presence and know that whenever you wish to call on them, they will be there for you. Breath deeply again and feel the change in your root chakra. Slowly count down from 10 to 0. You may wish to write your experience in your journal.

Celebration

Give thanks to the Creator. Spend time in celebration alone or with friends. Be open to receive the blessings of those who went before you.

Close Sacred Space

Using the prayer on page 137, give thanks and dismiss the great guardians and spirit-keepers of the directions and elements.

The root chakra facilitates the spirit's embodiment in a physical vehicle, for a limited time on the earth plane. The function of the root chakra, as its name suggests, is to maintain our connection to Mother Earth.

Root chakra work is a strong foundation for the chakras that follow. I suggest spending at least a month working on this chakra before ascending to the sacral chakra. Be aware of subtle changes, and keep notes on your progress. Energy flowing through the root chakra maintains health and keeps you safely anchored to the earth, our mother. You now have the potential to create a firm base from which to make your ascent through the chakras.

7

SACRAL CHAKRA

CELEBRATING SPIRIT, CELEBRATING SELF

'Ma Ferefún Ọ̀sun'
I give praise to the spirit of love, sexuality, fertility and abundance.

Prayer to the Yorùbá Goddess Ọ̀sun

THE SACRAL CHAKRA: CORRESPONDENCES

Sanskrit Name	Swadistana: Home of the Self
Meaning	Swa = one's own adisthana = dwelling place
Main Function	Provides a sense of Self. This is the sacred home of 'I'.
Quality	Centring
Location	Sacrum/lower abdomen

Spiritual Correspondences

Colour	Orange
Element	Water

Symbol	Crescent moon
Seed Sound	Vam
Petals	Six
Planet	Moon ☽
Esoteric Anatomy	Level of the gross physical body, which is at least 70 per cent water
Yoga Path	Tantra
Guna Quality	Tamas

Deities

Africa	Hathor, Yemoja, Òṣun, Nun
Akkadia/Sumeria	Tiamat/Ishtar
India	Rakini, Saraswati, Chandra Devi
Europe	Mary,[1] Demeter, Aphrodite
Mythology	Creation myths where all life is born from the fertile watery womb

Physical Correspondences

Gland	Gonads: ovaries, testes
Nerve Plexus	Hypogastric plexus
Body Parts	Womb, genitals, kidney, bladder, muscles
Water Energy Triad	Breasts, genitals, feet
Expression	Love and trust in Self. Responsibility to Self
Disturbance	Low Self-worth

Psychological Correspondences

Statement	'I can'

EMOTIONS

BALANCED	UNBALANCED
All emotion is allowed	Afraid of emotion
Ebb and flow of water energy	Hold on to water/tears
Creates mood changes	Damn up feelings and prevent sacral energy flow
Chronology	1 – 7 years

Rite of Passage	Developing a sense of Self. Leaving the mother to begin school. Blessed by water
Developmental Stage	Developing independence; strong physical presence and body awareness

Ways of Working

Foods	Leafy vegetables, salad leaves, cucumber, melon, mushrooms
Herbs	Damanian, Dong Quai, Black haw, Black willow bark
Oils	Clary sage, jasmine, rose, ylang ylang, sandalwood
Gems	Carnelian, amber, orange calcite, coral
Precious Metal	Gold

Main Function: To Know One's Self

When energy is free to move through the root chakra, it automatically flows up into the sacral chakra. The sacral chakra is responsible for emotions, sensation, sexuality, reproduction and creativity. From this centre we connect with our innermost selves. We are sensual, Divine creators, capable of Self-knowledge and wisdom. One function of this chakra is to introduce us to and let us come to know the inner beauty, strength and potential we harbour deep inside. The sacral chakra also governs sexuality and throws forth desire – the desire to share in one of the most beautiful gifts bestowed on us, sexual union. We learn that we can create love, ecstasy and life. The sacral centre offers the opportunity for us to fuse disparate parts of our being: self as individual human and self as Divine Spirit can be joined together in synergy. We thus create Self with a capital S. The more we are able to connect and resonate with the sacral chakra, the stronger is our sense of Self-worth and Self-love. This is not about overdeveloping 'I' at the expense of other people, or becoming egocentric, it is about recognizing Self as a blessed part of the Divine. When we see ourselves as Divine then we are truly ready to see God and the Goddess in everyone.

The sacral chakra is 'the sacred home of I'. We have all at some time asked the questions, 'who am I?' and 'what is my purpose in this life?' Answers to these mysteries can be found deep in the sacral centre. It is through working with this chakra that we come to know our individual beauty, creativity and wisdom. We learn that we belong in this world and that we are welcome here. Each one of us is here for a sacred purpose. According to the Ancients, we each made a pact in the spirit world before entering this incarnation. We agreed to learn certain lessons and carry particular gifts. Once in the physical realm, we seem to forget the agreements we made. The question of purpose arises because we long to remember. We long to find meaning in our lives. To help us remember, we are constantly guided by the soul. The soul knows the exact path we are to take, the lessons we are to learn and the innate gifts we have to offer. Fear, illness, pain, relationship troubles and all manner of issues are experienced, just so we will learn to question our existence and purpose in this life. Each question directs us towards the very core of our being, where the soul resides. In this core we find the chakras, and in the sacral chakra we find a sense of meaning and inner knowing.

Sacred Sex

The sacral chakra takes its name from the word *sacred*. In medical language this part of the body still maintains its sacredness; the spine in this area is called the sacrum, which literally come from the word sacred. The sacrum and pelvis protect the sexual and reproductive organs.

Sexuality and the ability to reproduce ourselves has been revered since the beginning of time. Women were held in the highest esteem by the Ancients because of our unique ability to give birth. Reverence for women gave rise to many early matriarchal societies. Early spirituality revolved around the Goddess, women's fertility and the fertility of the land. Sexuality was acknowledged as sacred and also respected for its role in reproduction. The life-force and sexual energy were known to be one and the same. Sex is not merely a physical act, but can also become a Divine ritual. In line with the laws of nature, sex can draw energy from the centre of our being out into the universal force-field. Our energy is replenished and returns to the core centre.

Today, sexual energy is misunderstood and abused. Many people no longer enjoy its spiritual significance. Sexual union is a sacred act. When we recognize ourselves as sacred, born from the sacred sexuality of our parents, we realize that sex is a beautiful way of connecting with and raising soul consciousness.

Sexual arousal requires the stimulation of the parasympathetic nervous system (PSNS). The PSNS has a relaxing and cleansing effect on the body, it reduces anxiety and gives way to a sense of calm. Sharing loving touch heightens sensation and nourishes the entire being. Pleasure and sensation are amplified through the sacral chakra. Orgasm is the experience of completely letting go and allowing the body/mind to surrender to the spirit and be flooded with ecstatic energy. All the cells in the body open to receive the Divine elixir and are realigned at the point of ecstasy. Climax is followed by spontaneous relaxation.

Sex can be a great healer. Pioneer of Western body psychotherapy, William Reich, found in his research on bioenergy that sex, and particularly orgasms, were crucial for the bioelectric current of energy to complete its circuit through the body.[2] This flow of energy he saw as essential for a healthy body/mind. He was not spiritually oriented, yet his theories relate closely to tantric yoga.

The sacral chakra is the centre of sexuality, responsible for the impulse of pleasure, sensation and sharing. For many people orgasm is the closest they will come to true spiritual bliss.

Celibacy is advocated in some spiritual traditions; this allows the life-force to accumulate in the body. Energy can then be directed up through the chakras, enhancing spiritual experience. Male ejaculation is thought to dissipate the life-force, while for women the life-force can be contained during sex.

Creativity

Like sexuality, creativity springs from the sacral chakra. The impulse to be creative causes us to develop innate personal abilities. Children, given paper and crayons, will have no difficulty drawing. On hearing music they sing and dance. When asked to tell a story their imaginations soar. We were all children once and we still maintain the same creative potential. The creative process is the act of 'bringing something new into being'. It is about communicating with Self and others. If you think back to your childhood you may remember enjoying one or more arts. I loved to dance and to play the piano. Movement and dance have remained priorities for me throughout my life. Learning to play piano is a gift I still intend to give myself. My latest excuse is that I need a good teacher. Writing this is helping me see how I hold back my own creativity. As a child I was not searching for a piano teacher, I just started to play. There is nothing really stopping me. I simply need to allow myself the time and patience to receive this creative gift. What holds you back and stops you singing, dancing, painting, acting, cooking, climbing, and enjoying your unique creativity? Commitment to ourselves is what really stops us. Tuning to the sacral chakra puts us in contact again with Self. That Self is creative. Be a child again, allow yourself time to take paints and enjoy, make music and dance. Like a child, do not look for perfection but take pleasure from the process, enjoy the mess, have fun, and as you do this rekindle your hidden talents and innate creativity.

Creativity can also gratify our desire to be of service to others. We all seek to belong and want to help others. To satisfy this desire, we must identify the gifts bestowed on us by the universe. You have been individually chosen to carry out a particular task for yourself, humanity and the planet. This could be raising the next generation, communicating, healing, making music, dancing, healing the planet, offering love and hope to people – there are so many ways you can be of service. The first step, however, is to observe what really heals you, what really lifts your spirit and keeps you up when the going gets rough. I sing and I laugh; this keeps me afloat – as long as I stay on the water and not under it I can continue my spiritual practice. Opening to Spirit really keeps me alive and allows me to share the blessings of spirit with others. As we discover our innate gifts and spiritual beauty, we suffer less in life. Suffering will always be present because pain keeps us searching for truth, and truth is found in the centre of our being where the soul resides. Once we recognize the leadership of the soul, we can relax and ask our spirit companions, Ancestors and guides for help. They will help us realign with spirit and identify our soul purpose.

If you are looking to create change in your life you can start right now by simply lighting a candle and saying a prayer. Ask for guidance, to be shown a sign, ask for light to shine from your soul and illuminate your purpose in life. Know your prayers will be answered. Wherever you are right now your soul is moving you towards its purpose. You are protected and ever surrounded by love and golden light.

The watery sacral chakra functions as a place of changing tides, mood swings and rocky emotions. In contrast, the waters of this centre can be still, offering a peaceful and harmonious place of rest. It is said that 'still waters run deep.' This is a very complex centre, connecting us on a personal level to the collective unconscious. Our guides, Ancestors and helpers from the spirit world can meet us here and help us on our journey through the chakras. It is not to be forgotten that this centre is one of the three personal chakras, resonating on a lower frequency than the upper four, universal chakras. It is, however, an extremely powerful chakra; strengthening this centre is essential before we continue our ascent. It is through this chakra that we learn to bring spirit down to earth. It is a centre of union; we learn to express our sexuality, develop creativity and bond the secular Self with the sacred Self, thus raising Self-esteem. We learn through silence to calm the waters and listen to the still small voice within, telling us we are beautiful, Divine beings worthy of love and light.

QUALITY: CENTRING

Centred, between the earth below and the sun above, lies the sacral chakra. The root chakra represents limitation, while the solar plexus chakra represents power and conflict. The sacral centre, amidst the two, can be a place of harmony and stillness. The body's centre of gravity is in the sacral area. It is from this point that we maintain physical balance. Not only is the physical body balanced here, but so are our e-motions. E-motions are movements of energy that we interpret as sad, happy, etc. These movements can be created from external and internal forces. Many hormones are housed in the pelvic region; they flood our system and can cause us to feel out of balance. We may experience a sense of being overpowered by our e-motions, out of control, constantly tearful or raging for no apparent reason.

Although many fragmented energies can meet at the sacral centre, its matrilineal power has the ability to nurture and heal the disparate parts of Self, making us whole again. The sacral chakra is therefore also an e-motional centre of gravity, a space where we can find balance and come into our centre. It is a place were we can be nourished and experience wholeness. From this sense of wholeness we are in a position to move forward. Being centred is the ability to stay in, or move from, a place of quiet wisdom.

The sacral chakra provides balance and equilibrium in relationships. When we are centred we act with response-ability. The root chakra is concerned with survival, and therefore acts mostly on impulse. The primary motivation for the solar plexus is maintaining power and can cause aggressive responses. Amid the two, the sacral chakra processes information which balances survival with the fiery will. A harmonious response is then delivered which takes into account variables, such as Self, others and the universe. Becoming centred requires an inner stillness which allows the body/mind to tap its potential for self-regulation. We cannot force the moon to be full, but if we wait patiently, sure enough the fullness of the moon will eventually be seen. The cosmic programme is already set in process. The same can be said of us (as above so below); there is a larger harmonious plan, already set in motion. It is when we stop and yield to this plan, even for a few moments, that the moon becomes full for us, and in its shining light we begin to see that which was previously masked.

We cannot force clarity; instead, by being centred and patient, we can tune to the universe and what it has in store for us. We can make suggestions in our prayers; it is good to let it be known what you want from this life, but essentially when this is done we need only be centred and let the will of the Goddess be achieved.

GODDESS OF THE LUNAR CHAKRA

The feminine sacral centre with its sensuality, beauty and flowing waters can be likened to the Goddess, the female Supreme Being, the all-powerful one with a thousand names. Patriarchy is responsible for alienating the Goddess, who was originally one with God. There are numerous Goddess archetypes, which relate to many different feminine qualities. These qualities are found in women and gentle-men. It is as important for men to resonate with the feminine lunar chakra as with the masculine solar (crown) chakra.

The Goddess of the moon is closely associated with the sacral chakra, which I also call the lunar chakra or, in Sanskrit, chandra chakra. The moon has been worshipped since the beginning of time. Numerous myths view the moon as the original creatress, the bright shining lady of the sky who existed alone in primordial time, until she eventually grew lonely and created the world and all life existing on it.[3] The moon is also accredited with the power to destroy and has been named 'the home of the dead' by the Greeks.[4] The same people believed the female Yoni (vagina and womb) was not only a gateway through which life begins, but also a passageway through which the soul returns to the stars. The moon was believed to have the ability to devour people, particularly men. Thus what began as pagan worship of the moon Goddess and sacred yoni turned to fear of both the moon and women's sexuality. This same fear penetrates Western society today, and all women exposed to patriarchy suffer its consequences.

Feeling our Goddess nature and really delighting in the lunar chakra can be difficult for women. Western society does not readily permit us to enjoy self-esteem, self-love, sexuality and women power. Powerful women, particularly those who remain aware of their sexuality, threaten the patriarchy we now live under. To rise above these difficulties we need to become familiar with 'the Goddess' who is all-embracing. All women and gentle-men can identify with and honour at least one Goddess. As familiarity with your choice of Goddess increases, let those of her qualities that are innate in you grow. Afford yourself the same love, respect and honour, for the Goddess is within you. All the Goddesses are within you. You are the Goddess. Again, this is not the ego speaking and must not be confused with ego. This is acknowledging your Divinity and empowering the spirit within. You may be residing in a physical body, but you are more than flesh and blood, you are more than thoughts and actions. You need not be afraid to accept that you are in essence Divine Spirit, ever part of and ever connected to the creatress.

The Goddess of the lunar chakra represents matter and spirit combined, thus creating balance. She is round and voluptuous, embodying a beautiful, gentle fullness. Grace and fluidity sway in her movements. Her beauty is not merely physical but encompasses a mind of wisdom, intuition and truth. She inspires moral justice and is the maker of love, which she gladly encourages. She is obedient to natural law, holding life, her creation, in the highest esteem. Creative energy springs from her waters, giving you the potential to express yourself through art, laughing and loving. When energy flows freely through your sacral chakra, you can access the Goddess nature which resides within.

Are you ready to realize your beauty? Ready to feel the Goddess flowing inside you, ready to rejoice in her wonders? Are you ready to see your reflection in the waters of your soul? You are beautiful, we are all beautiful beings. Can you take and give compliments? If someone says 'you look great', do you say 'thank you' and know they are right, or do you say 'Oh! This dress is only cheap,' reducing your Self to a cheap dress? The sacral chakra asks that you recognize your beauty in all its wondrous forms. When you feel low and unworthy, with other people's needs seeming to take priority over your own; when self-love and respect are lacking in your life, it is time to stop for a moment and resonate through the sacral chakra with the lunar Goddess.

The all-knowing, all-powerful Goddess of the lunar chakra has been with you since the beginning, she knows your strengths and weakness. She has answers for all your questions and surrounds you with light to help you see. She knows you are a Divine Spirit and returns you to that knowledge.

Element: Water

The sacred qualities of water are very apparent to us. People travel great distances to be close to the sea, or to visit hot springs and holy wells. Sunday afternoon strolls often take place by streams and rivers. Being close to water creates a gentle, calm feeling which most of us are familiar with. Water flows and soothes, nourishes and cleanses. The healing quality of water is as obvious to us now as it was to the Ancients. Water is a friend to all. She is held sacred and equated with peace in African traditional religions, because she maintains all life and therefore has no enemies.

Water promotes fertility and life. Creation myths abound, telling us how life springs forth from the watery abyss. We are each nourished and birthed from a watery womb. Fertility, reproductive organs, blood, semen, sexuality, emotion and self-image are all under the control of the water element. Rivers need to maintain their flow; likewise, water energy needs to move unrestricted through the body. Blood carries nutrients to cells and organs; it also removes waste products. Without enough circulation of blood and body fluids, stagnation and disease soon set in. If the emotions become dammed up, anxiety and tension greatly increase; this leads to stress, which we know can cause all manner of ailments, from backache to cancer. As we accept feelings of pleasure and pain, we allow the sacred waters to cascade deep inside. This movement of water stimulates spirituality and sexuality – both have the power to lift our spirits, refreshing and rebalancing the entire system.

As water flows through the body she awakens the senses and e-motions. Once awake, our senses seek gratification. The out-going motion of water provides the impetus that helps us become creative. We desire to please the senses, searching for food, beauty, sweet smells, lovers and pleasing sounds – all of which we can create and enjoy. The return movement to the core of our being carries pleasure as the senses are satiated.

Aside from motion, water energy is also responsible for stillness. As the waters within us still, the potential arises for reflection. We see our true spiritual nature in the depth of still waters.

The waters within can become turbulent when our desires are not met. Self-image suffers and we can sink in an emotional sea of our own making. Too much water energy, and quickly our emotions begin gushing out all over, creating changeable moods and depression. Other people's problems can overwhelm the watery person, who absorbs the troubles of the world. The addition of fire or earth energy will spur the individual into action, while water alone only causes saturation. Sensitivity to others, and poor personal boundaries, often allow watery people to be taken advantage of. On the other hand, the watery person also uses emotion to manipulate others.

Too little water energy can reduce the desire for sensual stimulation and creativity. A person lacking water energy may lead a rigid and overly analytic lifestyle, operating from the head, with little awareness of the body. For many people, Descartes was right when he said, 'I think, therefore I am.' The thinking mind takes precedence over intuition and the watery feeling sense.

Water is the greatest of healers: it purifies the body, clarifies feelings and enriches the spirit. When used well, water energy is truly a friend.

The globe consists of about 70 per cent water, as does the human body. These waters respond to the magnetic pull of the moon. It is well known that the moon's gravitational force creates motion on the seas, in the form of waves and tides. It is also known that our feelings and emotions respond to the moon's pull; hence the word 'lunatic'. Research shows that more accidents take place at the time of the full moon. Perhaps this is because we have stopped honouring the moon and recognizing her movement in the waters of our being.

Planet: Moon ☽

She maketh all Beautiful on which she smiles...

When looking into the moon's face, we see our own beauty reflected back. We see the creatress in whose image we are made. The moon is the great mother Goddess of the night sky. Her triune nature is to create, destroy and recreate. We see this in her dance, as she waxes and wanes, brightening the sky at full moon and leaving us in darkness before the new moon. The moon changes; as we follow her cycle, our moods change in rhythm with hers. For women, this is most evident in the menstrual cycle, where hormone levels wax and wane. Ovulation is akin to the fertile full moon,[5] whilst the progesterone-rich waning period brings darkness, out of which a new moon is born, carrying the potential of new life.

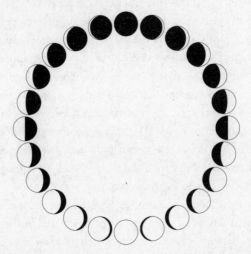

For 14 days the waxing moon swells towards her fullness, on the 15th day. These days are akin to the first half of the menstrual cycle, when the female egg ripens and prepares for ovulation. The 14 days of the waning moon represent the second half of the menstrual cycle, which carries the potential for new life.

When a new life incarnates, the sun keeps this life connected to spirit; earth supplies a physical body; the moon is responsible for providing it with a personality and a soul. 'Receptacle of souls' is a name of the moon, because she is seen to rule over reincarnation, creating a continuum between death and rebirth. When a soul leaves the earth, it goes out with the sea's tide and returns to the moon. The moon absorbs that soul in her brightness. In conjunction with the soul she chooses who or what it will be in the next life. Lessons to be learned are also agreed at this stage. She then provides the soul with the personality it needs for its journey and rebirths it, sending it back to earth with the incoming tide. She holds the power to create individuals, allowing each one to express uniqueness. When she returns us to earth, she imbues us with the potential to know everything that was, is, and ever shall be. This is the great power the moon has and shares with us.

Many people are afraid of this lunar knowledge, preferring to close down their intuition and stay with the scientific and rational. We should listen at all times and respect this intuitive wisdom, because it is the collective knowledge of all the ages.

The moon's receptive, female energy relates to the individual soul; whereas the masculine sun relates to universal spirit. The moon herself is the soul of humanity; she holds within her secrets the collective unconscious and the entire ancestral records. The sacral chakra houses the soul and resonates with the moon's force. The sacral centre, therefore, also provides access to the collective unconscious and ancestral records. We can readily tune to this part of our unconscious and feel a strong sense of connection to those who went before us. This happens sometimes – we seem to just know something, and credit it to 'women's intuition'.

The moon gives us our personality, supplying the energy with which we relate to others. When we resonate strongly with the moon's force, we are receptive to others and have many friends and easily create prosperous opportunities. If we do not have the moon on our side, we may have identity problems and low self-esteem; we may merge with others, going with the flow to such an extent that we drown in a sea of other people's desires and expectations.

It is useful to know where the moon is situated in your astrological birth chart. This is as important to know as your sun sign. It will tell you whether or not your moon is situated in a place of exaltation, which is a strong position, or a place of challenge. Wherever she rests, we can all learn to harness the moon's energy, strengthen the sacral chakra and enhance our connection to the universe.

MOON MEDITATIONS

Meditation is an excellent way of attuning yourself to the cycles of the moon. Try to get yourself a lunar calendar and follow the dance of the moon in the night skies. Watch the new moon as she emerges from the darkness and waxes towards her fullness before waning again into darkness. The three main phases of the moon provide inspiration for meditation.

Dark Moon Meditation

This is a time of replenishment, cleansing and healing. The moon is taking her rest and preparing for creation. In the darkness the seed of potential is planted. Take time to focus on what is changing your life. What do you need to put to rest? What do you have no further use of? As you look into the darkness of the sky, know that whatever you want to create is already taking root.

New Moon Meditation

The new moon brings creation and rebirth. Light is seen again in the dark night sky. This is the time to focus on what is emerging in your life. What secrets does the new moon hold for you? Listen to the energy in your sacral centre, awaken the lunar Goddess and ask for her blessing as you begin new projects and honour your own unique creativity.

Full Moon Meditation

The radiant full moon resonates with ovulation and fertility. This is a reaping phase, when the mature egg in its fullness is released, ready to become. You can take this time to celebrate your achievements throughout the past month. List them one by one, giving thanks to the lunar Goddess for each. Under the moon's light be still, absorb her powerful energy and feel her glorious beauty. Know that you and the moon are one.

Deities

Goddesses of water, sensuality and love rule the sacral chakra. They guard earth's watery realms and women's fertile wombs, creating tides and mood swings. Water Goddesses are found in all traditions, presiding over love, beauty, creativity and prosperity. In the depths of your waters lies a beautiful, intelligent, sensuous, Goddess. She awaits your call, ready and eager to amplify grace, love and riches in your life.

HATHOR (HET HERU)

Hathor is one of the most ancient deities of Egypt. A Goddess of fertility, who is mother to all Gods and Goddesses and queen of heaven. Hathor is depicted as the cow Goddess, and in human form she is seen wearing cow horns on her head. The shape of these horns resembles the shape of both the moon and the female reproductive organs. Hathor is also the Goddess of knowledge and wisdom. She is the female counterpart of the great God Thoth. Her patronage of the arts, dancing and merry-making are well documented. This beautiful and sensuous Goddess, whose own rhythm resembled that of the rising and falling of the Nile river, can be invoked regarding all issues of the sacral chakra.

THE CREATIVE WOMB AND FALLOPIAN TUBES

ANCIENT EGYPTIAN BIRD GODDESS

SYMBOL OF HATHOR

The regenerative quality of the sacral chakra is seen in each of these three related images. The ancient Egyptians' skill in embalming meant they had a very detailed knowledge of anatomy. Hence the creative womb and Fallopian tubes may have inspired these early images of the bird Goddess. Hathor wears two crescent moons embracing the sun on her head-dress. These moons resemble the horn-like arms of the ancient bird Goddess. Her arms open out and assume a position that looks very much like the female reproductive organs. In ancient Egypt the Ba (Soul) was depicted as a bird (the stork) – hence the popular myth that new babies – returning souls – are carried to earth by a stork. Again we see a relationship between a bird, the creative womb, and the regenerative quality of the sacral chakra.

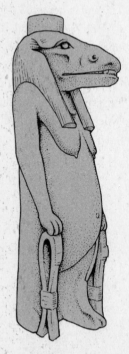

Taueret

TAUERET

Taueret is the ancient Egyptian Goddess of maternity and childbirth. She takes the form of a female hippopotamus, with large breasts. As a protectress of pregnant and feeding women, Taueret was sometimes depicted with the head of a roaring lion. Her energy can be called on to guard all pregnant women, especially those experiencing difficulty, from negative forces.

ÒSUN

Òsun, the glamorous river Goddess of the Yorùbá people, is one of Africa's most powerful and loved deities. Sweet, flirtatious and erotic, Òsun is seducing the world and gaining an international reputation. No party or festival is complete without the energy of Òsun. She is the force behind the arts, music, dancing and all forms of creativity. Òsun is in charge of conception and birth; once her children are born, she allows her sister, the Goddess Yemoja (*see page 157*) to mother them, freeing her to create wealth, which she is very good at. She also holds the power to see the future by reading the oracle with 16 cowrie shells. If elegance, prosperity, power and femininity are what you seek, then Òsun is the Goddess to ask.

One of the earliest known forms of Goddess. This ancient Egyptian bird Goddess is also known as Nathor.[6]

TIAMAT (NUN IN EGYPT, THE PRIMORDIAL OCEAN)

Tiamat is the Babylonian Sea Goddess from whose formless body the universe was created. Tiamat's first creation was a pair of serpents, called Lakhmu and Lakhamu. Tension between the serpents created the celestial realms above and the terrestrial realm below. This separation caused a loss of harmony which upset Tiamat and caused her wrath. Soon all her creation was in chaos. Marduk, son of Tiamat, turned on his mother and divided her body into many pieces. Having slain his mother he then took credit for her creation.

ISHTAR

Ishtar is the great Goddess of the heavens. She is the bright, shining star of morning and night. In her dual aspect, Ishtar is both a Goddess of love and a mighty warrior. She has the power to conquer over death. Ishtar enters the underworld and descends the seven steps to face Erishnigal, the Goddess of death. In her absence, plant, animal and human fertility ceases. Eventually the all-powerful Ishtar is released and rises again to restore fertility. If you deny your Self, and seem afraid of your own power and beauty, then tune to the healing energy of the Goddess Ishtar. She will bring strength and Self-knowledge.

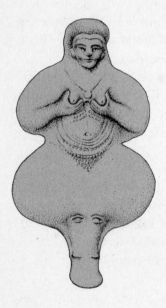

Ishtar, the Great Mother Goddess, was worshipped in relation to the morning and evening stars, hence her name. This ancient Babylonian Goddess was known as Astar to the Ethiopians, Astarte to the Phoenicians, Ashtart to the Caananites, and Esther to the Israelites.

RAKINI

Rakini is the emergence of Shakti in the sacral chakra, known as Rakini Shakti to the Dravidians. Rakini rocks the emotions, bringing both pleasure and pain. She bears in her four hands the arrow of erotic love, the skull – symbolizing romance and the emotions ruling the head – an axe, showing her warrior nature and ability to cut through all obstacles, and a drum that beats the rhythm of time. Rakini is also honoured for her music and art.

SARASWATI

Saraswati is the ancient river Goddess of India. She sits on a lotus flower (symbol of the chakras) and plays the vina (classical Indian stringed instrument). Goddess of knowledge, wisdom and the arts, Saraswati is attributed with creating the Sanskrit alphabet and language. This suggests she is older than her husband, the God Brahma. Saraswati has a fine intellect aided by intuition and a love of the arts. For help with exams and academic work, Saraswati can provide the balance that is needed for success.

CHANDRA DEVI

Chandra is Sanskrit for moon, and Devi for Goddess. Chandra Devi, then, is Goddess of the moon, the beautiful Divine mother. 'Devi' is often added to the name of women in India as a form of respect and recognition of the Goddess within.

MARY

Mary is the biblical universal mother, modelled on Isis, Ishtar, Aphrodite and other ancient Goddesses. Patriarchy stripped Mary of her Goddess nature and she became 'just a mother'. Do you recognize this expression? Yes, Mary was the first. Her fate has had a detrimental effect on women. Her status as an all-powerful Supreme Being needs to be restored. If you identify with Mary, then raise her and yourself up. See her embodied with the essence of the other sacral Goddesses, like Yemoja, who have never lost their power.

DEMETER

Demeter is the ancient Greek Goddess of fertility and motherhood. She symbolizes the creative energy of nature, which bears fruit and corn in spring. It is her joy at being reunited with her daughter Persephone that brings abundance to the earth. When Persephone returns to the underworld in autumn, Demeter's grief leaves the earth bare. Demeter knows the pain of a mother's loss and can be called on in times of despair.

APHRODITE

The Greek Goddess Aphrodite is associated with Hathor and Òṣun. She personifies love, wisdom and sexuality. Her name means 'foam risen', one who comes from the sea. She delights in sexual activity and creates a bond between lovers. In her time sex was considered sacred. The power of Aphrodite was much sought after by the Gods.

Mythology

THE GODDESS YEMOJA

Yemoja is Goddess of the seven seas, and she has as many aspects to her character. Affectionately called 'mami tutu', mother of the water, from her womb-like waters the earth is born, as we are born from the watery womb of our beloved mothers. Yemoja is mother to all that exists, and guardian of all seven chakras.

She is mother to Olókun, with whom she shares ownership of water. When upset by the Òrìshà or by people, Yemoja rages and begins taking over land. She can be placated with prayer and offerings of watermelon, her favourite fruit. Once appeased she quickly retreats. Although capable of destruction, Yemoja is happier giving life.

She is the beautiful, fertile, loving, maternal Goddess of the ocean. As she dances the lacy white ruffles of her turquoise skirt are seen as waves on the silver sea. Her curly black hair, which shines on the seabed, is the nutritious food, seaweed. Yemoja's treasure consists of many shells which reflect her beauty. The most precious is the cowrie shell, used to carry messages from the Òrìshà to beings on earth. When Yemoja walks on earth fountains and springs are born from her breasts. Rivers emerge that flow back to the sea, guided by Yemoja's sister, Òṣun.

Yemoja birthed the sun, moon and stars after a passionate affair with Olódùmárè. In thanks for the priceless children Yemoja produced, Olódùmárè gave her Ochumare, the seven-coloured rainbow, to wear on her head.

All women and gentle-men embody seven aspects of the Goddess Yemoja's character – the ability to express:

- beauty
- sensuality
- fertility and creativity
- motherhood/parenting
- turbulent emotions
- dance, allowing energy to flow through the sacrum
- treasures, including the seven-coloured rainbow of the chakras.

Expression

When energy is permitted to flow freely, through the sacral chakra, the essence of the Goddess will be present. If energy moves easily in your sacral centre you will know and experience:

a connection with the Goddess

Self-knowledge

how to be centred

a sense of peacefulness and harmony

love and trust in your Self

beauty within and around you

empathy and concern for others

a positive Self-image

confidence

inner security

independence

a balanced ego

---

your emotions easily roused

being able to cry easily

positive feelings about your body

sensuality

regular, pain-free menstruation

sexuality as sacred

the bliss of orgasm

well-functioning reproductive organs

creativity

the pleasure of the senses.

Disturbance

When energy is restricted in the sacral chakra you will feel:

a need for constant reassurance

extremely shy and lacking in self-confidence

that other people's opinions are more valuable than your own

insecure and jealous of others

manipulative

very emotional and over-sensitive

indecisive

a need for constant entertainment and sensual pleasures, possibly overindulging
in food, sweets, chocolate, drink and unsatisfying sexual activity.

You may also:

find it hard to be alone

harbour a sense of inadequacy.

Physically, insufficient energy in the sacral centre can cause:

cystitis

kidney problems

low libido and lack of interest in sex

cancer

prostate trouble

lower back pain

gynaecological problems

fertility problems

period pains and irregularities

problems during pregnancy and childbirth.

The sacral chakra, as the name suggests, is the sacred home of the Self. Energy emanating from this centre connects you to the Goddess within, enabling you to resonate with her creative power and exquisite beauty. To realize your own beauty, in the broadest sense of the word, is the lesson of this chakra. Once you truly recognize beauty in yourself, you see it all around: in nature, in others, even in those who wrong you. You enjoy the company of others, expressing love and knowing friendship.

As you increase the energy that flows through your pelvis, the mystery of sacred sexuality will be revealed to you. Your fertility and creativity will be enhanced. In Western countries many people, women especially, tend to restrict movement through the pelvis. This is a direct result of the many distorted views about sex and the prevalence of abusive behaviour. As you walk, the spine should be upright and the hips should swing. On the African continent and in many countries, women walk tall, balancing heavy items on their heads perfectly, with the weight evenly distributed through the spine and into the hips, which sway easily as they walk. A rigid pelvis is not a healthy one. Self-esteem, creativity, your emotional Self and all the pelvic organs suffer when you limit energy in the sacral centre. If your sacral energy is limited, the work below will be of great benefit. If your energy flows well, your connection to the Goddess within will be enhanced and maintained.

SEVEN WAYS OF OPENING TO SPIRIT AT THE SACRAL CHAKRA

Altar Work

Your altar for the sacral chakra needs to resonate with feminine watery energy. As you prepare to change your altar from earth (root chakra) to water (sacral chakra), remember to give thanks. Take time to acknowledge all you received from the earth. Be aware of the healing and growth you achieved during your earth energy work, and feel the enhanced flow of energy through your root chakra.

Sense the energy of water as you begin to prepare your new altar. Drink some water and feel it as it moves slowly around your mouth, into your throat, through your oesophagus into your stomach. Taste is the sense associated with the sacral chakra, so really be aware of how water itself tastes.

The colour of the sacral centre is orange, so use an orange-coloured natural cloth (cotton or silk) on your altar. Greeny-blue shades of water are alternative colours for your altar base. Reserve this cloth for use on your altar only.

Place four orange candles in the cardinal directions. Use sweet-smelling incense or essential oils such as ylang ylang, jasmine and rose. Fill your space with the soft smell of the Goddess. Put fresh spring water in a central position.

Orange-coloured gems are used to raise the sacral chakra vibration. Carnelian, amber and orange calcite can all be used; you may know of others. Add shells; they are gems of the sea which carry the voice of water energy. Take a walk along a beach and see which shells speak to you. Take them home for your altar; remember to thank Yemoja, otherwise you are stealing her jewels.

The sacral chakra is about coming home and meeting your higher Self. It is about generating self-esteem and inner beauty, and learning to express yourself sexually and creatively. Let your altar emanate beauty. Buy flowers, special candles, beautiful vessels for water. Splash out, you deserve the best. Know that what you give to the Goddess with love and trust in the universe, will return to you tenfold.

Journal-keeping

BODY MAP

This is a useful technique for increasing body awareness. Read the text through once first, and then practise with your eyes closed.

Begin by sitting comfortably, or lie down if you prefer. Be aware of your breath, its depth, which body parts move? Where does each breath reach? As you breathe, what happens to your feet, head, hands, etc.? Scan your body inside and out.

Now move your attention into your body and feel each part from inside. Start at your feet and work upwards. Be aware of any tightness, tension or pain. Feel the temperature of different parts. You may sense tingling or pins and needles. Are there any areas with little or no sensation? Stay still for a while and develop a visual map of your body.

When you feel ready, get up and take some time to draw a map of your body. It can be realistic or abstract. One way is to draw an outline first and then fill in the different parts as you see and feel them. This is not art in the classic sense of the word, so feel free to explore without judging yourself. When you have finished drawing, reflect on your body map and write a few key words – words that come to you quickly will be the most useful. Take as much time as you need. Remember to date your work – this is how you feel today.

Which parts of your body do you like and dislike? What do you love about your body? Where do you see your beauty manifested physically? How does your drawing reflect how you feel about yourself? There is of course no separation between body image and Self-image. Whatever you create on paper is an unfolding of your beautiful and unique Self.

Yoga Path

TANTRA YOGA

The ancient science and art of tantra,[7] created by the original people of India, is the mother of yoga. She birthed many paths of yoga, including hatha, bhakti (devotion to deities), Kundalini and nada (yoga of sound). She also created many vehicles for spiritual development, such as mandalas, mudras (hand gestures)[8] and rituals. Ayurvedic medicine – herbs, massage, breathing practices and elaborate methods of non-invasive diagnosis – is the child of tantra. Indian astrology – understanding the influence of the celestial realms – also claims tantra as a parent. The chakra system, with which we are now working, evolves directly from tantra.

Limestone carving of the Indian Serpent Goddess Kundalini

The Sanskrit word *tantra* means to expand and liberate. Shiva and Shakti are the male and female polarities of being. Shiva is the inanimate primordial source of pure undifferentiated energy. Shakti is the potent life-giving force which animates all energy. We embrace within ourselves Shiva and Shakti, the source and the force. Tantra aims to expand and liberate these energies, in order to create spiritual union. We each hold the potential to know and fully express both our male and female energies.

Swami Satyananda Saraswati, who is a leading exponent on all aspects of yoga and tantra, says:

> Tantra aims to transform every action of life into a ritual, so that the individual performs every action and thought with a feeling of worship and awareness.[9]

For the tantra yogi, everything is a manifestation of the almighty Goddess Shakti. When Shakti moves she awakens the God Shiva; they are one. There is no separation between the worldly and the spiritual, because Shakti is everywhere and everything. Tantra is a system of pleasure, excitement and joy. It challenges us to raise our awareness within the world to such a degree that we are able, through the manifest, to recognize the un-manifest, through the worldly to see the spiritual. We are invited to journey through the chakras, developing our unique Selves towards universal Beings.

Tantra seeks to expand and liberate all aspects of life, including the powerful sexual energy. Sexuality and the sexual act are not dismissed in tantra. They are, however, only one aspect of tantra. We live in a time and a society that has lost respect for the sacredness of sexuality. Sex has become abused, misrepresented, repressed and distorted. Tantra takes us back to a time when sexuality was not separated from other aspects of life, a time when both women and sexuality were revered. Tantra is not limited to sex, it is a **science and art for living**.

Tantra contains numerous practices and rituals for developing ourselves holistically. It has many levels through which it can be understood. This interpretation is brief and seemingly basic, but if you can incorporate this understanding of tantra into your life and truly transform each thought and action into ritual, then you will achieve the highest heights and greatest rewards right here, now, on earth.

Every day when you wake, give thanks for the gift of another new day, another opportunity to shine. As you meet the elements, say a prayer. They are with you all day – water as you bathe, fire as you cook and keep warm, the earth that always supports your movements, the air that allows you to breathe. We are truly blessed. To practise tantra yoga is to cease taking life for granted and begin to glory in the simple pleasures and joys of life. How much happier you will be when to breathe is recognized as a gift. How rich you become when food is a blessing from the Gods.

How full of love and grace you will feel when sexual union regains its sacredness. As all aspects of your life take on a spiritual significance, you will begin to slow down, stress will not hold you so tightly in its grip and Divine consciousness will grow inside you.

The lesson to be learned from tantra yoga is expanded awareness. We can embrace the very essence of tantra through honouring and celebrating ourselves, those around us and the world we live in every moment of the day. Through tantra you can grow to celebrate the unique unfolding of your life.

Mindful Exercise

DEVIASANA (GODDESS POSE)

Lie on your back with your legs stretched out. Then, bring your heels towards your pelvis, put the soles of your feet together and let your knees fall out to the sides. Relax in this pose, allowing energy to flow freely through your pelvis into your legs, and from your legs into your pelvis. Enjoy the sensation as energy floods your pelvis. Breathe deeply into your pelvis and hold the posture for 5 minutes or as long as is comfortable for you. Relax, with legs outstretched, then return to the pose. Repeat three times.

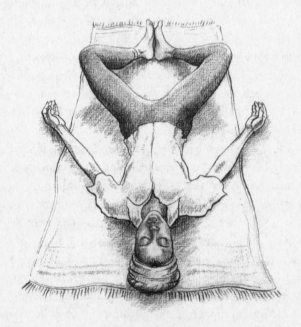

Deviasana (Goddess Pose)

EXERCISE TO CENTRE ENERGY

Sunrise

This can be done kneeling or standing.

Kneeling position – sit on your heels, your legs tucked under you, your spine erect. Rest your palms on your knees.

Standing position – feet hip-width apart; your body is upright, hips and shoulders are open, creating space across your chest and pelvis. Relax your arms at your sides.

From the position of your choice, take a deep breath. Feel contact with the earth on which you rest. Let go of any tightness, focusing your mind on the rhythm of your breath. Bring your focus to the centre of your body – 2 inches (5 cm) below the navel. This is where the sacral chakra, or Hara in martial arts, resides.

From this point of focus, visualize energy moving up through your belly, your chest, around your shoulders and along your arms to your hands. Feel the sensation in your hands.

Maintaining the focus and sensation of energy, inhale and begin slowly to raise your arms up in front of you. Lift them above your head, and turn your palms away from your ears. As you exhale, slowly lower your arms, taking them out to your sides as if drawing an arc. Remain sitting on your knees and rest for a moment.

Repeat three to seven times. Pay attention to your breath, open your body and feel the movement of energy inside. Imagine you are on a mountaintop and the air around you is fresh and full of life-giving prana. Take that prana into your centre and let it radiate through every part of your being.

This simple movement brings you in touch with the power of your own centre. It allows you to change consciousness at will. Extremely useful in stressful situations, it is calming, balancing and centring.

Butterfly Walk

Sit on the floor with your soles together, knees falling out to the sides. Hold your ankles. Your back and head are relaxed and falling forward. Keep holding your ankles as you move your feet away from you, as far as you can. Sit comfortably without straining. Now rock your pelvis and, still holding your ankles, 'walk' towards your feet. Once you arrive at your feet, begin walking the pelvis back again. Repeat three to seven times. Finish with the feet away from you, head down and back relaxed. Rest for a few moments, completely still. Feel the energy flowing through your pelvis and legs.

In this exercise energy is directed into the pelvis and legs. Energy can accumulate in the pelvis and restrict a regular flow between the upper and lower parts of the body. This limits development at all levels of our being. This walking unblocks energy in the pelvis and sacral chakra, which can then be distributed through the whole body.

Butterfly Walk

Meditation

Developing your meditation practice is a very important aspect of chakra work. It requires the discipline of the root chakra and a longing for Self-knowledge. When we direct our attention inwards, searching for the higher Self, like the Ancients before us we discover the secrets of the universe.

At the centre of the sacral chakra lies a crescent moon. The moon is a mirror, offering us the opportunity to see our true reflection. She is a symbol of our potential for growth. We can rely on the crescent moon to dance across the sky, changing her shape as she moves. She is wise and not afraid to reach her full potential. She is also prepared to fall and is willing to start the dance over and over again.

DHARANA

Prepare for your meditation as suggested in Chapter 5. We will practise dharana using the crescent moon. The colour of this symbol is orange. Lying within the crescent moon is the Black Dot. Close your eyes and see in front of you the dark screen, known as the *chidakash*. As you breathe deeply and evenly, allow the crescent moon, symbol of the sacral chakra, to appear on the screen. In your mind's eye see the soft lines of the crescent moon, the lower and longer line that holds the upper, shorter line in its embrace. Like a mother holds her child, the higher Self holds the developing individual soul. Keep the clearly defined image on your inner screen.

See the all-powerful Black Dot in the centre. Focus on the Black Dot. Maintain your practice for the desired length of time. Lengthening your practice will be a natural progression.

DYNAMIC

Visualize the crescent moon. Let yourself relax into the practice as you clearly define the symbol in your mind's eye. Now take your awareness to the sacral centre and feel the moon deep within. Slowly watch the waxing and waning of the moon, feel her as she changes shape. See her reflection in the ocean, feel the water inside you. Tune to the rhythm of moon and water. Be creative and let sensations flood through your system. Let the moon and her waters lift you; feel yourself supported, held in the sacred embrace of your higher Self. Let the waters of your soul overflow and unite with the ocean. She is your mother the Goddess, you are one. Stay with the experience and be present with whatever surfaces for you ... Gently return your awareness to the sacral centre, feel its gentle pulse. This is your unique dwelling place, the sacred home of I. In this place you can meet the inner Goddess and see yourself reflected in her beauty.

These meditations can be used to connect with your higher Self. As energy flows with ease through the sacral chakra you will experience a sense of who you are and what your real purpose is in this incarnation. You will begin to see beauty in your Self and beauty all around you. A sacred gateway will open inside, leaving you feeling at home in your Self. You will know through this sacred centre that whatever you can perceive you can achieve. There will be no stopping you in your newfound sense of Self and creativity.

Vibrational Work

COLOUR

Orange is the dominant colour of the sacral chakra. Its varies from soothing peach to a deep rusty orange, depending on the quality of your energy. It is a colour of inner strength and confidence. Its warm vibration can stimulate or calm. Harmonically, orange resonates with the earth and the moon; it also vibrates within one octave of our own DNA molecules[10] – this sonic relationship enhances self-regulation.[11] For thousands of years initiates in Asia have worn orange after taking renunciation vows. It is used because it can balance and charge the auric vibration. It is also a colour of sexual energy and is used to decorate the beds of newly married couples in Malaysia.

Take a moment to reflect on your feelings about this colour. Do you have it around you in your home, wardrobe, food? Could you use more of it? Orange can be used as a healing remedy; it will raise the vibration of a sluggish sacral centre. It is excellent for fatigue and exhaustion. The complementary colour of orange is blue, which can be used if you feel your sacral chakra is overcharged.

ESSENTIAL OILS

Orange and a range of other citrus essential oils are very good for reducing anxiety and stress because of their refreshing quality. Orange blossom is a luxurious oil that lifts the spirits and raises self-esteem. Mandarin is the main essential oil that can be used safely during pregnancy when the sacral chakra and water energies are extremely activated. Grapefruit, one of my favourites, has a soothing and balancing effect on the sacral chakra.

GEMS

Gems for the sacral chakra are carnelian, amber, orange calcite and coral. These all help balance sacral energies (for how to use, *see Chapter 6*). Amber is a resin that has been used as vibrational medicine since the time of the ancient Egyptians. One of its main uses is as protection: it can be worn as jewellery to purify negative energy.

The stimulating effects of gold have been known for a very long time. Traditionally in Africa gold was plentiful and worn in abundance. Gold is still used for wedding rings, which are worn on the water finger, in order to stimulate the sacral chakra and fertility.

Ritual

The root chakra ritual connected you to the earth and created an ancestral link with your foremothers. Once you are connected to the earth and your roots, you have a foundation to build on. You are ever free to receive gifts and guidance from your Ancestors. You can draw their powerful energy into your sacral centre and use it for self-healing and empowerment.

Ancestral energy focused in the sacral chakra strengthens Self. A strong sense of Self acknowledges inner beauty, wisdom, intuition and the ability to heal emotional wounds and grow in spiritual wealth. In this ritual I invite you to return to Yemoja and bathe in her beauty.

SEA BATHING

Plan a sacred visit to the ocean Goddess Yemoja. Take gifts of flowers, watermelon and light. Write a prayer for her and be ready to dance and play in her arms.

Most people appreciate the ocean. We love her beauty, her depth, her vastness and fluctuating rhythms. We close our eyes and soak up her loudness. We appreciate her calm and wonder at her wildness. The sea is without fear. She can hold us high on a wave, rock us gently in her arms and reassure us with whispers of wisdom.

Approach Yemoja with a prayer. Offer your gifts, and sail night-lights (without the aluminium) afloat on a large leaf. As they flow ask 'Mami water' for her blessing. Be specific – ask for the healing you need. Listen to her voice, dance with her waves and let her calming waters cleanse you. Absorb her powerful energy, drawing it deep into your sacral chakra. Feel your waters commune with hers as you return to the mother for nourishment. Know that she is always there for you, thank her for her welcome, her love and beauty ... Part when you are cleansed and full of her essence.

Let the waters of your soul be free, allow your energy to flow and let your inner light shine as you welcome the blessing of the sacred lunar chakra into your life.

> May you dwell ever with the Goddess
> May the Goddess dwell ever with you
> May all the dream seeds you planted
> Take root and flower and come true.
> *Shekkinah Mountain Water*

SOLAR PLEXUS CHAKRA

RAGE AND RADIANCE

Exalted is your power, O burning one, O sated one, O mighty one, powerful, skilful of flames, lady of the sky, mistress of the two lands, O eye of Horus and his guide ... lady of eternity, fiery one, O red one whose flame burns, Serpent Uraeus, who guides the people. O lady of fire, O searing one, O devourer, O scorching one, sovereign of thousands, may your awakening be peaceful.

Egyptian papyrus, 1600 BC[1]

THE SOLAR PLEXUS CHAKRA: CORRESPONDENCES

Sanskrit Name	Manipura
Meaning	Mani = jewel/gem; Pura = city: 'city of gems'
Main Function	Supplies energy in the form of heat, power and enthusiasm

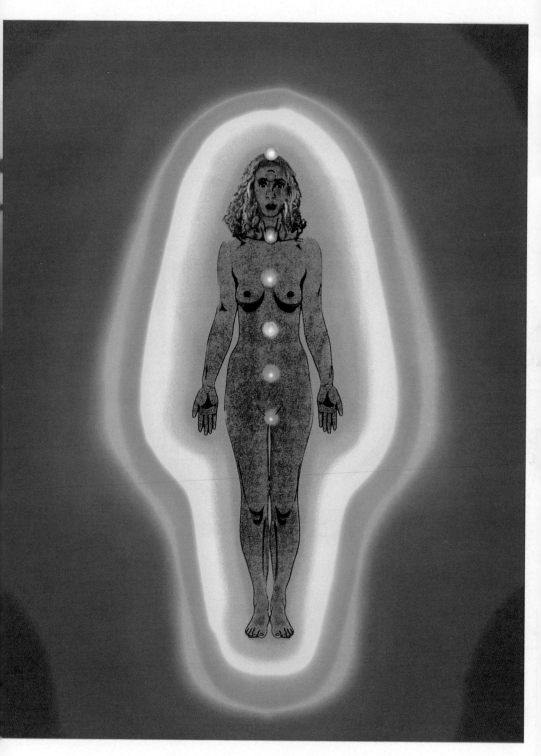

The seven major chakras and the aura.

Muladhara/Root chakra – showing Kundalini serpent energy.

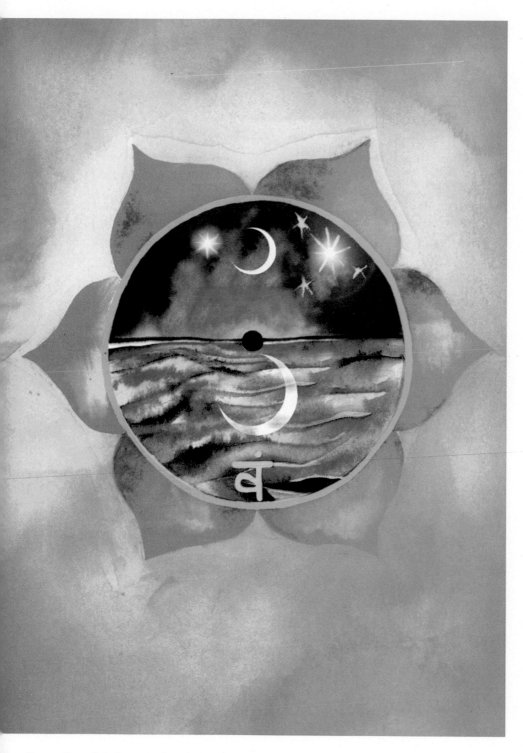

Swadistana/Sacral chakra – in this chakra the reflection of Self can be seen in the waters of your Soul.

Manipura/Solar plexus chakra – the fiery Sun which burns within each one of us.

Anaharta/Heart chakra – showing Maat, Egyptian Goddess of Truth.

Vishudda/Throat chakra – showing the 'Opon Ifá', the Yoruba Divination Tray. The 16 petals on this chakra resonate with 16 major Odu (Merindilogun Odu) of Ifá, the Yorùbá Spiritual teachings.

Ajna/Third eye chakra – the all-seeing eye of Horus.

Sahasrara/Crown chakra – the thousand-petalled lotus.

Quality	Feeling and Empowerment
Location	Base of the sternum

Spiritual Correspondences

Colour	Yellow
Element	Fire
Symbol	Inverted triangle
Seed Sound	Ram
Petals	Ten
Planet	Mars ♂
Esoteric Anatomy	Physical heat layer
Yoga Path	Karma
Guna Quality	Rajas

Physical Correspondences

Gland	Pancreas
Nerve Plexus	Celiac plexus
Body Parts	All digestive organs: stomach, small intestine, liver, gallbladder, spleen
Fire Energy Triad	Eyes, solar plexus and thighs
Expression	Full of energy and vitality
Disturbance	Hypoactive/hyperactive

Deities

Africa	Ra, Hathor, Ogun, Shango
India	Surya, Agni, Lakini, Rudra, Kali
Europe	Brigit
Mythology	Myths relating to the inner and external sun

Psychological Correspondences

Statement	'I feel'

EMOTIONS

BALANCED	UNBALANCED
Feel and express emotion easily	Controlled by emotions
Laughter	Unfeeling
Joy	Uncaring
Happiness	Quick-tempered
Passion	Flaring up
Rage, anger	Violence
Sadness	Despair
Conflict	Depression
Chronology	7 to 14 years
Rite of Passage	Puberty (ability to create life); blessed by fire
Developmental Stage	Creative and curious; ruled by will-power

Ways of Working

Foods	Starch, grains, legumes, sunflower seeds, sesame seeds, hot peppers
Herbs	Peppermint, cinnamon, liquorice (digestive herbs)
Oils	Rosemary, juniper, geranium, peppermint, black pepper, ginger, elemi, citrus oils
Gems	Citrine, tiger's eye, topaz

Main Function: To Generate Power

As we journey through the chakras, soul consciousness is raised. We become empowered and more of our potential is released. Ascending the chakras is magical: we return to the core and allow ourselves to enter the place of power deep within. At the root chakra we gained stability and courage from recognizing the innate gifts brought into this world. We enhanced this in the sacral centre, with self-knowledge and confidence. As knowledge increases we enter the solar plexus chakra.

The third chakra is concerned with the accomplishment of personal power and preparing for change. Balancing the solar plexus releases the abundance of inner wealth we have accumulated and moves us successfully towards the higher centres.

On a physical level, the digestive system is powered by the solar plexus. The stomach, liver, pancreas and other digestive organs are under its control. The fiery hydrochloric acid transforms food for life. The solar plexus is not only concerned with the digestion of food – feelings and emotions also need to be swallowed and digested. For example, *'how do we stomach our relationships with people?'* Some people feed and nurture us, others make us sick. These feelings are processed in the third chakra.

The solar plexus is a shining sun within the body. It functions as a generator and power house that fuels the entire organism. Too much fire and we overheat; too little and we are immobilized by a lack of energy. When this chakra is in balance nothing holds us back. We reign as kings and queens on the throne of our power. We are filled with warmth and express an abundance of passion and enthusiasm. We are assertive and quick to act, trusting in our ability to achieve.

Throughout time the sun has been recognized as the generator of all life. Without light from the sun, nothing would exist or survive. The Ancients recognized the power of the sun and accepted the bright jewel in the sky as the great creator. Manipura, the Sanskrit name for the solar plexus chakra, means 'city of gems'; it reflects the richness of the sun within this chakra.

QUALITY: FEELING

Feeling, which many of us fear, is the quality associated with manipura chakra. Our richness and power is often buried under a mountain of feelings which we refuse to recognize. Pain, frustration, anger and humiliation are juxtaposed with passion, joy, ambition and success. Many of us have learned to be afraid of our feelings, choosing to identify more with thoughts. Large amounts of energy are wasted in the effort to hold feelings down. Acknowledging them frees up energy and gives us a glimpse of our power. The more we accept and work with how we feel, the more empowered we become.

This chakra, by its fiery nature, is fraught with problems. It is known as *the seat of opposites* – a place where conflict arises. Our heads tell us one thing while our guts say another. The ensuing battle is felt in the solar plexus. Self-development tends to be most difficult at this stage because we fear power as much as our feelings. Rage or radiance, which is the sweeter? We need to feel our pain and experience our power. As energy balances in this centre we come to see that all life experiences, particularly the painful ones, have the potential to propel us forward.

I took a break from writing this section to watch a television documentary. I watched, surprised, by the synchronicity of what I was witnessing. People in the documentary were sharing their experiences of pain and torture. One man's story really moved me because he had manifested the power and passion to transform his pain and re-build his life. He had survived the horrors of Hitler's concentration camps. This man, of African and German parentage, told his story with tears in his eyes, pausing occasionally to wipe his face. I felt his pain yet it was his appreciation for life that struck me most. His passion is to sing and he was told by others in the camp, all of whom died, that if he ever escaped with his life he should sing professionally, which, by the grace of our creator, he went on to do. Though disturbing to hear his story, it demonstrated empowerment through pain. This man truly knows the richness of simply being alive. He had transformed rage into radiance.

Trauma, pain, loneliness, anger and fear can all be transformed once we are really willing to give them up. When we are honest with ourselves about our feelings, we can start to change them. Disturbances in the chakras often have secondary benefits. For example, holding on to pain may mean we don't have to forgive, or holding on to fear may mean we don't have to move forward. Whatever holds you back, is it time for you to let go of it? The solar plexus chakra is your centre of power; from here you can create whatever you want.

First be honest with yourself; take time in meditation to ask the universe for help and prepare to do the necessary work. Call on your will, which resides in this chakra. Will is conscious action; personal power has no direction without will. Like the sun and its rays, the solar plexus chakra equips you for brilliance and fuels you for success. It places your life in your charge.

Element: Fire

Close your eyes and visualize fire for a moment. See, feel and hear it ... I immediately sense its warmth, brightness and sparkle. I imagine both the fear and excitement felt when the Ancients first learned to make fire. Fire is both friend and enemy. It can protect you and keep you warm, but if it gets out of control it can burn or even devour you. Fire fuels laughter and joy, but it can also flare up, causing anger and violence.

Fire is one of the most abused elements. As children, we learn quickly that to be vibrant, excited and full of energy annoys adults. To maintain their love we dampen our fire energy. Adults often misuse fire energy by overpowering people, particularly children. Children are often humiliated and treated in ways that no adult would tolerate; yet children are expected to accept it. Fire energy is often damaged and distorted very early on in life. As we grow we may learn either to block fire because we don't like the way we have seen it used, or to express it angrily. Few people seem to learn the balanced use of fire energy.

When balanced, fire is an amazing element. It is full of vitality, fast, cleansing and forceful. It fuels the shamanic warrior, who uses the clarity and strength of fire to eliminate adversity. It possesses the Goddess Durga, who stands on a lion as both warrior and Divine mother. She uses fire to destroy ignorance and give birth to knowledge. We too can learn to channel our fire creatively. Fire is the element that provides the vision and drive needed to generate the change you dream about.

As a fiery centre the solar plexus is a great transformer. Working with the energy of this chakra changes followers into leaders, creates survivors from victims, and transforms the powerless into the powerful. A spark of motivation and a flame of will can swell into an all-powerful burning sun.

Planet: Mars ♂

The ancient Egyptians gave the name Heru Khuti to the planet we now call Mars. Heru Khuti was one of the many forms of the fiery sun God Ra. The Sphinx that guards the pyramids at Giza in Egypt is said to be a monument to Heru Khuti. From the power of the sun Heru Khuti created himself. This beautiful, protective God is also a mighty warrior.

To the ancient Romans Mars was the fiery God of war. He symbolizes the ego and destructive nature of the solar plexus. Pride and ego can be the cause of much inner conflict. Sometimes it is appropriate to let go of ego and selfishness in order to move forward. In martial arts the concept of yielding is primary. Learning to go with the flow will bring results, whereas fighting fire with fire will only create an explosion. In personal relationships, for example, what are the needs of those close to you? Can you learn to yield without feeling you are losing your power?

Mars in his creative aspect is the God of agriculture. He rules Aries, which is the first zodiac sign (21st March – 21st April). Spring is a good time of year to start new projects, as Aries is the sign of new beginnings and abundance. People born under this sign often use solar plexus energy with ease and make inspirational leaders. The ram, associated with Aries and the Egyptian sun God Ra, is the sacred animal of the solar plexus chakra. Rams represent ego and mind power. They are sacrificial animals, who have to be slaughtered like the Lamb of God to save our souls. The fiery ego must be controlled and occasionally sacrificed in order to reap the abundant riches of the city of gems.

Deities

RA

The ancient Egyptians called the sun God Ra. Ra is the great creator and sustainer of life. Ra's mother, the sky Goddess Nut, swallows Ra at night, embracing the sun in her belly; this creates darkness. Every day Nut gives birth to Ra, delivering light.

Solar energy is the powerful spirit deep within that we can birth each day to give us vision and direction. Pharaohs referred to themselves as 'sons of the sun' and inherited the power and wisdom of Ra. As we balance the solar plexus chakra we too can share this inheritance.

HATHOR

Hathor, of the sacral chakra, we meet again in the solar plexus. Here she is the fiery lioness Sekhmet, the embodiment of female rage, the fearless animal possessed by seven demons is ready to fight and kill all that stand in her path. As women we need not stand back and take all that comes to us. When you really need to fight for what you know to be right, don't be afraid to draw on the power of Sekhmet, protectress and keeper of Maat – the personification of Truth.

Hathor wears both the solar disc and crescent moons on her head-dress. She aims to unify the sun and moon. Hathor appears to give her name to hatha yoga – Hatha also means sun and moon. (In Sanskrit the sun is called surya and the moon is known as chandra.) Hatha yoga aims to unite the sun and moon. Hathor embodies lunar and solar energies and resonates with the sacral and solar plexus chakras.

SHANGO

Yemoja's son Shango is the Òrìshà of thunder. The spontaneous sounder of heavenly drums also produces lightning, a skill he learned from his wife Òyá. Shango is loud and temperamental; his energy is present during arguments. Fortunately he is a great problem-solver who can be both intuitive and emphatic. Like his animal, the ram, Shango knows sacrifice. He hanged himself after seeing his own wrong-doing, only to be deified by his followers. Much can be learned from the fiery wrath of Shango, whose energy is often very productive.

A head from a staff of Shango, traditionally carried by Shango's Priests. Fiery Shango is one of the most feared Òrìshà. He uses his double-headed axe to make war. Shango's axe also symbolizes the balance of force and wisdom.

SURYA

Surya is the great sun God of Indian spirituality. When an eighth of his radiant brilliance was removed to entice his wife to return, it was used to make weapons for war. Surya's radiance became the tools of rage. Surya is called by 12 names to reflect his many attributes; among these names are Indra – Lord of the Gods and destroyer of enemies, Dhata – Creator of all things, and Vivasan – who causes good digestion.

AGNI

Agni is the Indian divinity of fire. He appears in the heavens as the flaming sun, in the air as the fiery lightning rod, and on earth Agni is fire. As the hearth fire he is the protector and guardian of all homes. Agni the son of heaven and earth rides on a ram with his body radiating seven rays of light. Agni is a great purifier and rapid transformer of negative energy.

LAKINI

The Goddess Lakini is the triple-headed manifestation of Shakti energy in the solar plexus. She has four hands: in the first she holds the vajra (which is a thunderbolt); in the second an arrow shot from the bow of Kama, the lord of sex, symbolizing liberated sexual energy which can be focused and redirected; she holds fire in her third hand, and in her fourth she forms *abhye mudra*, the gesture of fearlessness. Lakini Shakti personifies courage and independence.

RUDRA

Rudra, the God of fire and storms, is the destructive aspect of Shiva.[2] He is no stranger to death, striking mortals and animals with his arrow. It is said that even the other Gods fear him. Yet Rudra, as we have come to learn of fire energy, is not all bad. He is the bestower of blessings in abundance, with the capacity to heal. From Rudra we can learn the control needed to bring balance to the solar plexus chakra.

KALI

Kali is the dynamic warrior Goddess, the mother who takes no nonsense, especially from husbands and children. She is a survivor who, having maintained her black skin colour, has met with much prejudice. Her character has been polarized into that of a ferocious, blood-thirsty black Goddess. Kali is fierce and, when necessary, will castrate and behead without thinking much of it, but she is also a compassionate mother who knows the pain of life and death and is not afraid of either. Kali is a powerful female who does not like ignorance and will go to any lengths to destroy it.

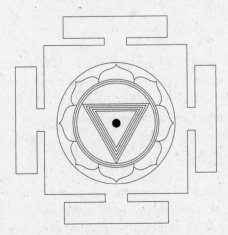

Yantra of primordial energy and creation. Kali is the Black Dot at the centre of this yantra. She is the womb from which all worlds emanate.

OPENING TO SPIRIT

BRIGIT

Like Kali, the Celtic Saint Brigit was originally a triple Goddess. She personifies the virgin, the mother and the crone. She is a teacher of martial arts and patron of warfare. As the Goddess of plenty, Brigit is at home in the solar plexus, which is our centre of abundance and richness.

Mythology

Ogun is a blacksmith and hunter who never tires of work. He is a warrior and guardian of the forest. He makes tools from iron and metal to cut through the undergrowth in the woods, preparing the path for civilization. A strong man with a passion for trouble and war, who acts quickly and therefore makes many mistakes, although troublesome he detests lies. In parts of Nigeria, oaths were sworn over a piece of metal in his name. This quiet but fiery Òrìshà is the father of technology, providing all kinds of transport, machinery and surgical tools. Ogun protects all those who work with metal.

One myth tells us that Ogun, who is a loner by nature, took himself off to the forest following a fight with his brother Shango. Shango was having an affair with Òyá, who was originally Ogun's wife. Due to Ogun's primary role in creating civilization, all the Òrìshà missed him. After he refused to return, the Òrìshà decided to go and get him. Òrúnmìlà, elder and master of divination, went first. The others were sure he would succeed, but Òrúnmìlà failed to persuade Ogun to leave the forest. Ogun insisted on remaining in the forest even after several Òrìshà went to fetch him.

As they were despairing and the work of civilization was slowing down, the beautiful Goddess Òṣun had an idea. She asked her elders for permission to enter the forest and return with Ogun. Unsure exactly how she would achieve this, after others had failed, she was granted permission as the elders felt that everything must be tried.

Òṣun went to prepare herself. She tied five yellow silk scarves around her waist, and placed a pot of honey beneath them. She ran singing and dancing into the forest. Ogun soon heard her songs and smelled the sweetness of honey. On seeing her, he was intoxicated with desire. Òṣun danced and Ogun followed. When he got close she wet his lips with her honey; Òṣun tied her scarves together and used them to lead Ogun back to civilization. Forgetting his resolve, Ogun followed his senses. As soon as he left the forest and greeted the Òrìshà, he turned to see that Òṣun, having achieved her goal, had disappeared.

From Ogun we can learn many lessons. We see that stubbornness can halt our creativity, and that desire can lead us off-track. The anger and isolation of Ogun hides his pain at losing his wife. Those who express fire easily often bury their feeling, fearing that no one will understand them. Ogun teaches the importance of balance, patience and justice. These qualities are needed for our ascent into the heart chakra.

Entrance gateway to the Ọsun shrine in Ọṣogbo, Nigeria, depicting Ọsun and Ogun, the hunter.

Expression

When the inner sun is free to shine, its rays will fill your being with light. You will not be afraid to strike while the iron is hot, forging ahead towards realizing your unique potential, and living abundantly. You will be free to:

feel full of energy and vitality

feel joy and abundance

express love, happiness and passion

feel in possession of inner strength

feel a strong sense of right and wrong

feel rage when abused

trust and own your feelings

feel and act on your intuition

know courage and fearlessness

know your warrior nature

know and own your personal power

be respectful of yourself and others

OPENING TO SPIRIT

enjoy clarity of mind

be full of curiosity and creativity.

Disturbance

When energy is unbalanced in the solar plexus chakra, you may be:

unfeeling and uncaring

controlled by anger

violent

hypoactive/hyperactive

lacking vitality, feeling depressed and despairing

fearful and mistrusting

prone to act before thinking

prone to accidents

full of ego and bravado

selfish

unaware of your own and other people's feelings

dictatorial

loud and aggressive

prone to cover your pain with anger

quick-tempered, flaring up easily.

Unbalanced energy in the solar plexus can cause the following problems:

eye problems

headaches

all types of digestive problems

liver problems

ulcers

diabetes

gallstones

exhaustion

fatigue and low energy

inflammation and skin rashes

eating disorders

fevers.

The solar plexus is the body's powerhouse – it generates energy in the form of heat, power and enthusiasm. It is one of the most misunderstood and abused chakras. When energy is blocked at this level, we witness a person who is self-centred, aggressive and capable of inflicting great damage to Self and others. Many politicians have a solar plexus disturbance and seek to control other people. Our prisons are also full of people with distorted fire chakras.

Another effect of solar plexus imbalance can be self-harm. People who are denied power may use the little power they have to harm themselves. Women often suffer from depression, self-mutilation and eating disorders because of this imbalance.

As we have seen, fire energy is not all negative but can be put to good use. It offers protection, warmth and rapid transformation. It is the force behind the person we see as fun-loving, creative and assertive, the person who is clear about what they want and determined to have it, a person of sharp intellect who is not afraid to destroy in order to construct anew.

In the body, the solar plexus governs the digestive system and the fiery hydrochloric acid needed to transform food for life. Too much fire and we overheat, too little and we are immobilized by a lack of energy. Fire's dynamic force is perhaps its most essential quality. The warm light and glow, the charisma and passion of fire can be recognized within each individual. The solar plexus is the rich 'city of gems' which provides the raw materials that we can wear as rage or radiance, weapons or jewels.

SEVEN WAYS OF OPENING TO SPIRIT AT THE SOLAR PLEXUS CHAKRA

Altar Work

You are now ready to replace your water altar with a fire altar. Give thanks as you change things around. Feel your sacral chakra strengthened as a result of the work you have done. Begin to create your solar plexus chakra altar. This will raise fire energy. A dynamic, warm, passionate ambience is to be created – a feast for the eyes, since sight is the sense associated with the fire element.

Lay down a base cloth, choosing yellow or another colour from the rays of the sun. You will need four yellow candles to place in the cardinal directions. Chunky candles with big flames are really good for this altar. Burn incense or essential oils that have a warm aroma – try rosemary, geranium or ginger. Refresh your water pot.

Crystals to be used are citrine, tiger's eye, topaz or other yellow stones that hold the sun's energy. In the summer you may find sunflowers which can be placed on your altar; they have absorbed lots of energy.

Fire energy is about rapid transformation. Ra, Shango, Ogun and Kali are deities of change; have pictures of them on your altar. Symbolize the sun and fire in any way that feels appropriate to you.

The solar plexus – shining sun within the body – is our Divine source of light and life. From this centre we generate our direction in life; from here we see our potential, and produce the power required to fuel prosperity and abundance. These concerns are not counter to spiritual development, quite the opposite. It is when we have satisfied our earthly needs that we look towards heaven. From the light of this altar, begin to clarify your vision in life. Start to see what is really unfolding in your life at this time. Where have you been and where are you going right now?

Journal-keeping

ABUNDANCE

Beneath anger often lies pain, and below pain, treasure. This is true in the solar plexus, as it is the very place where we store and then bury our hurts. The diaphragm is a sheet of muscle, much like an umbrella, that separates the chest from the abdomen. If pain rises up and reaches the heart, then it really hurts. We all know this and have learned unconsciously to store pain in the belly, under the protection of the diaphragm. This would be the perfect answer, only the pain also entraps our richness. A tremendous amount of energy is used in holding the pain down. If you are really to shine and fully experience your abundant capacity for fulfilment, then anger, resentment and pain must be transformed.

The Goddess Hathor holds a double-sided mirror in her hand. One side is clear, in which she sees her reflection; the other side is rough, to ward off negative energies. Negative energy often comes at us because we project it outwards (not always, but often). In Niger (West Africa) they say 'Ashes fly back in the faces of those who throw fire.' The more we can look in the mirror and see ourselves, the more we can deflect negativity. As we release some of our anger and feel our pain we gain access to the buried treasure of the solar plexus, the city of gems.

TRANSFORMING ANGER

If you are ready to begin transforming anger, answer these simple questions in your journal:

◎ What made you angry last week? **or**

◎ What could you have got angry about last week, but didn't?

◎ What does that remind you of from your childhood?

◎ How did you deal with the situation last week?

◎ How would you have liked to deal with it?

◎ What do you appreciate about what happened?

◎ What do you appreciate that has changed now you are an adult?

◎ What do you appreciate about how you dealt with this issue?

◎ What have you learned about yourself?

Before setting this exercise down here in this book, I completed it myself. As a child of Ogun (my ancestral father[3]) born under the sign of Aries, I love fire. Mostly I have learned to use it to my advantage, which I appreciate, but I can also flare up. This exercise helped me see that in some situations I am guarded and find it easier to shout than to say that I am hurting.

As children we develop coping mechanisms, which are no longer needed once we are adults. Once we understand this we can sit fully in our power. The simple yet powerful exercise outlined above prepares us for journal work on the next chakra (heart chakra), which is about forgiveness of Self and others.

Yoga Path

KARMA YOGA

As I write I am reminded of how broad and challenging yoga is. Hatha asks for discipline, tantra for awareness, and now karma asks for selfless service. Karma yoga is service without thought of reward. Mahatma Gandhi, Martin Luther King and Mother Teresa all demonstrated the epitome of karma yoga. They gave their lives completely to saving others. Humility is the key to developing the all-powerful solar energy, because it helps transmute rage into radiant spiritual power.

Karma yoga may sound as if it is reserved for the pious, but most of us have a need in some way to be of service to others. Karma yoga is the path of action. It provides the opportunity for your work to become your spiritual practice. We are accountable for our actions – this is the law of karma, which extends both before and beyond this lifetime. We enter this incarnation carrying karma from past lives, which affects us in this life. The bible says, 'as you sow, so shall you reap.' Experience proves this to be true. We each have responsibility not only for ourselves but also for the greater good of the whole. As we work with consciousness, our work can be offered in service to the community, the world, and the Divine. I often think that selfless service means I should not enjoy my work, and as I love my work I imagine it doesn't count as karma yoga. This is untrue, as it is the attitude with which the work is done that is important. To work to the best of your ability for the highest purpose is karma yoga. Karma yoga prepares us for fully activating the heart chakra.

If we are really to do karma yoga then the ego must be reduced. We must consciously seek to work towards the good of all people and our environment. Let us assume for a moment that each person is an individual cell, society an organ made from many cells, and the world a body made from many organs. The body functions as a whole within the cosmos. As an individual cell we have the choice to function for the greater good of the body or to behave selfishly, like a cancer cell, changing the natural order of things, creating havoc, destruction and possible premature death.

When our ego-centredness is added to that of millions of other people's, picture the tremendous disharmony that is imposed on the world. With a predominance of self-centred lifestyles in modern societies we are creating mass destruction on a global scale. We are each in a position to halt this destruction and choose conscious awareness.

The work we do, whatever it is, should always be done to the best of our ability, for the highest good and with compassion. All work brings power and we can use that power wisely. Work then becomes an active meditation through which the spiritual can be expressed. We are merely vessels with the ability to open to the Divine.

The lesson to be learned from karma yoga is selfless service. As we learn to reduce ego and to work in service, we are cleansed. Karma from past wrong actions is burned and no new karma is built. We are all here to make a difference in the world, no matter how insignificant our contribution may sometimes seem. We are all required to be of service and we must all remember 'what goes around comes around.'

Mindful Exercise

FLAME OF RA

This practice activates the inner fire. The abdomen acts like a bellows that fans the flame. In yoga this is a purification exercise called *kapalabhati*. It cleanses the digestive tract and lungs and increases the brain's supply of oxygen, leaving your entire system feeling invigorated and renewed.

The practice consists of a series of 20 breaths, followed by a slow deep inhalation and a short breath-retention. It requires practice, and possibly an instructor.

Begin by pulling the abdomen in sharply on the exhalation, and then allow it to relax on the in-breath. Repeat this quickly for 20 continuous breaths. Breathe audibly, through your nose and create a pumping action with your abdomen, like a bellows. On completion of the 20 quick breaths, take a slow deep inhalation and retain your breath for 30 seconds. Slowly exhale and relax your breathing.

This is one complete round; repeat three times. Practise daily, before morning meditation to raise energy levels and maintain the power of Ra within you.

WOOD CHOPPER

The Wood Chopper is a great way to release negative fire energy. When anger and frustration build up in the body and we just have to let it out, preferably without exploding, this exercise proves beneficial. It also has a stimulating effect that will warm the system and build a sense of confidence and assertion.

CAUTION

Avoid this exercise if you have a bad back.

The Wood Chopper is simple but powerful, so start slowly and build a rhythm that will gently warm up your body.

Position your feet slightly wider than hip-width apart, with your knees slightly bent. Expand your chest, clasp your hands and raise your arms up above your head. From this position, swing down as if chopping wood. Let your arms hang relaxed, breathe out and then slowly raise yourself back up. Repeat the movement several times, using a loud **ha!** sound as you go forward. To rest, let your body hang forward in a relaxed position. Stay for a couple of minutes, and then begin another round.

When you've finished this exercise, be still for a moment and feel the movement of energy flowing through your body. This exercise releases tension in the whole body.

Wood chopper

Meditation

You have journeyed from earth, to water and arrived at the fiery solar plexus. There are two main energy currents that emanate from this centre. One is the yellow downward-pointing triangle. The triangle of life is a symbol of the triple female. It is probably the oldest sacred icon. The triangle represents the yoni, which, like the sun, was seen as the source of all life. The lotus flower, which relates to each chakra, is also symbolic of the yoni. Sometimes triangles are depicted in this chakra facing upwards – this is a comparatively modern symbol for fire. The second energy current is the spiralling umbilical energy. It has the quality of warmth, movement and expansion. This current is used in polarity therapy and is seen to distribute vital energy out into the organism. This force is present during gestation and determines our constitution. Because it relates to the fiery sympathetic nervous system,[4] this current is also responsible for action. We will work with the triangle for dharana, and with the spiral for the dynamic meditation.

Spiralling umbilical energy, radiating out and embracing the body

OPENING TO SPIRIT

DHARANA

Prepare for meditation by making yourself as comfortable as possible. Close your eyes and follow the movement of your breath. When you are ready, gaze into the *chidakash*. Slowly bring the yellow downward-facing triangle into focus.

This is the sacred womb of the Goddess, she who gave birth to all.

The Divine woman who knows the mysteries of life, preservation and death.

She is the powerful one who is unafraid.

The destroyer of ignorance.

Feel the radiant energy of the Goddess surround you. Open wide, allowing your vessel to fill with her abundant force. Return to the protection and warmth of her womb. Feel yourself uplifted, revitalized and ever-blessed. Stay with the sensation as you bring your attention to the Black Dot in the centre of the triangle. Bring it clearly into your vision. Now rest your focus on the Black Dot, doorway to hidden knowledge. Continue your practice for as long as you find appropriate. As you finish, slowly re-focus on your breath.

DYNAMIC: RADIANT SOLAR UMBILICAL ENERGY MEDITATION

This meditation taps into the fiery energy of the solar plexus. It contacts the primal umbilical current, the spiral force that develops the foetus in the womb. After birth it continues to distribute healing energy throughout the body.

In your sacred space, prepare for meditation. Let your system slowly relax as you focus on your altar and absorb the yellow ray. Draw this colour deep inside, feeling yourself enriched with warm, revitalizing energy. Connect the warmth you feel with the heat of your inner sun. Visualize the spiralling umbilical energy beneath your navel. Allow this solar energy to spiral out, filling every single cell in your body.

The sun contains the power to create health and destroy sickness. Direct this solar energy where it is needed and programme its dynamic force. Guide the energy, say what you want it to do, ask for destruction of unhealthy cells, thoughts or negative energies. Ask for healing and repair. Ask for knowledge and wisdom. Be clear about what it is you need, and know that the universe will bless you. Let the golden spiralling solar energy radiate beyond your body, holding you, embracing you in light. Be open to receive the gift of fire.

When you are ready to complete your meditation, visualize the sun's golden rays returning to your centre. Feel the glow within, knowing that whenever you need to revitalize your entire organism, this powerful energy is always contained within you.

Vibrational Work

COLOUR

It is not surprising to find that the sun in the body resonates with the yellow ray. Yellow is the beautiful glowing colour of heat, fire and sunshine. When the solar plexus is open and vibrating harmoniously its inner radiance shines out. It can be seen in the eyes and the walk, and heard in belly-generated laughter. It is a joyful colour, the colour of confidence and contentment. Take a moment to focus on your use of yellow. Is it a colour you like or dislike?

The mind and nervous system are stimulated by yellow. It strengthens the sympathetic nerves and the motor activity of voluntary muscles. Yellow powers digestion and balances the liver and spleen energies. It is an important purifying colour that helps clear the aura and maintain a high vibratory frequency. It has a positive effect on the intellect. Too much yellow in the aura, however, can lead to over-activity, fear and panic attacks. It is just too much to cope with for some people. The complementary colour is violet – this should be used to calm excessive heat. Amethyst is a good stone for calming the solar plexus and can be carried by anyone prone to panic attacks.

ESSENTIAL OILS

Many essential oils have a stimulating effect on the solar plexus. Popular oils are rosemary, juniper, geranium, peppermint, black pepper and ginger. Rosemary is good to use in the mornings to add energy to your day. It stimulates the circulation and is a good 'pick-me-up'. You will notice most of these oils are culinary herbs. They can be used to stimulate appetite and regulate digestion. For this purpose the actual herbs are safer than the oils, which should never be taken internally.

GEMS

Gems for this chakra are citrine, tiger's eye and topaz. Topaz will calm the mind and sharpen the intellect. It is good when clarity is needed. Citrine is a powerful gem for healing. It aligns solar energy with imbalances in the body and helps to eliminate toxic energy. Citrine is useful during turbulent periods in your life. It helps you to keep moving but also provides a sense of security. Tiger's eye, as the name suggests, strengthens sight. It is used to enhance both physical and psychic vision. These are the main gems used to affect the yellow ray. Other yellow gems, such as yellow sapphire, yellow jade and periclase, can also be helpful in balancing the solar plexus.

VISUALIZATION TO RECHARGE A DEPLETED SOLAR PLEXUS ENERGY

Imagine a hot sunny day in a busy city. There is noise, hustle and bustle. You are in the centre slowly walking towards a high point. You begin to climb a sacred hill that overlooks the city. As you climb, allow your breath to deepen. Release some of the busy-ness from your day with the out-breath. Feel your body getting lighter as you escape the crowds and move into your own space. The noise of the city quietens as you ascend. Keep walking, slowly getting higher and higher. Feel the cool breeze as the warm sun begins to fade. As you arrive on the hilltop, the sun arrives on the horizon. Both you and the sun are ready to rest. Lie down and observe the colours of the sunset as they dissipate around you. Feel your own energy field relaxed and open ... let your yellow ray shine out and fill the sky, uniting with the radiant sunset. As they merge, feel yourself cleansed. Stay for a moment letting any toxic energy flow out and be neutralized in the sky. Open your solar plexus wide and allow your energy to be refuelled, revitalized and harmonized with the creative solar force. When you are ready, slowly get up, face the sky and spread your arms open wide ... feel your solar plexus recharged with abundance ... smile as you walk away uplifted and on top of the world.

> The Yogi, focusing always on manipura chakra, achieves all attainments. Pain and disease vanish, every desire is fulfilled, and time defeated.
>
> *Shiva Samhita 5: 106 – 107*

Ritual

FIRE RITUAL

Fire energy brings an abundance of power, passion and enthusiasm. This energy needs focus and direction. The rays of the sun, when focused through a magnifying glass, can create fire. Likewise, when the dispersed rays of your mind are focused through ritual, your fire energy can bring anything into being. Use this ritual to clarify your aspirations and goals.

You will need a journal, pens, drum or percussive instruments and fire, symbolic or real. If possible, invite some friends to join you. Fasting before this ritual increases its power, but if fasting is not possible, then cleanse yourself by smudging with smoke (*see page 79*).

Light a big fire outside, or have one in your home fireplace. Failing this, make a small fire in an old wok or metal pot. Traditionally cow dung is used, which burns slowly. You can use a little paper and wood. Be careful indoors; it is a good idea to light the fire outside and go inside once the fire is burning under control. Only a small fire is needed. Use mind power to visualize fire if you don't want a real one.

Create sacred space by visualizing a protective circle around you, and calling the directions as described in Chapter 5.

- Sitting down, quietly observe the fire. Gaze into the flames and be aware of the fire and its qualities. Feel its heat and light. Watch its passionate movement. See its capacity to consume and transform.
- Take your drum and begin to play. Be moved by the spirit of fire. Allow the drum to speak aloud. You will know when to stop and move to the next stage.
- Consider your goals in life. What are you trying to achieve? What are your dreams? Write your thoughts as they enter your mind.
- What stands in your way? Fear, lack of confidence, lack of money – whatever it is, write it down on a separate page. Whatever holds you back needs transforming to release energy. The resulting energy can be used to fuel your goals.
- Hold your list of goals. Take the other list and ceremoniously throw it into the fire. As you do so, ask the fire to consume and neutralize this negative energy. Feel weight lifting from you, as you watch the flames devour your obstacles and light the path of transformation. (If in a group, take it in turns to approach the fire, while the others continue drumming.)
- Without the great fireball in the sky, nothing on earth would exist. Fire is needed to create everything. To bring your goals into being, you need the blessing of fire. Fire energy helps propel you forward. It gives clarity, direction and enthusiasm.
- Take your list of goals and charge them with fire energy. Chant the solar plexus seed mantra *Ram* before repeating your individual goals. Clear statements, voiced loud, are the first step in making your goals a reality.
- Know the fire within has the ability to create.
- Return to playing your drum. Fade the drumming until all is silent except the fire. You will sense when the ritual is complete.
- Give thanks to the fire as you put it out.

Keep a copy of your goals written in your journal, with the date you performed this ritual.

Expect all goals to be realized.

Close Sacred Space
Give thanks and dismiss the great guardians and spirit-keepers of the directions and elements.

HEART CHAKRA

ENTERING THE LIGHT

O my heart, my mother, my heart, my mother, my heart whereby I come into being. (Rebirth) Stand not up against me as a witness nor oppose me in the council of judgement. Weigh not heavy against me before the keeper of the balance. You are my divine essence which dwells in my body, the divine power which makes strong my limbs. When you come forth in the place of happiness where we go, may you not cause my name to send forth an offensive odour before those who assign people to their rightful place.

Dr Maulana Karenga[1]
Translated from the Egyptian book *Coming Forth by Day*

THE HEART CHAKRA: CORRESPONDENCES

Sanskrit Name	Anahata
Meaning	Unstruck
Main Function	Transformation
Quality	Compassion
Location	Centre of thoracic cavity, behind the heart

Spiritual Correspondences

Colour	Green, rose pink
Element	Air
Symbol	Six-pointed star
Seed Sound	Yam
Petals	12
Planet	Venus ♀
Esoteric Anatomy	Pranic Sheath – permeates the entire body and extends beyond it, forming the aura
Yoga Path	Bhakti (devotion)
Guna Quality	Sattva (can also be rajasic)

Deities

Africa	Èṣù, Maat, Òyá, Shu
Asia	Kakini Shakti, Tara
Central America	Xochiquetzal
Europe	Aphrodite, Venus
Mythology	Moralistic themes that deal with truth and conscience.

Physical Correspondences

Gland	Thymus
Nerve Plexus	Cardiac plexus, brachial plexus
Body Parts	Heart, lungs, arms, hands
Air Energy Triad	Shoulder, kidneys, ankles
Expression	Truth, vocation, responsibility to others
Disturbance	Confusion and frustration

Psychological Correspondences

Statement	'I love'

EMOTION

As we move into the fourth chakra the emotions become more subtle. Heart chakra love asks for nothing in return. It differs from the sacral centre, where love holds many expectations. Emotions of the heart centre seek balance. When emotion ceases to be in balance, energy falls to the solar plexus and is experienced as personal feeling.

Chronology	14 – 21 years
Rite of Passage	Adulthood, key of the door (to your heart); separation from family group. Blessed by air.
Developmental Stage	Love for a significant other may develop, and/or true compassion for all people which can draw an individual into selfless service.

Ways of Working

Foods	Fruits, nuts, avocado
Herbs	Kelp, mistletoe, echinacea
Oils	All floral oils, angelica, palmarosa
Gems	Rose quartz, Green tourmaline, emerald, green jade, green aventurine, pink carnelian

Main Function: Transformation

The heart chakra, found in the middle of the seven centres, represents transformation. This is symbolized by the six-pointed star, which demonstrates balance and the equal importance of heaven and earth.

As we travel up the chakras, awareness of the root chakra develops grounding and a sense of embodiment. We learn to take up residence in the physical body and embrace our mother the earth. Consciousness is further raised as we develop centring in the sacral chakra and feeling in the solar plexus. Work on the three personal chakras prepares us for transition into the universal realms, which begin with the heart chakra.

Transition occurs between all the chakras. As we integrate teachings and gain knowledge at one centre, we then make a transition to the next chakra. The transition between the solar plexus and the heart centre is major. This is the transition from **Embodiment to Enlightenment**. We move into the universal realms, and before us lies the potential for rebirth. Just as birth into a physical body manifests at the root chakra, birth into a light body manifests at the heart chakra.

The light body is a vehicle that resonates at a higher frequency. To move on the physical plane we require a physical body; likewise, to move in the finer vibratory realms of light we need a light body. We enter the light body through the heart chakra, and move towards enlightenment. As soul consciousness is raised we are transformed by light. We reconnect to the cosmic wheel of life and remember our soul purpose. We are spiritual beings here for a reason, and we are not afraid to love and learn. Inner wisdom is a sacred friend and guide, in whom we trust. We are seriously back on track, with our soul consciousness returning towards the Divine universe. We are lifted by spirit to another dimension and blessed with the gift of universal love and light.

A vibrational quickening is taking place on our planet right now. This means that evolution on all planes is speeding up. We are Opening to Spirit and learning our lessons quickly. We are reincarnations of the Ancient Ones. Their life-force moves within each one of us. The chakras are our spiritual archive. From this ancestral memory bank we can access knowledge of everything that was, is and ever will be. It is here in the centre of love and compassion that we acknowledge the unity of all beings. We are one people, each born from the Divine source of our creator. Chakras are not limited by time and space. The knowledge of past, present and future vibrates simultaneously within these wheels of life. That is the power we are opening to. We are bearing the fruit of spiritual seeds planted in previous lifetimes. As consciousness is raised we learn to use the knowledge we gain with compassion and love for a developing universe.

QUALITY: COMPASSION

The quality of the heart chakra needs little explaining; it is known to everyone reading these words. The heart is associated with love, truth and compassion. Ancient secrets are held in popular sayings of today, such as:

I love you with all my heart
I give you my heart
Let's get to the heart of the matter (truth)
Cross my heart (truth)
Open your heart (compassion)
My heart was touched (compassion)

These common sayings confirm our knowledge of the heart chakra and its wisdom.

Touch is the sense linked to the heart chakra. Touch has one of the longest entries in the dictionary. This is due to the breadth of the heart's energetic qualities. Love and touch are two powerful healers. They both contain the potential to open the energy field and allow an increased flow of vital energy. We all need love; we search for it because we know it has the power to hold everything in balance. To the ancient Egyptians the Ab (heart) was the conscience, the self-judging aspect of ourselves that seeks truth and frees us from limitation. In the Yorùbá language of today, Ọkàn is still the word for both heart and conscience. 'Ọkàn mi á jè mi lèrìí' is the strong belief that 'my heart will be my judge'. When the conscience is clear, the heart will not be heavy. Shackles of guilt and fear will not hold us back. Instead we will be able to spread our wings of compassion, open our hearts and send unconditional love flying through the air.

Element: Air

Air is lighter than all the other elements – so subtle, yet so vital. We can survive for weeks with no food (earth), days with no water, hours without heat, but only minutes without air. Breath is life. We begin life with inspiration: our first breath. Life ends as we take our final breath: we literally expire. Re-spir-ation comes from the Latin word 'spiritus'. Spirit means both breath and prana/energy. The Ancients knew the relationship between prana and breath; this knowledge remains in the language. Air travels from the heart and pervades the entire body. Prana follows a similar route through the nadis. Prana fuels the spirit of light that resides in the heart, known as the *akhanda jyoti*, the eternal flame. Meditation on this light develops compassion.

The air element moves through the heart chakra, carrying the winds of change. We can be inspired, moved or blown over by this element. Thoughts have an airy quality; they are boundless and travel freely. Thoughts are powerful and, like the wind, they can change everything in their path. Positive thinking followed by right action can change this world.

Air is the element behind all movement. If you are feeling stuck, then heart chakra work is essential. A surge of love will soften the most rigid heart. At times love can be overwhelming, we are literally 'blown out' by it. It may seem easier to give love than to receive love. When this happens, we must remember that love is like the air we breathe. We cannot expect only to exhale. We must also open our hearts to receive the abundance of love that is our birthright. Each one of us is deserving of love. No matter how hard it may be to acknowledge, you will always remain worthy of love.

Birds fly freely through the air. They were viewed by the Ancients as carriers of messages from the Gods and symbols of transformation. Winged Goddesses of ancient Egypt are the original guardian angels; their wings demonstrated their power as protectors, keepers of higher knowledge and great female healers. Auset's gathering of the scattered remains of her husband Ausar's body and her ability to heal and re-member him are symbolic of the female power of love and transformation. Auset's wings are an extension of her heart chakra. Our shoulder blades and arms are our wings. They extend from the heart centre and should move freely, allowing us to give and receive love and compassion. The more we breathe deeply and spread our wings, the more air energy we flow through the body.

Planet: Venus ♀

We experience the earth's energy at the root chakra; the moon reigns in the sacral centre, and the sun shines in the solar plexus. There is also of course the influence of the ruling planets: Saturn at the root chakra and Mars at the solar plexus. As we journey through the sky we meet Venus, who rules the heart chakra. Venus is the moon's daughter. In the dark sky, her light shines bright; only the sun and moon can outshine her. Venus is the ancient Roman Goddess of love and beauty; she guides us to a place of peace and harmony within.

Venus is a manifestation of the feminine, of woman, love and relationships. When the soul awakens at the heart centre it resonates with the planet Venus. Venus develops in the soul a longing for peace and harmony, a desire for love and happiness. She bestows on us the gentleness and empathy of a mother. Her energy connects the heart to the sacral chakra, creating love within sexual union. Venus brings joy to all relationships. She is humane and forgiving, seeking equilibrium always. Compassion and unconditional love can be shaped from the pure energy of Venus.

Venus controls circulation. Blood flows out from the heart, feeding and cleansing all the cells and returning through the venous system (veins). The thymus gland is a major organ of the lymphatic system (the body's defence mechanism), which is also ruled by Venus. Energetically, prana is circulated through the nadis to animate the entire body and maintain health. Venus is also responsible for circulating love. Love is available in abundance – we can be sure that the love we freely give out she will return to us tenfold.

When we go inside and search our hearts, we feel the warmth of Venus, we see the light of the eternal flame. Each breath we take is an act of grace that fans the flame of the soul. When your heart is hurting, speak with Venus, the bright star that shines in the morning and evening. She can bless you with forgiveness, healing and love.

Deities

Numerous Gods and Goddesses exude heart chakra energy. Deities are the very essence of love and devotion. Earth Goddesses of the root chakra birth us onto the physical plane, but as cosmic mothers they also receive us as we are reborn into the light. The sensuous Goddesses of the sacral chakra also embody the love and compassion of the heart centre. These deities provide a continuum of life, death and rebirth. As you rise beyond the personal realms and open your heart, invite the indwelling deity to fill you with love, truth and compassion. Let the secrets of the rainbow be revealed to you.

ÈSÙ

Èṣù, Yorùbá God of the crossroads, is a trickster and messenger of the Òrìshà. He is the keeper of 21 roads, who clears obstacles and opens the path to success. The crossroads symbolize transition where Èṣù the holder of aṣé (prana) has the power to help us progress or hold us back if we fail to honour the sacred. In the Ifá tradition, Èṣù must always be contacted before invoking the other Òrìshà. In the same way we must contact the essence of the heart in order to raise awareness and open the path to the higher centres.

ÒYÁ

Òyá is the Yorùbá Goddess of wind. She can cause havoc in our lives through brewing up mighty storms. She demands that old patterns and habits which hold us back and no longer serve us be given to her so she can carry them away and bring forth change. Like Òyá, breath holds the secret of change. Welcoming the Goddess Òyá and breathing deeply may bring emotional storms, but it also brings the opportunity for transformation.

Shu – seen here separating the sky goddess Nut and Geb, god of the Earth.

SHU

Shu is the ancient Egyptian God of light and air. He is always mentioned with his sister Tefnut, Goddess of rain and gentle wind. Together they develop balance. It is said that they possess only one soul between them. Shu is the principle of air, breath and life. He is responsible for separating heaven (Nut) and earth (Geb), thus creating the universe. It is through controlling Shu, the breath, the essence of life (pranayama), that we are able to unite our internal heaven and earth.

KAKINI SHAKTI

Kakini is the four-headed Shakti that resides in the heart chakra. She sits on a pink lotus flower and is the embodiment of higher consciousness. As she directs energy upwards she inspires visionary arts, such as music, poetry and dance. Her art is pure bhakti (devotion), straight from the heart. Meditating on Kakini Shakti in the heart chakra brings balance to the body, mind and emotions.

TARA

Tara is the tantric Goddess of Ancient India and Tibet. She is the benevolent Goddess of wisdom and spiritual transformation, the destroyer of ego and bestower of compassion. Tara is a *boddhisattva*, an enlightened being who chooses to remain on the earth plane to ease suffering and guide each of us towards our Divine home. The most popular of 21 forms of this Goddess is Green Tara.

XOCHIQUETZAL

Xochiquetzal is the Mexican Goddess of love who lives on the mountaintop. Her peaceful spirit is found in symbols of rebirth and transcendence, such as doves, flowers and butterflies. She has the ability to transcend ordinary reality while continuing to hold the dancing body sacred. This beautiful Goddess shares the secrets of love and sacred sexuality. At death, those of us who have lived a life of love and devotion can join her on the mountaintop.

Mythology

MAAT

The Twa people of central Africa still know Maat by her original name, Matu,[2] meaning 'mother of the underworld'. This ancient African Goddess is the personification of balance, justice and truth. Like Auset, she can be seen wearing wings of transformation. Maat's main symbol, however, is a single green ostrich feather which she wears attached to her head-dress. Maat's feather is used to weigh the hearts of the deceased in the hall of judgement.

Coming Forth by Day is one of the oldest spiritual texts. It guides the soul's journey through the underworld to the next life. To come before Maat, the deceased must be able to utter words of power. These words are keys to open the door of the hall of judgement. Once beyond the gateway and in the hall, 42 negative confessions (such as 'I have not committed murder') are recited before the same number of judges. Each judge represents one of Maat's 42 sacred laws. When the confession is complete it is time to impress upon the presiding deities the positive qualities that ruled the living heart, such as love and compassion. The heart of the deceased is then placed on the scales and weighed against Maat's feather. Have the worldly lessons symbolized by the gatekeeper Anubis and the wisdom of Tehuti been learned in this lifetime? Is this the heart of an honest, loving person who lived life according to the wishes of the Divine? If the heart weighs heavy, then the soul will reincarnate and return to the world. If the heart is as light as a feather (hence the popular saying), then all lessons are learned and the soul may return to the stars.

We have inherited a great legacy from the African Goddess, Maat. We still talk of hearts being heavy or light. Someone with a heavy heart is an anxious person striving to learn the lessons of life; while a light-hearted person knows the secrets of love and laughter. Symbolically the key of the door is given to people at the age of 21. This age is associated with the heart chakra. Twenty-one is the magical age of transformation, when young people are finally initiated into adulthood. Green, the colour of Maat's feather, is also the healing ray of the heart chakra. Her negative confessions precede the Ten Commandments and the yamas and niyamas found in yoga. Her scales are seen today in courts of law as symbols of truth and justice. Maat became synonymous with that which is honest and straight, to the degree that the Egyptologist Budge gave the definition of her name as 'straight', which is still common language for honesty today.

The Goddess Maat is not only the upholder of truth but a way of being. She guides us towards enlightenment. The way of Maat can be achieved while still alive. Every day we step towards rebirth and deliverance into the light. We must make this journey a conscious one, by examining our actions and moving forward in truth and harmony. We are each held accountable for our own conduct. When we choose to live according to Maat she helps heal our conscience and grants change. The ancient Egyptians strived to live a life of Maat, a life filled with balance and universal truth. This Goddess opens the gateway to spiritual achievement and transformation. She is the energetic quality of the heart. Maat is the love we hold dear to our hearts and the truth we seek to live by.

Expression

As we move into the fourth chakra, the emotions become more subtle. Love of the heart chakra asks for nothing in return. It differs from the love of the sacral centre, which is reciprocal. The heart chakra is concerned with balanced emotion. When emotion ceases to be in balance, energy falls to the solar plexus. Commitment and compassion spring from the heart. Love of a significant other develops here, as does universal love.

When the heart is truly open you will experience:

compassion

love of Self and others

loving personal relationships

balance

a commitment to truth

inner transformation

a deep sense of pain at times

respons-ability

a calling/vocation

desire to be of service to others

movement towards social action for change

respect for Ancestors, elders and those who made it possible for you to be where you are now

free movement of your breath

what it is to reach out and touch

being touched

a lack of fear and faith in the Divine.

Disturbance

If you limit the energy that flows through your heart chakra you may:

feel confusion and frustration

act unlawfully

lack clarity and direction in your life

lack commitment to essential mundane matters

be tricked into thinking you are operating from the heart, when really you seek power and reward

abuse love

abuse alcohol (spirits)

fear your great capacity to give love

fear your great need to receive love

be afraid to reach out and touch, paralysed by past hurts

stay hurt, thereby causing yourself physical ailments.

Physically you may suffer:

immune disorders

cancer

heart problems

chest infections

disorders of the nervous system

depression.

At this time in our cyclical evolution as human beings, many of us have strong heart chakra energy. Our souls are speeding towards the Divine. We want to move into the heart chakra and love unconditionally; we want that so very much. We want to communicate with spirit and heal ourselves and the world. We want to live in unity. We are at the stage of development which I call aspirational – we are **aspirational humans**. We have visions of a harmonious planet and are beginning to take the necessary steps needed to create change.

Many of the problems we face stem from trying to run before we can walk. Before we can truly open to the universal, our personal stuff has to be dealt with. The Ancients survived intensive, often potentially fatal initiation rites, which illuminated the transition between the worldly and the Divine. Some became shamans or entered the priesthood, monasteries, the wilderness, and undertook long periods of spiritual practice. If we are to experience transformation of the heart, then we too must face our fears, remove all obstacles and commit to our spiritual practice. We have to be prepared to stop kidding ourselves and really change.

When we look round we see poverty, racism, war, and the study of objects taking precedence over study of the Self. We are not living in an enlightened age. This is the technological age, *kali yuga*, a time of great struggle. But through opening the heart, it is possible to make a difference in the world.

When we take respons-ability, things change. As we allow ourselves to breathe fully, the pranic sheath and the nadis are slowly cleansed. As prana flows freely the heart chakra awakens, bringing love and compassion. Change is inevitable; we cannot open the heart and at the same time remain stuck. Opening your heart and allowing your love to show transforms you and changes the world.

SEVEN WAYS OF OPENING TO SPIRIT AT THE HEART CHAKRA

Altar Work

Sit for a moment and give thanks to your fire altar. Feel fire energy as it moves more freely through your body. See before you the vision created as a result of your work with fire. Let the purpose of your soul's journey be clarified. Maintain this clarity as you move on from the solar plexus chakra and begin to focus on the heart chakra.

We are now going to work with air energy. This is the first of the higher energy centres. Our work now is less personal and more universal. Our concern is to generate an environment of love and compassion. This love and compassion will disperse through the element air and touch people everywhere.

You will need a green altar cloth, preferably in silk. Silk has a fine vibration – but if you cannot get silk, use cotton. Four green candles are to be placed in each of the four directions. Use a green vessel for spring water, if you have one. For incense or essential oils, use floral aromas such as rose, jasmine, orange blossom or melissa. They are all sweet-smelling and pleasing to the Goddess. Gems to use are those that harness green or pink rays, such as rose quartz, green tourmaline and emerald. Statues of Buddha, Maat or any Goddess of love will lift the energy of this altar. Some rounded wooden figures are particularly pleasant to hold and stroke; this will heighten your sense of touch. Place pictures of loved ones around that lift your vibrations. As before, use your creativity to develop your altar. Feel love as you attend to your altar. Let universal love be all around you.

Working from the heart chakra means working for the good of all beings. It means asking the Goddess Òyá to blow the winds of change and light the lives of those who live in ignorance. Air transcends all boundaries. Think not of yourself or of personal gain, but let your love flow through the air as a gift to the universe and all who dwell in it.

Journal-keeping

FORGIVENESS

The ability to forgive is truly a wonderful gift, and a great blessing for those on whom it is bestowed. As we work with heart chakra energy it is time to turn passion into compassion. Passion is a charged emotion. When passion fuels positive experiences we feel excited and high; we can remain uplifted for weeks. When it fuels negative and painful experiences it can drain energy, leaving us exhausted and depressed. To forgive is a gift we can allow ourselves. As you journey through the chakras and allow healing to embrace you, forgiveness will come more easily. Working with heart chakra energy means working for the good of all beings. This exercise can be used for forgiving yourself or others.

Cultivating Forgiveness

Begin by creating sacred space. Cleanse the room with a smudge stick made from sage, which is a purifier of negative energies, and sweetgrass, which brings blessings and grace. If you cannot get a smudge stick, then use incense or burn essential oils. Cleansing with air is recommended for heart chakra work, but another element can be used if need be. Cleanse your aura by surrounding yourself in smoke from the smudge stick. Fan the smoke up the front of your body, pausing over your heart, and down the back. This prepares you for the sacred work that follows.

You will need your journal and a pen.

After cleansing, light the candles on your altar, then kneel down and say a prayer.

Give thanks for the life you live and choices you are free to make. Ask to be blessed with the strength, insight and blessings you need to create forgiveness. Forgiveness that is everlasting. Forgiveness that will free you of the pain you carry. Forgiveness that will heal each person involved. Forgiveness that will change your passion into compassion.

Sit in quiet meditation for 10 minutes, focusing on your breath as it moves through your heart chakra. Allow your heart to open wide; let it fill with grace and receive healing energy from the Goddess Maat.

❀ Write down the name of the person or people you want to forgive.
❀ Write down what it was that hurt you.

Four Stages of Forgiveness

1 **Regain your power.** In your mind's eye, visualize what this hurt is doing to you. How is it draining your energy? How is this destructive force of fire (anger/rage, etc.) affecting you? Make a note in your journal.
2 **Reflect back.** Close your eyes and allow the negative energy to lift from you; feel it become light and fuse with the air element. Let this energy go – it is not yours, direct it back. See where it is going. Where did it come from? How was it created? Make a note in your journal.

3 **Recognition of universal love.** Be aware that we are all children of the universe, we each have lessons to learn. Close your eyes, open your heart and feel universal love flood through you. We are all connected through the heart and through the air we breathe. Inhale love, peace and harmony deep into your being. Now extend that love out to all beings. Write down your feelings.

4 **Forgiveness.**
> Feel yourself fully embraced in the spirit. See the person/persons who hurt you fully embraced in spirit.
> Let go completely, leaving it in the hands of the Gods/Goddesses.
> Reclaim your power, reclaim your energy, reclaim your love and compassion.
> Write down your feelings.

As you forgive, the energetic charge that was holding you back is released. You can feel compassion instead of rage. You can allow yourself to understand. You may forget, you may not, but the charge will slowly dissipate, leaving you free.

Remember to give thanks for all blessings received.

Yoga Path

BHAKTI YOGA

Bhakti yoga is the way of the heart, the path of devotion. Like all yoga, bhakti is to be felt and experienced. I have always loved singing, and the place I was encouraged to sing most was at church and Sunday school; to this day hymns touch me deeply. Sharing devotional hymns, prayers and chants is pure bhakti. I recall a very special moment in my life. I was walking through the Sivananda Ashram in Rishikesh, taking a short-cut into the town. As I walked I found myself being drawn towards sweet-sounding voices. I sat at the back of a large hall and listened to several women singing *bhajans* (devotional songs). I cried, something burst inside me and flooded out. I realized something deep inside me was missing. I didn't know what it was but I knew these women had a love, a joy, something so beautiful. I knew I needed to find that which was missing in me. Their devotion was a precious gift to me, a gift I absorbed into my being, allowing movement to take place.

Bhakti is not for everyone. The Krishna Consciousness Movement, well-known proponents of bhakti yoga, have done their part to encourage many people onto this path, but they have also put others off completely. Opening to Spirit, however, means opening the mind. Yoga suggests that we 'take everything in, chew it over and then spit out what we don't need'.

The practice of bhakti requires surrender based on the understanding of Divine law, as expressed in the following adage: **'Not my will but thy will, not my will but thine.'**

Bhakti yoga honours many deities. This is done through chanting prayers and puja – devotional rituals. Many deities are mentioned in this book. Choose one or two that you resonate with and find out as much about them as you can from books, myths and museums. Establish their favourite colours, foods, position in the house, numbers, seasons and specific days they predominate over.[3] Then go inside yourself and experience their qualities from within. Learn from internal and external sources. Create an altar using the information you have gathered, following the guidelines of altar work. Meditate with and honour the deity regularly, sing his or her praise-songs if you are able to learn them.[4] Keep company with other seekers and visit exalted ones – the presence of the wise will raise your vibration and bhakti will come easily.

You can ask deities for help. Like our Ancestors and guardian angels, they are here to assist us in our spiritual growth. Using the chakra correspondences, attain a knowledge of which deity presides over which problems. For example, Òṣun helps us deal with personal problems such as self-esteem, while Maat brings harmony and illumines truth. The deities you resonate with will change as you change.

Bhakti yoga opens the heart and teaches the lesson of devotion. It is a calming and soothing yoga that releases an abundance of compassion and love from deep within. Through bhakti your life can unfold to fulfil your sacred destiny.

Mindful Exercise

SPHINX

The Sphinx, which is half-animal and half-human, symbolizes unification between our instinctive Self and our higher Self. It blends the strength and magnificence of a lion with human consciousness. The Sphinx represents the integration of the higher and lower chakras.

Sphinx Posture. The Great Sphinx.

In this posture the chest is lifted and the heart area opened. Prana is encouraged to flow freely through the body.

Lie face-down on the floor, then bring your hands directly under your shoulders. Keep both elbows on the ground and let your forehead touch the floor. Now, slowly raise your head, shoulders and chest. Keep your feet together on the floor. Continue to lift up into a Sphinx-like posture. Lengthen your spine and breathe deeply. As you open your heart, allow it to fill with love and wisdom. Let the knowledge of the Sphinx be known to you.

ISIS, POSE OF IMMORTALITY

In this posture the heart is opened wide, the rib cage, arms and wings of the body are extended in a universally receptive gesture. As the body twists the full length of the spine is massaged. The spine is stretched, cleaned and refreshed, bringing elasticity and youthfulness to the spinal cord. The spinal cord communicates with every cell in the body. The bones, muscles, organs all have a relationship with the nervous system. Yoga tells us that if the spinal cord is kept healthy we will enjoy a long and fruitful life, hence the name of this Egyptian posture.

Begin by sitting comfortably over your heels. Now place your right foot alongside your left knee. Take a deep breath and extend both arms out to the sides, as you breath out, soften your arms, letting them slightly curve into a universal embrace. From this position turn first to your right, keep your arms outstretched and twist your spine as far as is comfortable. Turn your head and look to your right. Take a full breath. Keep your legs positioned and turn your upper body around to the left.

Twist your spine, breath and look left. Return to the centre sitting over both knees, relax your hands onto your knees.

Isis, Pose of Immortality

LOVING TOUCH

I had a wonderful experience recently while visiting the bank. I was in a hurry and became increasingly frustrated at the length of time I was kept waiting. When finally an assistant came to help me, I got upset with her and she got upset with me. Once the transaction was completed and tension released, we apologized to each other. The assistant then intuitively offered me a hug, which I happily accepted. I felt so uplifted to find human contact in this place of bars, locks and officialdom. This was an unexpected gift I both needed and appreciated.

At the time this felt so natural, that it was not until later that I realized the real power of what had taken place. We all have the power to offer loving touch. I invite you to follow your intuition. Next time you feel like reaching out to touch some-one's hand, or have the urge to smile open-heartedly, or hold a loved one in your embrace, don't hold back. Let your loving heart energy flow. I am not suggesting forced contact, I am simply saying when the feeling is there, let it show. Remember, when touch is offered honestly from the heart, it will always be received.

Keep your heart in wonder at the daily miracles of your life.

Kahlil Gibran

Keep your awareness tuned for what is being offered to you each day. Every day is full of miracles and blessings. It is your responsibility to recognize these gifts. They come in many guises – it may be a felt sense, an answer to a prayer or the sighting of a rainbow. Life is a Divine blessing. Be mindful of the many miracles unfolding right now in your life.

Meditation

This is where you transcend the personal into the universal realms. To gain most from meditation on the universal chakras, purification of the pranic sheath is necessary. This is achieved through fasting and pranayama (*see Chapter 5*). As energy becomes more subtle, meditation practice needs to be less dynamic and more still. We will therefore omit dynamic meditation and focus on dharana for the remaining chakras.

We will continue dharana on the chakra symbols. Anahata chakra has at its centre a six-pointed star. This symbol of transformation is made up of two interlaced triangles. The downward-pointing triangle relates to involution and the movement of spirit into matter. The evolutionary shift of matter back towards spirit is pictured in the upward-facing triangle. Together they represent the marriage of opposites, the merging of heaven and earth, male and female, Ida and Pingala, Yin and Yang. This is one of my favourite symbols because of its significance. The six points represent the six chakras in balance. Lying in the middle of all the chakras, the six-pointed star does not discriminate, instead it upholds the equal importance of all the chakras. ✡

DHARANA

Start by raising energy in your environment through cleansing and lighting candles on your air altar. Practise pranayama before meditation. You can use alternate nostril breathing, discussed in Chapter 5, or this simple cleansing breath.

CLEANSING BREATH

Sit upright with your eyes closed and your mind focused on your breath. Let your abdomen rise on the inhalation and fall on the exhalation. Focus attention on anahata chakra. This centre controls the heart and lungs and, consequently, the breath. Now prolong the out-breath. Inhale to a count of four and exhale to a count of eight. Continue this breathing pattern for at least 10 minutes ... The lengthened-out breath has a cleansing effect on the whole system. Return to your natural breathing rhythm.

Continue to breathe gently and repeat the word 'compassion' with each breath. This plants a seed in your mind. Now move your attention to your mind's inner screen and visualize a six-pointed star ... tune to the pulsation of the star ... see its light and feel its love. Slowly move the star to your heart centre. See its form, feel its vibration and colour (green or pink) within. Let the love, compassion and unity of heaven and earth fill your entire being.

Gently shift your vision to the Black Dot in the centre of the star. Concentrate solely on the dot – gateway of consciousness.

Vibrational Work

COLOUR

Green is the dominant ray of the heart chakra. Many clairvoyants also see rose pink in the heart and aura at this level. Green is balancing and cooling, with many healing qualities. It is probably the most widely used colour in healing. We find an abundance of green in nature; it is the colour of spring. Green propels new growth, change and transformation. Its gentle energy helps heal the 'emotions of change', such as pain, loneliness and jealousy. These emotions cause the heart centre to close down – the chest collapses and we are literally starved of oxygen. Heart energy can become clogged, leaving the green colour grey and cloudy. We know that green in nature cannot exist without oxygen. The same applies to us: the heart is the air centre which fuels the whole body. When the heart aches and we cut off the green ray, we invite all manner of ailments to invade the system. Raising the green vibration is therapeutic. It lifts the spirit and harmonizes the body. Green stimulates the thymus and lymphatic system; it can be used for cancer patients, HIV and other ailments associated with immune deficiencies, alongside conventional medicine. Green is said to be antiseptic, having the ability to destroy viruses and infections. It helps lower blood pressure by its calming and balancing nature. It is also good for inflammation of the joints and reducing physical pain.

Consider your relationship to the colour green. Do you need to increase its use in your home, your food, clothes or environment? Green energy can easily become depleted. Women, especially mothers, often ooze green energy. We are nurturers, naturally giving, loving and compassionate, often to a point where our own energy suffers depletion. Surrender is a skill women must learn. Let some of the control go and allow someone else the pleasure and satisfaction of taking care of you. Each time you do for yourself you deprive someone of the honour of doing for you. (Even if you can do it better!)

Turquoise is the colour band between green and blue. Although it doesn't relate directly to the major chakras, it is an important vibrational energy for healing. It helps unite the heart and throat chakras, facilitating the expression of love and compassion. Turquoise (the gemstone) is widely used by Original Americans for its healing qualities, and was also known to the ancient Egyptians, who used it to balance heaven and earth energies.

ESSENTIAL OILS

Sweet-smelling oils open the heart and lift the spirit. Rose, jasmine and geranium are all useful oils for the heart chakra. You may have offered roses to sweeten the heart of someone you love. Rose oil is also used as an aid to meditation and prayer. Rosary beads were originally scented with rose oil to calm the mind. The beautiful aroma of jasmine is used during ceremonies in India. The flowers are picked at night and worn in the morning. Unlike rose and jasmine, geranium is a stimulating oil, which lifts depression and reduces stress. Massage is an excellent way to use essential oils to raise heart chakra energy, because it incorporates touch, the sense associated with the air element.

GEMS

Emerald, green jade, green aventurine, green tourmaline, pink carnelian and rose quartz all have balancing effects on the heart chakra. Take some time to find a stone that you resonate with. You can set the stone in a piece of jewellery to wear around the heart area, or carry the stone in a pouch. Larger pieces can be placed in your environment and used to enhance your meditations. Always cleanse your stones and create an energetic relationship with them.

Ritual

SACRED JOURNEY (PILGRIMAGE)

Life is a journey with many destinations. There are achievements, disappointments, mundane rituals and celestial highs along the way. At this junction you are invited to make a sacred journey. The Ancients travelled for days, even months on foot to reach sacred sites. People arrived, performed rituals and asked for healing. They would celebrate the harvest and other sacred times together. Holy water, stones and amulets would be taken away in exchange for a prayer of thanks. Today sacred sites are mostly frequented by tourists, but the energy of the Ancients can still be felt if you enter deep meditation.

As personal energy is transformed at the heart chakra and you open to the universal realms, make a promise to yourself to visit the place of most spiritual significance to you. It may be the home of your Ancestors, a temple or a sacred mountain. Take time to prepare yourself for this sacred journey; be sure your vehicle is cleansed and open to receive fully the healing this visit will bring.

Sacred sites are created either naturally or by humans on the Earth's chakras, for the Earth has major and minor chakras just as we have. She also has a system of nadis – ley lines on which sacred sites are aligned around the world. Her energy charges these sites. Mount Meru, the Pyramids, Uluru (Ayers Rock), Glastonbury Tor, Machu Picchu and numerous other sacred places are ancient initiation sites.

Before you travel, find out as much as you can about how the Ancients received blessings at your chosen site. A dark, narrow tunnel, resembling the birth canal (rebirth canal), forms the entrance to the Great Pyramid. The Tor at Glastonbury was circumambulated seven times. The Kaaba (Black Stone) at Mecca is also walked around seven times. Make your visit a time of personal initiation and rebirth. Use meditation to help you understand what you need at this point in your life's journey. Create a rite of pass-age (*see Chapter 6*) or another ritual to perform at the site which will harness the energies you require, or just be still and meditate. Always offer a gift in return for your healing. You can light candles or incense, or give food, money and praises.

Planning is a significant part of the journey – the doubts and fears, the waiting, the excitement, the miracle of bringing your sacred journey into being. It is something we all deserve and the universe is waiting to help you make it happen. So allow your next holiday to be truly filled with holy days. Take your journal and start planning straight away.

The tree of eternity has its roots in heaven above, and its branches reach down to earth. It is Brahman – pure Spirit, who in truth is called the immortal. All the worlds rest on that Spirit and beyond it no one can go:
This in truth is that.

Katha Upanishad[5]

THROAT CHAKRA

POWER OF COMMUNICATION

It was the Egyptian priest-scribe, Tehuty, more familiarly known in myth and legend by his Greek name, Hermes, who was first credited with defining the elementary nature of the chakra system fifty thousand years ago.

Rosalyn L. Bruyere

THE THROAT CHAKRA:

CORRESPONDENCES

Sanskrit Name	Vishuddha
Meaning	Purification
Main Function	Communication
Quality	Vibration, sound, voice
Location	Throat C3 – C5 (between the third and fifth cervical vertebrae)

Spiritual Correspondences

Colour	Blue
Element	Ether
Symbol	Inverted triangle surrounded by a circle
Seed Sound	Ham
Petals	16
Planet	Mercury ☿
Esoteric Anatomy	Etheric body
Yoga Path	Mantra
Guna Quality	Sattva

Deities

Africa	Tehuti/Thoth, Òrúnmìlà
India	Shakini Shakti, Saraswati
Europe	Hermes, Mercury
Mythology	All that relate to divination-oracles

Physical Correspondences

Gland	Thyroid
Nerve Plexus	Pharyngeal plexus, cervical plexus
Body Parts	Throat, ears, mouth
Ether Reflex Areas	Fields and spaces in the body, joints, cavities, lumen (inside of vessels), endocrine glands
Expression	'Open to Spirit' – Awareness of and Communication with Spirit
Disturbance	Limited spiritual awareness

Psychological Correspondences

Statement	'I speak, I hear'

EMOTIONS

BALANCED	UNBALANCED
Stillness, peacefulness and harmony	Restlessness, anxiety

Chronology	21 – 28
Rite of Passage	Childbirth; creation of that which will remain after your death (art, music, writing). Blessed by Ether.
Developmental Stage	Wisdom and creativity

Ways of Working

Foods	Aesthetics and presentation of food
Herbs	Kelp, camomile, benzoin
Oils	Frankincense, camomile, sandalwood
Gems	Blue lace agate, lapis lazuli, blue quartz, turquoise, lazulite

Main Function: Communication

From the Ancients we learn that the universe was created from a single sound. That sound was *Aum* – ॐ. Sounds are responsible for bringing everything into being. The universe is created from pure vibrational sound. Sound travels through the ether and gives rise to the other four elements: air, fire, water and earth. Vishuddha chakra is situated in the throat region, the vocal centre of the body. Spinning of the throat chakra brings forth communication, which in the broadest sense of the word is the function of this chakra. Sound and hearing from all planes of existence come together in this centre.

Vishuddha means purification. As we ascend the chakras, purity of the nadis and energy bodies becomes increasingly important. This is due to the higher frequency of the chakras. If toxic energy exists, it will cloud communication and limit experience at this level. Fasting, cleansing, pranayama, a pure vegetarian diet, positive thinking and extended time spent in spiritual practice all enhance throat chakra work and help develop psychic abilities.

Many people experience blocks in the throat chakra. Time and space for spiritual practice is often limited, resulting in alienation from spirit. This causes deep grief and longing. We often reach outside of ourselves to try and fill this gap. It is only when we re-connect with spirit and remember the soul purpose of this incarnation that we feel whole again and grieving ceases. Opening the throat chakra and resonating fully with the ether element helps us re-connect and communicate with spirit. The throat chakra connects us to our Ancestors and the collective unconscious. We can communicate with the etheric realm through dreams, meditation and divination.

Hearing is also a function of this chakra. Sound and hearing have a close relationship; they resonate in the same etheric field. Sound travels out until it meets resistance and then returns as hearing. Listening is a characteristic of the throat centre, a skill we can all develop. Listening is not merely hearing, listening is hearing with the addition of awareness and presence. On a subtle level, listening becomes clairaudience (extra sensory hearing). This is when we are able to communicate with invisible beings and energies that surround us. The voices of our Ancestors speak to us through nature. Trees, birds, flowers and the wind all carry messages, if we only stop and listen to them.

QUALITY: SOUND AND CREATION

> Those who come to understand the power of vibrations will hold the scepter of power in their hands.
>
> *Temt Tchaas Egyptian proverb*

Sacred sound is the quality of this chakra. From sacred sound, form is created. Research in cymatics[1] (the study of sound waves and matter) demonstrates how sound can organize matter. Dr Hans Jenny conducted a series of experiments in which he scattered sand, water and earth on steel plates. Sound was then channelled through an oscillator under the plates. The results were amazing. The subtle vibration organized the sand and other media into beautiful symmetrical shapes that resemble flowers and mandalas.

Hans Jenny's images show proportion and symmetry. Mandala-like circles and waves are perfectly created when sound is introduced to randomly arranged liquids.

Ancient African civilizations were familiar with the creative force of sound. The Egyptians had power words, called *hekau*. These are 'mantras' in Sanskrit. In English we use affirmations. Sacred sounds were seen as the language of the Gods because of their ability to raise consciousness, create form, and heal. Sound is still one of the greatest healers in the world. *We all know that something as simple as a kind word lifts the spirit and can brighten a person's outlook – try it today. Say a kind word to as many people as you can. Notice their reactions and be aware of what is created in you. Giving away a kind word costs nothing and leaves you and the recipient feeling rich.*

There is not a culture alive that does not have music. Music is the pounding of our mother's heartbeat, the whisper of her soothing voice, the rhythm of a sacred drum and the vibration of a didgeridoo. Since the beginning of time music has been fundamental to human existence and the maintenance of health.

Everything comes into being through sound. To the Dogon people, words are fertile; they contain *nummo*, the very essence of life. The force of the creator travels through the breath of each spoken word, which has the ability to create or destroy life. The original people of Australia believe their ancestors sang everything into creation. Nothing exists until it has been sung into being. I mentioned earlier that before I wrote this book, I talked about it a lot. I was literally singing it into being. I continued to speak about it all through its development, that way other people began to help me by talking about it too, and together we created the energy that formed this book.

Sound by its very nature is creative. Sound organizes complex pictures. When we image things we immediately want to give them names. If I show you a picture of something green, crisp, round and edible, on seeing it you will automatically think 'apple', not 'green, crisp', etc. The word 'apple' organizes all the other information. A baby must be named; the name will then become imbued with the unique quality of its owner. In Africa the vibration and meaning of names are extremely important. A name refers not only to the lineage of the person but also to the unique quality that this soul has carried into this life. The name Babatunde, for example, means 'father has returned from the spirit world'. Omoshalewa acknowledges the child's decision to be born into a particular family, since it means 'this child chose my family.' People with Christian names, who are not Christians, often change their names to reflect a chosen path and enhance their spiritual aspiration and destiny. Many of us within the African diaspora, whose names were changed due to slavery, or who were given Christian names because of migration, have changed our names to resonate with and reflect the energy of the motherland. Ifakunle, for example, means 'Ifá is in abundance'; an African-American diviner might adopt this name to develop his art. Name changing is also popular in the West, especially when people become initiated into ancient spiritual traditions such as yoga and shamanism.

Ifá Divining Stool

What is the meaning of your name? Does it resonate with your destiny and spiritual aspirations? Are you honouring the meaning of your name in your life, by recognizing your soul purpose? If your name has no spiritual meaning for you, you may consider giving yourself an additional spiritual name or changing your name completely so that when people call you they constantly affirm the spirit of your soul.

Several years ago it became important for me to be known by one of my Nigerian names. Olushola means 'she or he who is blessed by Olódùmárè'. After many years I have come to realize that, like all souls, I am truly blessed by the creator.

The vibration of the throat chakra is responsible for the creation of visionary arts. Music, painting, writing and dancing are all ways of communicating with the higher Self and providing inspiration to others. (Art of a more personal quality is created from the sacral chakra.) The Ancients used art to heal. They recognized the unifying quality of sound, for example, which could create order from chaos. When things get difficult we speak about 'falling apart'. We speak of 'trying to pull ourselves together'. Shamans use the magical quality of drumming to retrieve fragmented parts of people's troubled souls. An open throat chakra and flowing ether energy are essential for self-healing.

Element: Ether

Ether, the most subtle of the elements, is closely aligned with pure spirit. This primary boundary is an interface between our creator and us. Although we carry the gift of divinity (God) within and always remain connected to the creator, we still long to return and be fully united with our source. We experience deep grief at our temporary separation and loss. We know in our hearts that we are pure Divine beings, who are merely experiencing life in a physical vessel.

Ether is a vibrational field that unites all the elements. It is the original space from which life evolves. New discoveries in physics refer to this space as the 'Quantum Vacuum' – energy-filled space-time. Science once believed space was completely empty and that solid mass was the only true reality. Now science, like the mystics of old, is beginning to recognize that matter arises from vibrations in subtle energetic space.

This quantum vacuum, or ether, is an abundant creative force. In spiritually advanced parts of the world this knowledge has been utilized for thousands of years. Ether has been seen as our connection to spirit and container for health. The ether that flows through the throat chakra was present in the very beginning, a neutral energy that is invisible yet all-pervading. From the sound of ether came the mountains and trees, the rivers and seas. Everything is created from the essence of ether.

As a neutral element resonating with the neutral source of life, ether is a great healer. It is this element that we draw on to create an internal and external environment that is conducive to healing. When ether is flowing, the other elements have space in which to move. As healers of ourselves and others we must be able to harness the stillness and mystery of ether. This is done through purification. Meditation is a great clearer of internal space. The altar work below will lift the energy around you. Cleansing and preparation transform negative energy, develop a peaceful milieu and channel ether for healing. In the right space we can hear the messages from our spirit guides and helpers.

The body has many spaces, in the form of cavities such as the cranium, chest, pelvis and the joints; these are all governed by ether energy. For the body to function fully, we must allow ourselves internal space. Disease occurs when there is restriction, i.e. lack of space. As you take up room in your body, ether flows and health improves. Posture, digestion, immunity and the nervous system all benefit from having increased inner space in which to operate.

Ether energy is all around us and we can transfer our thoughts directly through it. This is telepathy. Some people are extremely skilled at telepathy and can intuit all manner of factual information. Increasing and trusting our higher intuition can develop this skill. (Personal intuition exists at the sacral centre.) To a certain extent telepathy is something we take for granted, yet when it is presented as esoteric power we find it hard to believe. We communicate telepathically more than we realize. Mothers often communicate directly with their children. We sometimes sense that a friend is in trouble or suffering, only to find out later that we were right. We can go to phone someone and find they were holding the phone ready to call us. The same thought occurs to you and a friend, you both speak at exactly the same time, and then laugh – you may not think that what is happening is a form of telepathy, but it is. Intuition can be useful in many situations. I went on a retreat at Findhorn attended by over 100 people. While there, I found a silver chain. As I walked through the corridor I saw a woman and out of the blue/ether, I realized the chain was hers. Hesitantly I asked her and, sure enough, she had lost it the previous week. It is important to listen to your intuition and not be afraid to use it.

Planet: Mercury ☿

The planet Mercury, to quote the astrologer Alan Oken '... is the hottest, quickest, closest and smallest of the sun's cosmic family'. Due to its close proximity to the Sun (28 degrees), whatever astrological sign your Sun is in, Mercury will also be in that sign or close by, either proceeding or following your Sun sign. Both my Sun and Mercury are in Aries. You can apply the characteristics of your Sun sign to your throat chakra. For example, Aries people are said to be sharp and enthusiastic. At the throat this can translate into clear, dynamic communication. We are also known to act impulsively; at the throat chakra this can result in speaking before thinking.

Mercury, Hermes and their Egyptian predecessor, Tehuti (also known as Thoth) are the Gods from whom this planet gets its name. Tehuti is the multi-talented messenger of the Gods. In his role of communicator Tehuti is involved in writing, speaking and teaching. It is Tehuti who governs knowledge and intellect. He helps us to process information on all levels, whether it is from the senses, dreams, the ether or our higher consciousness. He provides the wisdom needed to solve problems, make decisions and express feelings clearly.

As lawmaker and lord of 'Divine words', Tehuti stands with Maat in the hall of judgement. His powerful words are known to come to pass. Not even the Gods overturn his decision-making. His words are responsible for creating both the heavens and earth. His wisdom is responsible for natural law and the maintenance of universal equilibrium. It is from Tehuti that we get the expression 'As above, so below.' Trimegestus, the term used to describe Hermes, originates with Tehuti, who was known as thrice-great. This was due to Tehuti's ability to harness the great creative potential of ether. He was heralded as the inventor of astronomy, astrology, theology, mathematics, medicine and botany.

Tehuti is, however, best known as a scribe to the Gods; he has the ability to use words as prayers and tools for creation. Mantras, hekau, and the song-circles of original Australians all hold within them the power of creation. It is through the throat chakra and its alignment with Mercury that we too can access this power. We can tune to the planet Mercury and become, like Tehuti, a multi-talented master of knowledge.

Tehuti is the original bearer of the caduceus, which symbolizes balance and healing. His words of power aided Isis in the re-membering of her lover Osiris. Osiris, after being scattered and strewn, was able by the love of Isis and the healing words of Tehuti to become whole again and give life to a son, Horus. Words and music hold healing power. They help us remember our true spiritual nature and, as a result, become whole and creative again.

Tehuti was the ancient Egyptian scribe of the Gods and Lord of Divine words. He is seen here carrying his wand with a single entwined snake. Tehuti is the original bearer of the caduceus.

Deities

ÒRÚNMÌLÀ

The Yorùbá deity Òrúnmìlà was a wise prophet, who once, like Thoth, walked the earth. He now dwells in the sky, where he keeps a record of each person's individual destiny. Although he has no visible image and refuses to return to earth, he gave his people the Ifá oracle with which to communicate with him. Through the oracle Òrúnmìlà reminds us of our forgotten truth and destiny.

SHAKINI SHAKTI

Shakini is Shakti as she manifests in the throat chakra. She is the embodiment of purity and can be seen wearing a blue sari. Shakini is the bestower of *siddhis* – psychic powers that are achieved as we ascend to this level of consciousness. She carries scriptures in her hand bestowing visionary arts and higher knowledge. Shakini speaks to us through dreams.

SARASWATI

Saraswati is the ancient tantric Goddess of knowledge and wisdom. She is patron of all the arts, especially music. She is seen sitting on a lotus flower playing her vina. The creation of letters, mathematics, magic and learning are also attributed to this Divine river/water Goddess, who was originally known as 'the stream of speech'. She is commonly known in Hinduism today as the consort of the creator God, Brahma.

HERMES

Hermes is the well-known Greek God of esoteric truths (renamed by the Romans as Mercury). His attributes and qualities are the same as those of the Egyptian God Thoth. He was seen to embrace both masculine and feminine principles. He was knowledgeable in divination, magic, medicine and alchemy. He carried a caduceus (staff of Hermes) which transformed whatever it touched into gold. Hermes was known as the enlightened one and, like all deities of the throat chakra, was a communicator of truth and wisdom.

We can see that deities in many cultures share common traits. This demonstrates the spiritual unity of all human beings. We are one people. Deities responsible for communicating the wisdom of higher knowledge resonate with the throat chakra.

When we have decisions to make or reach times of confusion and despair, asking for help from the etheric realm, through an oracle, can provide answers to the great mysteries of life and direct us on our path towards spiritual evolution and fulfilment.

Mythology

THE VOICE OF GREAT SPIRIT

This tale is from the oral tradition of the Original[2] Australian people. It is told to children while still young so that they maintain knowledge of the spirit within nature.

Long ago, Great Spirit spoke directly to people every day. People gathered together in the mornings to hear the wise voice. They could not see Great Spirit; they only heard his words. Eventually they grew tired of listening to the voice with no face and decided to enjoy themselves and to gather together to dance and sing. They refused to listen any longer.

Great Spirit was very upset about losing his connection to the people. He immediately sent for his messenger, Nurunderi. He asked Nurunderi to call all the people from every corner and let them meet together under a large old gum tree. He told his messenger that he would never speak to his people again, but wished to give them a sign. When the message from Great Spirit reached the people they were very frightened. Nurunderi ordered them to sit around the tree and be silent.

Through the silence a loud roar was heard. The gum tree was split open by a powerful, invisible force. A huge tongue came down from the sky and entered the tree. When the tongue could no longer be seen, the tree healed itself as quickly as it had become wounded. Nurunderi dismissed the people, telling them they were now free to continue enjoying themselves with corrobberies (community gatherings that involve ritual and dance). They need not worry about Great Spirit, for he would not bother them again.

The people were happy at first and had much fun, but they soon began to tire of endless pleasures and longed to hear the voice of Great Spirit again. They called Nurunderi but he had nothing to say. They asked the Ancestors, who said nothing. They looked to the sky and begged the Milky Way to help them. Wyungare, the old man who lives in the Milky Way, heard their requests. He gathered them around the gum tree again and reminded them of what they had seen before. The tongue of Great Spirit resides in all things; if you listen carefully you can hear his voice whenever you choose.

When we listen closely to nature's creations, we too can hear the voice of Great Spirit. This is the lesson of the throat chakra. To hear the voice of spirit we must always be ready to listen.

Expression

As energy spins at the throat chakra it creates a sense of connection with all life-forms. An appreciation evolves for minerals, plants, trees and animals; all life becomes sacred to the individual who can tune in to throat chakra energy at will. As energy balances in this centre, it is expressed through communication. Through the throat chakra and ether energy we talk to spirit in all its manifestations. We are free to commune with the birds and the trees. We can connect with those who went before us and we can be here now communicating fully with ourselves and those around us.

When the throat chakra is balanced and resonating strongly, you will experience:

the ability to tune to energy

the ability to sense energy

contentment

congruence – you can say what you think and feel

creativity

being artistic

discipline regarding spiritual practice

being reliable

a broad voice range: loud, soft, gentle, assertive, clear, confident as appropriate

you may be clairaudient (hear voices from discarnate souls)

you may feel other people's energy and pain.

Disturbance

Limited energy in the throat chakra results in:

limited awareness

lack of creativity

insensitivity

rudeness and bombastic behaviour

tactlessness

self-righteousness

loneliness

isolation

verbosity.

Physically you may suffer:

thyroid problems

metabolic disorders, weight loss/gain

eating disorders

exhaustion

hyperactivity

repetitive sore throats

ear, nose and throat disorders

toothache

hearing problems (including selective hearing)

muteness (including 'elective mute' – being mute by choice).

When energy is balanced and flowing through the throat chakra, spiritual life becomes increasingly important. Space is made through which to receive and express spirit. Subtle energetic vibrations, which would once have gone un-noticed, are felt, seen and heard. The ability to recognize and draw energy into your system – from the elements, the atmosphere and people around you – becomes second nature as the lower chakras vibrate fully and the throat energy extends.

The desire to spend more time in nature, to move out of the city, to increase your spiritual practice and spend time alone are all expressions of balance in the throat chakra. Ether, remember, is about space. The chronological age of this chakra is 28. You may already have children or reproduction may well be on the agenda; this chakra influences conscious parenting. It creates the awareness required to provide an environment that nurtures a child's physical, emotional, psychological and spiritual needs. Work may be a high priority at this age and throat chakra energy will bring creativity and caring to your chosen profession. You will be conscious of how your actions affect the planet and its people. When the throat centre is balanced, personal power can be used constructively.

When energy is allowed to remain in the lower chakras, limitation continues. The beautiful body temple becomes a prison and we cannot see beyond earthly reality. As energy ascends through the heart into the throat, our horizons broaden. Our sense of awe and wonder increases, our path in life is illuminated and our direction becomes clear. It is time to be creative and make changes. Family, work or home, they may all change when energy moves freely through the throat. Don't be afraid, listen closely to your guides; let all voices be heard and reshape your destiny in accordance with the Divine essence that flows through you.

SEVEN WAYS OF OPENING TO SPIRIT
AT THE THROAT CHAKRA

Altar Work

You have now ascended to the throat chakra. As you replace your heart chakra altar, demonstrate your appreciation to the universe with a moment's silence. Feel the air energy in your heart centre and let the love you have magnified flow through and around your body. Be aware of your developments regarding heart chakra energy.

As mentioned above, the throat centre relates to communication and the element of ether. Ether resonates with the etheric realm, which is the home of our Ancestors. This altar should be created to harness ancestral energies and spirit guides.

Hearing is the sense associated with this chakra; listen carefully and you will receive guidance.

Decorate your altar blue. Again, make use of a silk altar cloth if possible. Position four blue candles in the cardinal directions.

Frankincense is the oil or incense to burn for this chakra; it will also spiritually cleanse the environment. A purified environment is important to create energy that attracts loving guides and Ancestors. Put fresh water in place and gather the appropriate crystals: blue lace agate, lapis lazuli or turquoise are ideal.

Sound is also necessary for this altar. Drums, rattles, bells, chimes and shakers can all be used to raise energy and speak to spirit. Arrange photographs on your altar of anyone you wish to communicate with, incarnate or discarnate. They may speak to you through your dreams, so be prepared to write them down as soon as you wake up. Enlightened masters, mothers, teachers and deities can all be pictured on your ether altar. If you do not possess the images you require, write names on pieces of paper and place them on your altar. Remember, this is not about worshipping images but about raising particular frequencies of energy. An altar is a sacred space where the physical and spiritual worlds meet. A well-cared for altar, as you may have already discovered, helps uplift your spirit and focuses energy on specific issues.

Focused work on the throat chakra provides answers to many of life's questions. Now is the time to really Open to Spirit and be aware of spirit as it speaks to you. Communication can occur in any medium – images, sounds, dreams, feeling or intuition. We receive messages from spirit all the time, but we simply do not hear or trust the information. If you doubt that what you receive is from spirit, ask for a sign. If the communication is genuine then the sign will reveal itself to you. This is a time for trusting in your intuitive ability and accepting fully your everlasting connection to spirit.

Journal-keeping

COMMUNICATION

The throat centre relates to communication in the broadest sense of the word. The ether element resonates with the etheric realm, which is the home of our Ancestors and spirit guides. Through this chakra we can tap into the akashic records. This is a subtle, expansive version of the Internet, the original cyberspace. It records everything that has taken place since the beginning of time, on all planes of existence. It is the greatest library and archive. In order to access and 'download' information we need to be spiritually 'on line' – that is, Open to Spirit.

When difficult decisions arise it is easy to feel pressured and alone. By asking the Ancestors for guidance we realize we are not alone and a burden is lifted. Hearing is the sense associated with the ether element and, therefore, with this chakra; when you listen carefully, with your entire being open, you will receive guidance.

FREE WRITING

Free writing is a technique that involves writing without stopping to judge, censor or correct. Simply take your journal and allow words or symbols to flow on to the page. Be totally honest with yourself and release your inner feelings and creativity. If you have questions, ask them and continue to write. Let the energy flood through you, keep writing. If you don't know what to write, say so – whatever comes to mind, write it down. Do this for as long as feels comfortable.

I find this a very illuminating process. It appears that through channelling energy into writing, without conscious intention, it is possible to tune to the ether and gain personal insight.

You may receive a message immediately or you may wish to continue free writing on a daily basis. It is very useful when done before or after meditation. It can sometimes feel as if you are not the source of the words. I have found this technique quite magical.

End your free writing by giving thanks to your ever-present guardians.

OPENING TO SPIRIT

Yoga Path

MANTRA

Mantra is an aspect of yoga associated with the throat chakra. As we begin to understand the power of sound we realize that nothing exists without motion. The Ancients say everything in life is created through vibration. Quantum physics proves this to be true. Our Ancestors tuned directly to sound vibrations, which hold the ability to create, maintain and destroy.

The creative sound vibrations of hekau and mantra rearrange thought patterns and re-channel energy. 'Energy follows thought,' and through the power of the mind we can direct our energy to create whatever we desire. Unfortunately, negative energy programming is more common than the use of mantras. We often repeat the words 'I can't do ...', 'I am no good at ...', 'I hate ...' We say these things because we lack knowledge of the power of vibration. The Dogon say that the creative word passes through the liver. This is the body's largest organ, responsible for purifying toxins. This suggests that all words should be purified before we utter them. Words and thoughts are sparks that hold the potential to destroy or give light. It is up to us to harness that potential and use it creatively.

The repetition of mantras or affirmations are keys that unlock treasure chests of pure consciousness. Each chakra has a seed mantra that awakens its presiding deity and liberates the natural forces of the chakra. Mantras can be used for protection from negative energy, for healing, spiritual development, raising soul consciousness, and as a form of prayer. As you repeat mantras you become still, your concentration and focus gradually increase and your energy is harmonized and aligned with the cosmos.

Mantras can be said aloud or in silence. They are usually repeated during meditation while focusing on the appropriate chakra. They can, however, be used at any time to calm and centre you. They can also be written – this is known as *likitha japa* and is a very powerful practice.

Repetition of mantras is very important. When we sing or hear a song it often stays with us all day. We find ourselves repeating it, even when we no longer want to; this is how a mantra operates. It gets caught in the grooves of the mind and works its magic. Repeat your mantra for 10 to 15 minutes in the morning and it will create a harmonious frequency that you can tap into consciously and unconsciously for the rest of the day. Use the seed mantras below to resonate with particular chakras, or create positive affirmations and use them like mantras.

BIJA MANTRAS (SEED MANTRAS)

Chakra	Mantra	Sanskrit (to use for likitha japa)
Root	Lam	लअम
Sacral	Vam	वअम
Solar plexus	Ram	रअम
Heart	Yam	यअम
Throat	Ham	हअम
Third eye	Aum	अुम
Crown	silence	

It is always preferable to take initiation into mantra from a teacher. This helps you get the pronunciation correct and provides the added benefit of the teacher's energy (*darshan*). But do not be held back if you don't have a teacher. It is your devotion and attention to practice that really bring results.

When voiced, the bija mantras are pronounced using a soft 'a' like the 'u' in 'bun', and a lengthened 'm' as in 'mother'. They follow the natural flow of the out-breath. When done silently the mantra is repeated on both the in- and out-breaths. It is traditional to say the mantra out loud to begin with and then continue in silence. The silent period should be the longer of the two.

An example of likitha japa:

वअम वअम वअम वअम वअम वअम वअम वअम वअम वअम वअम वअम वअम वअम वअम वअम
वअम वअम वअम वअम वअम वअम वअम वअम वअम वअम वअम वअम वअम वअम वअम वअम

Creation through sound is the secret learned from mantra yoga. Mantras work directly with ether energy to positively shape your life.

Mindful Exercise

NECK ROTATIONS

This simple practice removes tension in the neck and throat area. It creates space for sound to resonate fully through the throat. When the throat chakra, our ether centre, is healthy, energy flows more easily through all the other chakras.

Centre your head over your shoulders and lengthen your neck. Make your neck at least 1 inch (2.5 cm) longer. In this exercise we rotate the neck seven times, moving systematically down the seven cervical vertebrae. Begin with an almost imperceptible rotation towards the right; allow each rotation to increase slightly. Rotate seven times in all, starting with small rotations and finishing with a large circle around your shoulders. Now return, this time rotating to the left, starting with large rotations and slowly getting smaller until your head sits upright over your shoulders. Breathe evenly and focus on the release of each individual cervical vertebra.

When this round is complete, repeat in the opposite direction, rotating down to the left and then coming up again to the right. Remember to breathe evenly as you rotate your neck.

Occasionally taking 5 minutes to release the neck while sitting at a computer is also beneficial. It will help enhance communication as energy is freed to flow between the body and the head/mind.

SHOULDER STAND

This posture directs prana to the throat area and has a balancing effect on the throat chakra.

CAUTION
Because some pressure is placed on the neck, take care when trying this exercise.

Inverted postures should be avoided during menstruation.

If you suffer from neck or back problems, seek advice from a qualified yoga instructor.

You will need a blanket to support your shoulders and protect your neck. A blanket reduces pressure on your neck. Fold the blanket until it is about 2 inches (5 cm) thick and wide enough to accommodate both your shoulders and elbows. Place the blanket on the floor and lie with your head off the blanket and your shoulders and elbows on it. Place your arms by your side. Have your legs stretched out, feet together. Now slowly raise both legs and hips and use your hands to support your back. (Your neck should be resting comfortably on the edge of the blanket.) Close your eyes and lift your legs, straightening them as much as you can. Lift and hold for about 30 seconds.

To come down, slowly round your back and let your feet fall towards your head. Place your hands, palms down, on the floor behind you – they act as levers to gently lower you down. Exhale and come down slowly, massaging the spinal muscles as you move.

BHRAMARI PRANAYAMA (HUMMING BEE)

Music is the voice of the universe and the voice of humanity.

Yehudi Menuhin

Sound has the power to restore the vibratory frequencies of the body and harmonize them with the vibrations of the universe. The sound of a bee humming was used by sages to induce *pratyahara* – relaxation through withdrawal of the senses. This retuned the body/mind to the universe. Bees have long been associated with the Goddess and her powers of healing and transforming consciousness.

The benefits of bhramari pranayama are far-reaching. Dr Singh In 1993[3] carried out a clinical research project with 448 pregnant women at the Munger Hospital in Bihar, India. All the women practising bhramari normalized their blood pressure, reduced the effects of stress and seemed to have regulated their hormones, which aided the births of healthy children.

To practise bhramari, take up a squatting position if comfortable – if not, sit cross-legged, or upright in a chair. All the senses are to be blocked, so place your thumbs in your ears, first fingers lightly over your eyes, middle fingers gently on your nose, ring fingers over your mouth and let your small fingers rest on your chin. Hear silence for a moment, then allow your face to relax. Take a deep breath in and begin to 'hum'. The sound should continue for the length of your exhalation. Experiment with different speeds and pitches: slow, low sounds resonate with lower chakras, high, faster tones resonate with higher centres. Feel the sound as it vibrates through the spaces in your head and body. Find the healing sound you need, right now, to retune your-Self to the universe.

Bhramari pranayama

LOVING KINDNESS

As you go about your business today, let your kind thoughts be heard.

- When you appreciate what someone has done – make sure you tell them.
- When you see someone who looks radiant – compliment them on how they look.
- When you hope someone is successful – take time to wish them success in their endeavours.

– whatever positive thoughts you have about people today, make an effort to let them know. Kind words have enough power to uplift both the giver and the receiver. Of course we do this all the time, yet I am sure with this reminder we will utter affirming words even more often.

Meditation

> God is a circle whose circumference is nowhere, and whose centre is everywhere.
>
> *Joseph Campbell*

Vishuddha chakra is the last centre relating to the physical body and the elements. The remaining two are more subtle. Vishuddha is symbolized by a circle. Circles express wholeness, completion and protection. Many rituals are performed in the safety of a sacred circle. This chakra offers communication through ether; hence meditation can be very powerful. There are always messages specifically for you. We each have angels and helpers in the spirit world that are there to guide us. We need to develop the ability to enter an altered state of consciousness, where we can communicate with our guides. Through meditation we can Open to Spirit at this level and tune directly into the etheric realm. It is important to reduce mental input as much as possible, so psychic awareness can be enhanced.

Cleanse your sacred space, to remove any negative interference. Burn frankincense, which is an excellent purifier (it has been used for this purpose for thousands of years). Sit quietly in front of your altar with the candles glowing. Practise bhramari pranayama to help you enter a meditative state. If you have a question, ask the universe for an answer. As you begin this meditation, let all thoughts go.

In your mind's eye see a circle, a line that has no beginning and no end ... at its centre see the Black Dot ... Be still and aware of all sensations ... Gently re-focus on the Black Dot in the centre ... then sense the circle of your throat chakra, feel its resonance ... Be still and let spirit speak to you ... Guidance can come in many forms. It may be an image, sensation or a sound. Be receptive, not active; be still and welcome the blessings of ether.

Vibrational Work

COLOUR

Sky blue is the dominant colour of the throat chakra. It is the colour of peace and tranquillity. We all know how uplifting it is to stare at a cloudless blue sky on a hot sunny day. The range of sky colours is broad, and any tone can be found in the throat chakra. Blue is a cooling to cold colour. It has powerful healing potential. Many physical ailments are characterized by heat and inflammation, therefore blue is widely used. It is slow in frequency and therefore balancing where too much speed and stress are the causative factors of illness. Because it balances the throat chakra and reduces inflammation, it can be used effectively for sore throats, laryngitis and other throat infections. Like the sky and the ocean, blue is an expansive ray.

Blue also balances problems related to the root and sacral chakras. It offers space and expansion where the root is contractive. Blue is often lacking in the aura; it is an energy that becomes depleted easily in stressful environments. Blue walls or decorations help maintain the blue ray and reduce stress in the home or workplace.

Practitioners, having charged their own energy fields, can draw on the blue ray and channel it into a client's physical heat layer. This can be done through the hands if the client is present, or directed through the ether if the client is absent.

ESSENTIAL OILS

Cleansing oils are used for this chakra. Frankincense and sandalwood have a long history as aromas that banish evil spirits. They are very useful oils for purification and protection. They have a calming quality and help to clear the mind. The Egyptians used sandalwood as oil for embalming; it is also burned at funerals in India to cleanse the soul as it is released.

GEMS

Blue lace agate, blue quartz, lapis lazuli, lazulite and turquoise all help regulate the throat chakra. They can open internal space and raise energetic frequency at this centre. Blue lace agate is a peaceful and soothing stone. It neutralizes heat and redness and helps reduce fevers. Turquoise is a very powerful gemstone that is used in many cultures. Blue of the sky and green of the land come together in this gem. It is therefore seen to unite heaven and earth, the spiritual and the physical, the head and the body. It is a great healer because of its ability to unite fragmented parts of the soul. Turquoise is said to absorb negativity and protect its wearer. Gems for the throat chakra can be used to uplift the spirit and enhance spiritual alignment.

Ritual

STORY-TELLING

Much of what we know today of how the Ancients lived and worshipped was passed on in oral history. For thousands of years people gathered together to study, teach the children and enjoy 'edu-tainment'.[4] We should not let the art of story-telling die because we have books and 'tel-lie-vision'.[5] Story-telling is a way of keeping records and passing information to the next generation.

Have you thought about telling your own story or part of it? I'm sure you have at some time. Story-telling is throat chakra work in more ways than one. It is purifying; it can cleanse the soul and help you to move forward. It calls on creativity and vision. It provides an opportunity for real communication with Self and others. And most of all it is medicine, the healing art of story-telling.

We tell stories all the time: we gossip and embellish the stories with anecdotes for maximum effect. We need to tell our stories, and define ourselves. We all have stories to tell. This is not gossip or creative writing, it is reclaiming ritual. Your transformation story has archetypal energy that shapes form. It has made you who you are. Your story is a tale of healing. You have found a way out of no way. If you are reading these words, you have a story to tell. You have not reached this place alone. You have been blessed.

When we trace our ancient-story (ance-st'ry) distant or near, we gain valuable insights into who we are genetically and spiritually. In Yorùbá tradition we have what is known as Égúngun festival. This celebration of luminous spirits can last up to seven days. It is ritual theatre where stories of our Ancestors (Égun) are retold and enacted. The 'Ara Òrun' – person from heaven – parades the streets covered from head to foot in swirling attire. No flesh is visible. The Égúngun of notable people wear elaborately carved masks. The Égúngun is praised in song and dance. They are greeted with gifts, as people are reassured that the Ancestors are still with us and we can seek guidance and wise counsel from them.

I invite you to write your story of transformation. It can be as long or short as you like. Prepare yourself energetically: create sacred space around you, so your story comes through the ether. Reflect on your journal, starting with the statement on the first page; the pages that follow can form the basis of your story. It need not take long if you don't want it to, or it can become an epic. It is your story, so allow yourself as much space as you want. Many people have done this with me in my workshops. After just two days of chakra work the most incredible transformation stories are written and told. The energy we create in the workshops really helps this happen, but before people arrive they are ripe, over-flowing with messages from spirit that have no direction, dreams that need interpretation, pains that are signalling the need for change. All these chaotic rhythms create harmonious music as we begin to understand the chakras. A new purpose shines on the horizon. You have a story of courage, love and transformation waiting to be told.

Yes, you guessed, writing your story is only the beginning. Story-telling is the real art that gives life to your story and ensures that it lives on not only in the ether but also on the physical realm. When you have written your story, it doesn't have to be perfect, tell it to somebody. Read it to a loved one, preferably from the next generation. Tell it in the third person, *'there once was a woman ...'* Let the story unfold, it has its own life now.

The throat chakra marks the boundary between the head and the body. You are now prepared to move beyond the centres in the body and ascend to the higher chakras in the head.

It is said that a person who opens this chakra knows all the scriptures without needing to read them. That is, a person at the level of understanding comprehends the meaning behind the scriptures through his/her own experience and intuition. He/she becomes compassionate, peaceful and full of bliss.

Swami Satyananda Saraswati

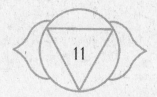

THIRD EYE CHAKRA

EXTRA-ORDINARY VISION

Ancient African scientists found that as a person develops a soul-eye consciousness, the powers of perception become vastly magnified. With an operative soul-eye the individual was reported to have developed god-like powers of intra- or extra-sensory perception. It was with these thoughts in mind that the Ancient Africans, particularly the Ethiopians and the Egyptians, placed the serpent upon the crowns of their royalty.

Richard King, MD

THE THIRD EYE CHAKRA: CORRESPONDENCES

Sanskrit Name	Ajna
Meaning	Perception or command
Main Function	Seat of wisdom, centre of inner vision
Quality	Vision
Location	Slightly above and between the eyebrows

Spiritual Correspondences

Colour	Indigo
Element	Light
Symbol	Two snake heads and eagle wings
Seed Sound	Aum
Petals	96, which is the sum total of all the petals below, times two. (Usually depicted as two)
Planet	Jupiter ♃
Esoteric Anatomy	Astral body
Yoga Path	Tantra focusing on Mandalas and Yantras
Guna Quality	Sattva

Deities

Africa	Horus, Utcheat/Uraeus, Òsumaré, Dan
India	Ardhanarishvara (Shiva-Shakti)
Prophets and great teachers	Buddha, Jesus, Mohammed
Mythology	Myths pertaining to snakes, visions, eagles and prophecy often correspond with Ajna chakra

Physical Correspondences

Gland	Pineal
Nerves	Autonomic nervous system
Body Parts	Left and right cerebral hemispheres, mind function
Expression	Insight and knowledge
Disturbance	Dismissive of own personal spiritual experience

Psychological Correspondences

Statement	'I see/I know'
Emotion	Stillness of body/mind
Chronology	28 – 35 years
Rite of Passage	Vision quest
Developmental Stage	Increased spiritual practice and accumulation of wisdom

Ways of Working

Foods	Fasting
Herbs	Marijuana, ayahuasca, peyote, mescaline
Oils	Frankincense, sandalwood, benzoin, amber, myrrh
Gems	Sapphire, lapis lazuli, sodalite, jet, black opal, azurite

Main Function: Wisdom and Inner Balance

Awakening Ajna chakra, our highest psychic centre, is the main purpose of all spiritual practice. Ajna chakra is the gateway to the soul and the link between the many subtle bodies. It is the home of higher consciousness, healing power and psychic perception.

At Ajna chakra, three streams of consciousness meet: Ida – eye of the moon, Pingala – eye of the sun, and Shushumna – eye of the Divine. These three paths lead to liberation; this is known as *mukta triveni* in Sanskrit. Inner balance is born from the meeting of Ida and Pingala. Their union creates a stillpoint, a moment of freedom. In this stillness the serpent Goddess Kundalini is free to rise up the Shushumna. Kundalini (or Uraeus, to the ancient Egyptians) is a symbol of higher consciousness. When higher consciousness is awakened, the serpent Goddess gently dances up the Shushumna, creating undulating movements. As she raises her head at the point of the third eye, she grants wisdom and vision beyond time and space.

The third eye and Ajna chakra are not the same. Ajna chakra is the force that generates the third eye on the spiritual level. On the physical level Ajna generates the pineal body, cerebral hemispheres, limbic system and the eyes. The individual mind and intelligence are the psychological aspects of Ajna chakra. Spiritual practice focused at this centre aims to raise the level of conscious awareness, release an abundance of healing energy and open the third eye.

Elédàá in Yorùbá refers to the force of the creator that manifests from the third eye. The closeness of the Sahasrara (crown) and Ajna chakras is recognized in this force. Ajna chakra is connected to the pure undifferentiated energy of the crown chakra. It is pure energy separated into two – the creator and the created. This chakra marks the first movement away from the Divine, the beginning of duality. It is therefore also the final point before reunion with the Divine source.

Ajna chakra is known as the seat of the soul. It is here, close to the creator, that the soul is thought to reside.

Work on Ajna chakra is of utmost importance because it is through extending our perception that we lift the veil of Isis. We learn to see beyond the illusion and limitations of ordinary reality. Ajna chakra allows us to embrace darkness and enter the light. The play of darkness and light creates time and vision. Once they are under our command we experience true expansion. When Kundalini rises, we see with her eye and she sees beyond duality. She is not bound by time or space. It is said in Hatha yoga pradipika[1] that 'the sun and moon regulate day and night, thus creating time.' It also tells us that Shushumna swallows time. Hatha yoga pradipika is saying that when we open Shushumna nadi through intense spiritual practice the limitations of time disappear. This is the secret of Ajna chakra. At Ajna chakra we see through the eye of the Divine.

QUALITY: VISION

All life is created from the darkness of the oceans, and all people from the darkness of the womb. Sacred darkness is the source of all light. This creative abyss was symbolized as the Black Dot – seed of all creation – by ancient African scientists. It came to be known by such names as the eye of Horus, soul eye, elédàá, bindu, Rasta far I, third eye, and the seat of the soul. The Black Dot is the doorway to expanded states of consciousness and extra-ordinary vision.

Psychic perception is the quality bestowed at this level of ascension. It is the ability to see into the outer realms and other dimensions. It also includes gifts such as thought transference, remote viewing, precognition and teleportation (out-of-body experience). These special abilities are called *siddhis* in the yogic system. Obtaining these powers is not the goal of yoga. Psychic powers are, however, a sign of development; if not abused they aid us on our path towards enlightenment. These powers provide a glimpse of the natural laws and workings of the universe.

Seeing with the psychic eye differs from ordinary vision. Subtle vibrations are registered through the subtle senses: ears – clairaudience, eyes – clairvoyance, and touch and felt sense – clairsentience. These vibrations are then interpreted by the higher mind. To see clearly, which is the meaning of the word clairvoyance, is to see more than the material world. It requires that we energetically dismantle objects with the inner eye and sense only the space, field and vibration. We need to look into, through and around. With practice we learn to see outside our limited reality. A telephoto lens is able to bring a distant image close. With our telephoto third eye we are able to see the past and future, bringing them into the present.

Seeing involves **attention**. This is often lacking, and is necessary if you are to advance your spiritual practice in order to influence Ajna chakra at will. With experience you learn actually to alter the chemical composition in your body. The parasympathetic nervous system is stimulated, triggering a release of hormones and neuro-chemicals. Brain waves reach a relaxed alpha rhythm. The cerebral membranes and cerebro-spinal fluid are positively influenced, thus stimulating a relaxation of the third ventricle, which is said to be the actual seat of the soul. This can induce a trance state that will transport you to the outer realms and astral and causal planes (sixth and seventh layer of your aura and beyond). It is at this stage that you begin to experience extra-ordinary vision.

We literally have the power to tap into universal and ancestral archives of wisdom and knowledge. As we advance our skills we can access any information; everything that was, is and ever will be is available to us. Attention and focus are the key factors. For example, if I think, 'what am I going to have for dinner?' I must focus my attention in the past and memorize the foods I like. I then have to project my attention into the future and visualize the meal I will prepare. Without attention and focus, I cannot achieve my desired aim. Extra-ordinary vision requires the same principles, attention and focus. Only this time our attention is asked to focus into more distant parts of our memory, to access ancestral and universal data. You may never have asked yourself to do this and therefore think it is beyond your capability. If you try, you may surprise yourself.

In creating your future, again it is the third eye, aided by Ajna chakra, which can travel anywhere unrestricted. We know from our daydreams that anything is possible. You can make your dreams reality. Anything you perceive you can achieve, as long as you use your gifts of attention and focus. Learning to use Ajna chakra is a case of discipline and trust in your self-knowledge and creative abilities.

Element: Light

> The light of the body is the eye;
> if therefore thine eye be single,
> the whole body shall be full of light.
> *Matthew 6:22*

Light is the visible band of electromagnetic energy; ultra-violet being the band above and infrared the band below. The electromagnetic spectrum includes many kinds of waves such as X-rays and radio waves. Variations in frequency of light give rise to different colours, moving from red, found at the root chakra, to violet at the crown. Light travels at a speed of 186,000 miles per second. Sound, which resonates at the throat centre, moves at approximately 331 miles a second, over 500 times more slowly than light.

Ajna chakra is the body's conduit for this powerful energy known as light. It receives light and channels it as colour through the chakras and aura. Visualization on light and colour are effective tools for healing.

The pineal gland, which is the physical aspect of Ajna chakra, processes light. This small neuro-endocrine gland, the size of a pea and the shape of a pine-cone, has baffled modern science for a long time. It was said to have no known function. Yet when we turn to ancient science we find an abundance of oral history, folklore and written texts pertaining to the pineal gland, Ajna chakra and third eye. The Ancients understood the complex workings of Ajna chakra from having direct experience of its power. They realized that it is possible to alter consciousness and shape reality through influencing Ajna chakra. The pineal's creative function led the Ancients to refer to it as the creative 'gene of Isis' (genesis).[2] Its partly crystallized nature and ability to absorb, store and transmit light energy suggests it is the body's inner crystal.

The pineal gland works closely with the pituitary gland. This is because the energies of the Sahasrara and Ajna chakras are linked. Where the pituitary is known as the master gland, because it has a stimulating effect on various bodily systems, the pineal we could usefully call the 'mother gland' because it appears to calm the body's systems. The pineal releases two neuro-hormones, serotonin and melatonin. Serotonin, which is dominant in the day, helps to keep us active and awake, while melatonin encourages rest and is dominant at night. Together they regulate the body's circadian rhythm, which is the biological cycle responsible for maintaining balance in relation to light and darkness. If we stay in darkness for several days, serotonin and melatonin levels continue to alternate. If, however, we are exposed to constant light or we stay awake for several days, the rhythm is disrupted. Changes in exposure to light are implicated in seasonally affected manic depression, where people get accustomed to being high in the summer and experience lows when the system normalizes during the dark winter months. It is in the winter when people experience this problem. Melatonin is being used as a cure for jet lag, where lack of sleep and change of time zone disrupt the circadian rhythm.

In meditation and other spiritual practices it is customary to focus on Ajna chakra. Meditation is also said to be more powerful if done during Brahmahurta, which is between the dark hours of 4 and 6 in the morning. During these hours levels of the hormone melatonin are at their highest. Melatonin is associated with the release of innate hallucinogens. Research shows that high levels of melatonin are present during altered states of consciousness and psychic visions.

MELANIN, LIGHT AND THE CHAKRAS
Melatonin is also active in the production of melanin. Melanin, like the pineal gland, has attracted little scientific research until recently. African American scientists have pioneered research on melanin and its benefits on our physical, psychological and spiritual health.

Melanin, the light-sensitive black pigment found in the skin, brain, eyes, ears and other organs, is present in almost all living organisms, including the celestial realms. Dr T Owen Moore states:

Melanin in the surface of the skin, in the internal organs and the nervous system, can enhance a person's connection to the spiritual world and act as a battery charger for the chakra system.

The Ancients had a profound knowledge of the Eternal Spirit, Ajna chakra and the chakras in general. Maybe our African Ancestors respected their relationship to the creator and geophysical phenomena such as the sun, moon and the elements because of their blackness. Dr Moore points out that 'melanin is a critical link between our human bodies and the elements in nature, enabling us to optimize our health.' People from cultures in tune with Divine law and adhering to strong spiritual traditions tend to have high concentrations of melanin in their skin. Melanin tests on Egyptian mummies carried out by Cheikh Anta Diop during the 1970s in France were used to verify the ancient Egyptians as African.

Melanin has many functions. Physically it protects the skin and helps to neutralize free radicals,[3] which slows the ageing process. In the brain it can heighten awareness and speed reactions. It facilitates energetic motility in the nervous system, and stores energy in the form of memory.[4] Melanin absorbs light and transforms electromagnetic energy. The release of neuro-chemicals, such as serotonin, norepinephrine and dopamine, is enhanced by melanin. These chemicals are found in the pineal gland.[5] The characteristics of melanin optimize spiritual and physical health.

Dr King, researcher of African spiritual science, locates the Black Dot – doorway to dreams, ancestral memory, past-life regression and extra-ordinary vision – in the melinated areas of the brain (neuro-melanin is common to all people regardless of skin colour). King refers to this neuro-melanin nerve tract[6] as *Amenta*, meaning underworld. These nerves assist the release of innate hallucinogens and communicate with the third ventricle, which has long been termed 'the vault of initiation' and 'the seat of the soul'.

Pyramids are temples of initiation where ancient Egyptian Godkings and priests became masters of inner science. They also symbolize mountains, chakras and consciousness. The upper chamber of the great pyramid is completely made from black granite. This is symbolic of night, dreams and Amenta, the underworld. Entering this black chamber or level of consciousness activated the pineal gland, bringing illumination and knowledge of the essence of life. Like the ancient Egyptians we have the potential to develop soul-eye consciousness. Work on Ajna chakra amplifies spiritual awareness and raises energy to the heights of Mount Meru.

Melanin is one of our many blessings, and we should learn to understand the spiritual significance of this beautiful gift. We have at our disposal an innate channel for processing vibrational energy. Melanin can receive light and distribute it through the chakras and aura. During spiritual practice we can focus on light (Ra) travelling through the vault of initiation, raising soul consciousness and awakening ancestral memory.

Planet: Jupiter ♃

The planet Jupiter resonates with the very essence of Ajna chakra. To the ancient Egyptians it was known as Heru-Wep-Sheta, meaning 'Horus reveals the mystery'. It was also known as the light of wisdom and planet of expansion. As the largest planet in the solar system, Jupiter was regarded as king of the heavens. He acts as guardian and protector of law, truth and justice.

Ajna chakra is the gateway to expanded consciousness, truth and spiritual illumination. When we tune to this chakra we gain freedom and liberation. This is depicted in the glyph for Jupiter ♃ where the soul (half moon) is raised above the + cross symbol of earthly limitation. As you ascend to this chakra you will notice the change in your vibration. Those around you will begin to see the light that shines from your heart. At Ajna chakra the planet Jupiter becomes your teacher and guide.

The chronological age for this chakra is around 35 years. At this stage in life many foundations are set in place, work and family are often established, and it becomes important to find time for personal and spiritual pursuits. Both Jupiter and Ajna vibrate at the level of the higher mind, tapping us into the astral and philosophical realms. It is here that our greatest inspirations can be fertilized and directed down the chakras towards manifestation. Jupiter aids the generation of ideas. He channels energy from heaven and sends it down as prophecy. He stimulates your inner genius; your prophetic 'gene of Isis'. When your awareness is raised, your senses turned inward (pratyahara) and your full attention focused on the vibrations of Jupiter at Ajna chakra, good fortune and abundant blessings will be yours. The inner crystal that holds all memories will be stimulated and the way opened for the mysteries of Horus to be revealed.

Deities

HERU (HORUS)

Heru, the hawk-headed son of Ausar and Auset (Osiris and Isis), is the personification of light. His is the face of heaven. His right eye is the sun and his left eye the moon. He favours those who, like him, seek to destroy negative influences, liberating truth and wisdom.

The winged solar disc – symbol of Horus in heaven and the expansive essence of the Soul.

URAEUS

Uraeus is an ancient African Goddess with numerous characteristics. When Uraeus is found at the sixth chakra she represents power over all external and internal forces. Developing serpent power puts us in control of our lives and prepares us for oneness with the Divine.

ÒṢUMARÉ

Òṣumaré is the beautiful cosmic serpent who manifests as a rainbow. Opposites are merged in this male and female deity. Òṣumaré provides continuity. Lying between heaven and earth, the rainbow unites the creator with the created. By swallowing her tale she links the present to the past, forging a smooth way to the future. As rainbow Goddess, Òṣumaré is known universally. She unites the seven colour rays of the chakras, offering us peace, hope and harmony.

Òṣumaré and Dan (*see below*) may well predate traditional Yorùbá religion as it is known today. Òṣumaré is often seen as an aspect of Olódùmárè, the creator.

DAN (FON PEOPLE OF DAHOMEY)

Dan is another cosmic serpent and rainbow deity. The serpent represents earth and the rainbow is symbolic of light and heaven. Dan is also depicted swallowing his tail, showing his ability to overcome duality and create unity. Dan then revolves around the earth, causing the universe to spin. This rainbow serpent creates the constant movement of the life-force.

ARDHANARISHVARA

In the deity Ardhanarishvara, Shiva and Shakti conquer duality and become one. Their merging energies symbolize unity between the lower three chakras – personal realms, and the upper three chakras – universal realms. Just as their forces unify, we too can know harmonious union with our creator.

The Divine union of Shiva and Shakti forms the deity Ardhanarishvara, who is male on the right and female on the left.

OPENING TO SPIRIT

Mythology

THE WINGED SERPENT

The frequency of energy at each chakra is symbolized by an increasing number of open lotus petals (root = four, sacral = six, solar plexus = ten, heart = twelve, throat = sixteen). This beautiful flower blossoms from dark, muddy earth. Only two petals are depicted at Ajna chakra. They represent duality. The entire manifest world is part of this duality. In the body feminine energy flows through Ida nadi and masculine energy flows through Pingala nadi. Teachings from many spiritual traditions indicate that we transcend ordinary reality when Ida and Pingala are balanced. At Ajna chakra we have the potential to fly beyond duality and unite with our creator.

An ancient Egyptian papyrus reads:[7]

...Goddess Uatchet cometh unto thee in the form of living Uraeus to anoint thy head with flames [light the inner flame]. She rises up on the left side [cognitive hemisphere] and she shines down on the right side without speech [intuitive hemisphere]. They rise upon the head during each day and every hour of the day.

Here the Goddess Uatchet relates to the negative and positve currents of Ida and Pingala, where energy constantly maintains the rhythm of life. Ida and Pingala relate to the two cerebral hemispheres: sun on the right, which drives our masculine, linear, cognitive force of intellect (Pingala) and moon on the left, which drives our feminine, spatial, intuitive force of intellect (Ida). Balancing these polarities creates the neutral force, in which dwells the message of the prophets.

The papyrus goes on to say:

I am Uatchet [serpent power] I come forth from Horus, I am Horus [wisdom] and I fly upon the forehead of Ra [light] in the bows of his boat, which is heaven.

The serpent Uatchet (Uraeus-Kundalini) flies like Horus the hawk and delivers the prophet's message of unity. The message of Ajna chakra is known in many traditions. We see heaven and earth merge, Shiva become one with Shakti, Buddha wearing a jewel on his forehead to symbolize his open third eye and enlightenment. The Goddess Hathor unites the sun and moon, Uraeus becomes winged and the cosmic serpent Òsumaré swallows her tail, creating Ouorborous, the circle of pure consciousness.

When serpents can climb no more, they develop wings. Wings carry us the final distance home to our creator. Wings symbolize liberation and transcendence. Ajna chakra is our direct link to the astral planes. Astral travel includes many experiences, from the simple daydream to full-out of body travel. On the astral plane, space and time are no longer operative. The soul can go anywhere to gather information. We receive thoughts, emotions and intuition from our higher consciousness and we can communicate with all life-forms; plants, animals, trees and invisible forces whisper their secrets. We reach these celestial heights through flight when we have the ability to tap into Ajna chakra.

Birds fly from the celestial realms to earth and from earth they return again to the heavens. They soar freely through the air, connecting the physical with the spiritual. Like the all-seeing eye, wings transport us beyond spirit and matter, beyond dark and light, returning us to the blissful realm of pure consciousness.

Expression

At this advanced level we are awakened to infinite possibilities. By now, your spiritual practice should be well established and then experience will propel you to the realm of knowing. It is now that we really begin to see the fruits of discipline, commitment and an ever-increasing desire for truth.

As energy flow increases at Ajna chakra you will experience:

spontaneous spiritual awakening

trance states

profound insights

knowledge of past lives

understanding of, and therefore no fear of, death

meaning and clarity in your life

extra-sensory-perception

healing abilities (of the Self/others)

increased balance of left and right hemispheres

contentment

inner mastery

knowledge of nature

ecstasy arising from sexual energy (this can be achieved via sex or celibacy).

Disturbance

If Ajna chakra is out of balance you may experience:

grief

mental slavery

staying imprisoned by lower energies

dogmatism

abuse of the higher powers you have gained

scepticism

being dismissive of your own spiritual experience

overactive Ida or Pingala nadis.

Your health may suffer:

SAD (seasonal affective disorder)

skin cancer (over-exposure to sunlight)

headaches, migraine.

When energy flows freely through Ajna chakra and the third eye, our perception of reality changes. We see the universe as it truly is. As Gerber clearly states, 'All matter is an expression of the crystallized light and energy of the creator.' ESP is simply a matter of seeing and believing, or seeing and trusting. We see all the time, but we don't believe. We allow ESP to remain beyond our 'normal' frame of reference. If I ask, 'What colour dress is Tayo wearing?', you will answer, 'Green'. You easily believe what you see with the physical eye. If I ask, 'What colour is her aura?' you may not answer, simply because sight is limited to two eyes. When we look with the third eye we see on a more subtle level. First we require trust, which can later be replaced with belief based on knowing.

When energy is restricted at Ajna chakra, knowledge will be limited. A person may experience feelings of grief and alienation. Questions about the meaning of life will remain unanswered. Some people try to understand all life through using the rational intellect, leaving creative and intuitive abilities untapped. Such people will be dismissive of other people's spiritual growth. If you are around people like this, don't try to change them, let your energy embrace them and teach by example.

On the other hand, someone may have raised energy to this level, achieving a high degree of inner power, which is then abused for personal gain. There is no awareness of the creator's greatness; instead it is mistaken for one's own.

With awareness we learn to use the pure light of Ajna chakra directly. Light knows no bounds – we can guide it into the body, stepping it down through the chakras. Through meditation we can direct light into the world for personal and global healing.

SEVEN WAYS OF OPENING TO SPIRIT
AT THE THIRD EYE CHAKRA

Altar Work

As you move through the chakras, ascending towards pure spirit, your practice will become second nature. As you prepare to move onto the third eye chakra, as usual take time to honour the energies that helped you achieve your previous work. I am sure ether work was a powerful experience for you. Feel the experience in your energy field right now. Acknowledge your spiritual development.

The third eye chakra is the centre of wisdom and insight. The colour is indigo, the bluey-black of midnight. During the stillness of night a healthy person undergoes a process of self-regulation. This corrective activity creates healing of the body, mind, spirit and emotions. The element here is light. Both darkness and light play an important role in true wisdom. Therefore both should be represented on this altar.

Your altar cloth should symbolize the night sky, with four black candles, each providing the light of a shining star. From your altar, let the aromas of frankincense, sandalwood, benzoin, amber or myrrh fill the room. These resins have been used for centuries by the wise to clear the mind, and enhance our connection to universal knowledge. Water is a great amplifier of energy and, as usual, should be placed on your altar. Gems that vibrate with the third eye are sodalite, jet, black opal, sapphire and azurite. Position them in a way that magnifies their energy: create a power symbol such as a triangle, or circle. As this chakra reflects inner sight, keep this altar simple. The light emanating from darkness signifies the duality of Ajna chakra.

At this level of chakra awareness, information is largely received through visualization. The dark mental screen seen before closed eyes lights up like that of a movie screen, and events are played out before your eyes. Tuning to higher vibrations should be easier for you now. If you have consistently followed the practices of the previous chakras, then only a few focused moments are needed in order for you to Open to Spirit and connect with Divine order.

Journal-keeping

CREATING A DREAM DIARY

Dreaming is a familiar experience of expanded consciousness. Space or time does not affect dreams. They transport us into another reality, a reality that contains symbolic language and archetypal images. The Ancients saw dreams as direct messages from the Gods; much later, Jung referred to them as the royal road to the unconscious. Before dream prophecy can be understood, dreams must be interpreted.

The first stage of interpretation is to start keeping a dream diary. Write down your dreams as you remember them. Keep your diary and a pen by your bed so that when you wake, you can write immediately. Begin to make a personal dictionary of dream symbols as they appear to you. A personal dream dictionary is useful, as the symbols in dreams can hold unique as well as universal meanings. The symbols can be drawn or described in words. The language of dreams can provide information about external events, as well as personal themes.

For example, *death* may forewarn you of the termination of life, or it may refer to a part of yourself that is coming to an end. A *snake* may tell of approaching danger, or it may refer to the rebirth of an aspect of yourself.

As you keep your diary and personal dictionary, many things will be repeated. Patterns will be revealed to you. The mystery will start to unravel. Dreaming is a very individual experience and no one interpretation will be appropriate for everyone. It is better to take the time to really get to know your own psyche and dream language.

The second stage of interpretation is analysis. This can be done in many ways:

- You can simply speak with friends about your dreams, as you probably do now, and gain some useful insights.
- Your dictionary of dream images can be re-drawn, exaggerated and animated if you want.
- The dream can be made into a story to give it more power. This is also a good way of changing dreams. Maybe you behaved in a passive way and want to repeat the dream, so that this time you can be more assertive.
- You can re-enter the dream through creating a trance-like state. Relax yourself deeply and then use the dream as a guided visualization. You can then extend the dream if you wish.
- Ask questions. How does the dream relate to your life now? What do you like or dislike about it? What do you love about the dream? What do you fear?
- One of the most important aspects of dreams are the feelings they provoke. How did you feel during your dream? How did you feel when you woke up?

All these methods can provide insight into the meaning of your dreams.

Working with dreams can be very inspiring and creative. We all dream, although we may not always remember them. If you have difficulty recalling dreams, work on Ajna chakra will create improvement. It is also helpful to avoid being awakened by alarm clocks. Instead, set your unconscious mind before you go to sleep. Ask to be awakened at a specific time. This is very effective with practice.

Try to avoid speaking before you write or draw your dreams in the mornings. As you tap into the pool of knowledge and wisdom that awaits you, remember to have fun and don't take everything in your dreams too seriously. Dreams provide the opportunity to take a break from ordinary reality.

Yoga Path

MANDALAS AND YANTRAS

Mandalas are circular images that bring apparent chaos and complexity together into a pattern of wholeness. They are magic circles used for meditation and healing. The sand paintings of India, Tibet and Original America, and rose windows in Gothic cathedrals are all mandalas. The Earth herself is a mandala. Nature produces them abundantly, in the form of snowdrops, shells, breasts, flowers, cobwebs and the swirling energy centres we know as chakras. Your body, together with your aura, forms a sacred circle.

Naturally occurring mandalas: The gentle spiralling of new hair on the crown of a baby's head forms a perfect mandala, as does a woman's breast – the nipple sits in the centre with the milk ducts perfectly surrounding this central point.

A yantra is a specific mandala used in tantric yoga. The power of the universe, the Shakti energy, is retained within them. It is said that as the body contains the soul, so the yantra contains the deity. These symbols of pure consciousness are used for trance-form-ation. Together with mantras they invoke deities and illuminate great mysteries.

OPENING TO SPIRIT

Yantras and mantras are forms and sounds of pure consciousness. In chakra dharana, the meditation practice given below, the chakra mandalas are used as yantras.

ADVANCED CHAKRA DHARANA

Dharana (concentration) is the sixth stage of raja yoga (as mentioned in Chapter 6). It is an effective technique that induces deep meditation. Using your 'felt sense' and the chakra correspondences, ascertain which centre needs balance and healing. Position the relevant chakra symbol (*see colour plate section*) against a wall in front of you. Sit in a meditative posture, arm's distance from the wall with the centre of the image directly opposite you. Be aware of your breath and start to relax. Begin staring into the yantra. See the bija mantra in the centre ... the inner symbol (square, crescent moon, etc.) ... the circle ... number of petals ... colour ... see each aspect individually, and then as a complete whole. Maintain the image in your mind's eye ... Now take your awareness to the chakra location within your body. Visualize each aspect individually and then as a whole. Tune to the pulsation and energetic rhythm of the chakra as it begins to vibrate. Feel the sensation expand and fill your entire being. Absorb the powerful healing energy and receive the many gifts that are bestowed on you. You are embraced in pure spirit, one with the universe ... When the time is right your meditation will end ... visualize the chakra symbol within ... see all its aspects before you open your eyes. Deepen your breath and be aware of the ground supporting you. Bow your head and give thanks for the blessing you have received.

The lesson here is unity. Through expanded consciousness the limited becomes the unlimited, the finite infinite.

Mindful Exercise

THE SQUAT

For many people in Africa and Asia, squatting is as natural as sitting. The benefits of squatting are well known, and therefore it is performed regularly throughout the day. Cooking, waiting in queues, going to the toilet, resting and other general daily activities are all carried out in a squatting position. According to Dr Stone, the founder of Polarity Therapy, no other exercise equals this one for minimum effort and maximum results.

This posture calms and focuses the brain and nervous system by stimulating the parasympathetic nervous system and circulation of the cerebro-spinal fluid. The pelvis is opened, as are the nadis and chakras. The overall flow of energy through and around the body is enhanced by this simple yet powerful posture. This posture benefits all the chakras.

You can be creative with this posture, finding a position that suits you. If your heels don't touch the ground, roll a towel up or place a book under them.

Experiment with the:

◇ narrow squat: feet 6 inches (15 cm) or less apart
◇ wide squat: feet 12 inches (30 cm).

Try the Pyramid squat too. Stand with your feet apart and facing outwards. Lean forward placing your hands just above your knees, thumbs on the inside. Knees are directly over your ankles. Now lengthen your spine and straighten your arms. Shoulders are up towards your ears. Breathe deeply and let your neck relax. This posture stretches your whole body. You can rock gently in squat postures, breathing deeply and rhythmically. If the posture is difficult at first, please persevere, it is well worth the effort. Dr Stone continued to practise the squat into his eighties; he called the wide position 'the youth posture'.

Narrow squat

Pyramid

CHAKRA SCANNING – RAINBOW MEDITATION

Now you have raised your awareness and ascended to the brow chakra, mindful exercise will be easier. From this chakra the inner eye can be used to scan the chakras below. With experience gained through regular practice, it is possible to assess accurately the energy levels of your chakras. You can scan your chakras daily using this simple practice.

Relax in a meditative posture and focus on the movement of your breath. When your mind is still, turn your attention to your root chakra. See the red ray and assess its quality. Is the colour dense or fading? Is the energy vibrant or weak? Is the pulse strong? Scan the root chakra body parts. With practice this can be done quite quickly. Once you sense the energy levels, you are ready to move on to the next chakra.

Move through all the centres, focusing on the colour rays, assessing the energetic quality.

This practice takes around 15 to 20 minutes.

Motion is the nature of energy; it seldom stays the same. Chakra scanning is an excellent way to tune in to your core energy and receive an update on how it is moving. A deeper knowledge of your higher Self develops as you become familiar with the subtle changes that occur. When you know what is happening at a core level, you can tune your day to the spirit that moves you.

Meditation

Your chakra ascension is almost complete. You have reached the stars, the celestial realms. The dark night sky is spotted with shining light. The brow chakra takes you into the darkness, where all the colours of light reside. This meditation is practised as a ritual for 21 days. It circulates consciousness through the chakras, bringing illumination, vision and insight.

ASCENDING MOUNT MERU

This meditation is more powerful if done during Brahmahurta, which is between the dark hours of 4 and 6 in the morning. The Ancients always favoured this time, and it has now been explained by science. During these hours, levels of the hormone melatonin, which is produced by the pineal gland, are at their highest. Research states that high levels of melatonin are present during mystic experiences and psychic visions.

Each day prepare your sacred space. Remember, this daily ritual balances Ajna chakra, so maintain an altar that resonates with the night sky. Use indigo or black candles. Gaze into your candle and see all the colours of light – blue, green, violet, red, orange and yellow – as they radiate out from the black centre. Spend about 10 minutes practising anuloma viloma pranayama (alternate nostril breathing – *see page 86*) to prepare for meditation. The meditation can take between 10 and 50 minutes.

To begin dharana, focus first on Ajna chakra. See all the colours of the rainbow merge on the black screen ... after a few minutes of tuning to Ajna chakra, continue with the daily practice as outlined below.

This aspect of the meditation is practised for seven days and repeated for the next two weeks (21 days in all). Once you reach Day Seven, begin again at Day One.

Day One	dharana on a red square	muladhara chakra
Day Two	dharana on an orange crescent moon	swadistana chakra
Day Three	dharana on a yellow downward-facing triangle	solar plexus chakra
Day Four	dharana on a green six-pointed star	anahata chakra
Day Five	dharana on a blue circle	vishuddha chakra
Day Six	dharana on the Black Dot	Ajna chakra
Day Seven	dharana on Pure Spirit	crown chakra

Dharana is practised by focusing the image first on the chidakash (mind's blank screen) and then sensing the image in the chakra location. During your meditation, absorb the vibration and powerful energy ... fill your being until it overflows ... hear the whispers of wisdom as spirit speaks to you.

> And Jacob called the name of the place Peniel, for I have seen God face to face and my life is preserved: And as he passeth over Peniel the sun rose upon him.
>
> *Genesis 32:30 – 31*

Vibrational Work

COLOUR

Indigo, colour of the night sky, dominates the brow chakra. It is composed of bluey-black and violet. The violet gives indigo its warm electric glow. Black brings mystery, the unknown darkness of night. When it is not feared, this ray aids in our development of inner vision and psychic energy. It fuels our quest for knowledge. It holds hidden truth and great potential within its stillness. Like black, indigo absorbs energy – we need to be careful what energy we are around when we open to this ray or wear indigo-coloured clothing.

Indigo's ability to draw energy makes it a good purifier. It can balance negative energy, but may not be the first choice of colour. Its components blue or violet should be used first; if they don't work, then indigo, which is more potent, can be tried. It is a healing ray that helps balance the third eye. It is especially good for clearing psychic overload. Strong indigo in the aura filters psychic interference. This colour resonates with the astral sheath and guides purified energies from the celestial realms down to earth. When the indigo ray is strong, energy flooding through Ajna chakra can give rise to mystic experiences. When the indigo ray is weakened (and the nadis blocks) the same energy flowing through Ajna chakra can cause mental disturbance and mental illness.

ESSENTIAL OILS

Essential oils of sandalwood, frankincense, amber, myrrh and benzoin clear the atmosphere and raise the vibrations of the spiritual triad (the throat, brow and crown chakras). These oils have been used in temples for thousands of years and still serve us today. Catholic churches burn frankincense to create sacred space before services. Have these oils in your home so you can cleanse the air if negative energy starts to accumulate. They can also be burned on your altar to aid your meditations and bring insight.

GEMS

Sapphire, lapis lazuli, sodalite, jet, black opal and azurite can all be used to balance the third eye. Lapis lazuli reduces pain; it works on the physical, emotional and spiritual levels. The pain of spiritual longing can be alleviated as lapis lazuli opens the user to the spiritual triad of the throat, brow and crown chakras. It is a protective gem that was used by the Ancients to ward off evil and bring good fortune. It affects all the chakras, probably because it helps to balance the nerves and endocrine system. Lapis lazuli is said to clear the mind and order thoughts. Artists can benefit from wearing lapis lazuli, as it aids creativity through developing visionary insight. Expression can be enhanced in whichever artistic medium you choose. Its powerful energy heightens meditation. Having stood the test of time, lapis lazuli is a gem we can all find a use for.

Sodalite, which vibrates at a lower frequency than lapis lazuli, has many of the same qualities. Try holding gems from the blue range, to sense which work for you.

Ritual

CHANGE AND VISION

You have arrived at Ajna chakra, celestial realm and gateway to the sacred sanctuary of the crown chakra. Here you can create a vision of purpose that will connect you to spirit and carry you forward in your life. Ancient cultures recognized the power of the third eye, the chakra of vision and creation. What we see we can be.

This ritual is to be done during the dark nights that precede the new moon. You will need your journal, a pen, sunflower seeds, some earth and a candle.

Create sacred space by cleansing your environment, preparing your altar and calling the directions (*see page 136*).

✺ Sit in front of a candle and stare into the shining flame. Watch the colours of light dance to the rhythm of your breath. Close your eyes and raise your energy up through the chakra colours of your inner rainbow. Focus your attention on the Black Dot of your third eye.

✺ With your inner eye, visualize a typical day in your life now. Begin with waking and see everything – where you are, who is with you, what you do, what it means to you and how you feel. Use one or two words to describe where you are now and write them in your journal.

✺ This time, close your eyes and envision what you wish to create in your life. Let your imagination be free – remember, what you see you can be. Visualize your-Self getting up, see where you are, whom you are with, what you are doing. Be aware of how you feel. Find the words to summarize where you are going and write them down.

◈ What are the differences between the first visualization – your typical day – and the second, your idealized day? What has changed? What do you need to do to realize this new reality?

◈ This is the time of profundity; the new moon will be born from the dark night sky. Hold the seeds in your hand as a symbol of new beginnings and spiritual growth. As you plant the seeds in the earth, have a clear image of what you are now growing within. Ask for the blessing of the new moon; she will replace struggle with ease.

◈ Walk outside and look up at the dark sky and give thanks.

Close Sacred Space

Give thanks and release the great guardians and spirit-keepers of the directions and elements that have assisted your ritual.

Watch the sky each night and, as you see the new moon appear, know that as she grows, so too will you.

CROWN CHAKRA

THE PEAK EXPERIENCE

I am the one that transforms into two
I am the two that transforms into four
I am the four that transforms into eight
After that I am one
Coffin of Pentamon, Cairo Museum

The Crown Chakra: Correspondences

Sanskrit Name	Sahasrara
Meaning	One thousand – Infinity
Main Function	Liberation
Quality	Fulfilment
Location	Anterior fontanel – top of the head

Spiritual Correspondences

Colour	Gold, violet or white
Element	Pure spirit
Symbol	Circle

Seed Sound	Silence
Petals	One thousand
Planet	Sun ☉, Uranus ♅
Esoteric Anatomy	Anandamayakosha – bliss sheath, universal force-field, infinity
Yoga Path	All paths
Guna Quality	Sattva

Deities

Africa	Amen Ra, Olódùmárè
India	Shiva, Aditi
Europe	God, Zeus
Supreme Gods and Goddesses of all cultures	
Mythology	Creation and cosmological myths

Physical Correspondences

Gland	Pituitary
Nerve Plexus	Central nervous system
Body Parts	Transcends the physical body and controls esoteric anatomy
Expression	Satchitananda: Truth, knowledge, bliss
Disturbance	Ignorance of one's spiritual nature

Psychological Correspondences

Statement	'I am (Divine)'

EMOTIONS

BALANCED	UNBALANCED
Peak experience	Disorientation
Peace	Constant worry
Oneness	Fragmentation
Chronology	35 – 42 years
Rite of Passage	Acceptance as an Elder
Developmental Stage	Wholeness, Individuation

Ways of Working

Foods	Fasting
Herbs	Comfrey, golden seal, camomile
Oils	Lavender, bay laurel, hyacinth, spikenard, valerian
Gems	Amethyst, diamond, selenite, clear quartz, pearl

Main Function: Liberation

As we fly high above Ajna chakra we reach the home of our creator, Sahasrara (crown) chakra. Here we can truly rest. Sahasrara is the still quiet place of oneness. The realm of *anandamayakosha* – bliss sheath. This is the destiny of all spiritual practice. It is our birthright to know and dwell, at our will, in a state of peaceful bliss.

I believe we have all experienced oneness at some point in life. I believe we know peace and bliss intimately, and that we search for their return in everything we do. It is this inner knowing that leads us towards liberation. Each step we take on life's journey brings us closer to home. At the lowest times in our lives we reach out to touch hope, we seek the helping hand of our creator, begging to be lifted from our pain. Despair is a lesson that teaches us to move closer to our creator. The joy and laughter, the pain and tears, all experiences can help us remember our destiny and realize that we and the creator are one.

My work has led me to understand that liberation can be experienced on three different levels. The first is when an elevated being raises soul consciousness to the level of Sahasrara chakra and enters the indescribable realm of *Mahasamadhi*. Mahasamadhi means 'great absorption in the Divine'. The soul that evolves to this level never returns again to the earth plane. Mahasamadhi is the highest level of consciousness. This is attained after thousands of incarnations, when all karma is completed and the soul is totally purified and enlightened.

Death is another level of liberation. Yogis believe that when we have finished our personal supply of prana we expire. Life is measured in breaths instead of years. During life we have a quota of breaths to use at will. We can use them quickly, through anger and stress, or we can stay calm and relaxed, lengthening each breath and extending life. When the time comes for us to leave the body, it is like being awakened from a dream. In a dream everything feels real, until we wake up and realize it was just a dream. We are taught in yoga that life is a dream, an illusion – death is waking up and finding yourself liberated from life. At the time of death, prana leaves the body through the *Brahmarandhra* ('hole of Brahma' – anterior fontanel, the soft spot on a baby's head). This is the same spot where the soul first enters the body and takes up its residence in the third ventricle.

The remaining level of liberation is a temporary experience, where the soul can activate a high level of consciousness. This level is not Mahasamadhi, nor death, but an opportunity to glimpse enlightenment. I use Abraham Maslow's term 'peak experience' to describe this heightened state of awareness. This felt sense of liberation is, by its very nature, beyond explanation. I can, however, try to guide your memory to a time when you have felt the freedom of Sahasrara chakra.

Try to remember a time when you felt totally at one with your creator and all around you. This happens when the cares of the world are no longer on your shoulders and you have time and space in abundance. It may be during meditation or when you are in nature. You may be by the sea, on a mountaintop, or in a beautiful forest. The sun may be setting or the full moon offering its guiding light. You feel uplifted, ecstatic and glad to be alive. Loved and loving all rolled into one. The vibrant life-force is flowing freely through your body and you feel 'spirit' filling your hungry soul. Do you recall such a time? This is an extremely powerful experience, summed up in the mantra *Soham soham* – 'I am that I am.' Peak experience is the place where the experience and experiencer merge. In yoga this may be termed *Sarvikalpa Samadhi* – absorption in the Divine with form. In this state a high level of soul consciousness is attained and we come to know our creator, yet the experience of duality remains. This is in contrast to a higher level of Samadhi known as *Nirvikalpa Samadhi*, where there is no form, no experiencer, no duality. In Nirvikalpa Samadhi there exists only oneness.

The crown chakra is the home of liberation. As we evolve spiritually we progress through the different levels of liberation, until the soul eventually attains Mahasamadhi.

QUALITY: FULFILMENT

> Having reached that place supreme, the seers find joy in wisdom, their souls have fulfilment, their passions have gone, they have peace. Filled with devotion they have found the Spirit in all and go into the All.
>
> *Mundaka Upanishad*

Fulfilment is the quality of Sahasrara chakra. It is the realm of completion, and realization. All knowledge resides here at the home of our creator. I need say little of this quality because it is beyond everything. Words cannot convey you to the realm of Sahasrara. Discipline and a love of truth will lift you onto the eagle's wings and grant you insight. Spiritual practice is the only vehicle that will carry you here.

Element: Pure Spirit

You are pure spirit. Pure undifferentiated spirit is your very essence. This **gift of divinity** lies within you and all things. It is the source of our origins, to which we will return. Spirit unites and animates all life-forms. Without spirit no-thing exists, with spirit everything is no-thing but pure energy. Impossible to describe, pure spirit just IS.

Life is a journey; it asks you to Open to Spirit as it floods through you. It asks you to raise your energy through the chakras, seeking truth and wisdom. Spirit bestows gifts and grants beauty. Spirit is – and therefore you are – the very essence of love and wisdom. Your nature is Divine. As you Open to pure Spirit, you will be guided and ever-blessed.

Planet: Uranus ♅

Uranus, Neptune and Pluto form a triad known as 'the higher planetary octaves', planets of higher spiritual evolution. Although the Ancients did not name Uranus, some astrologers believe they were familiar with its force and attributed its characteristics to the Sun.[1]

When energy floods through your open chakra system it will gravitate towards the crown, opening in you a profound experience of higher consciousness. Individual consciousness is affected by the oscillating rhythms of planetary energy. The crown is aligned with the vibrations of Uranus. Uranus is the planet of liberation. In its symbol ♅, the crescent moon of your soul meets with the soul of the Divine and together they embrace matter. The small circle is the animating life-force which fuels the soul.

Uranus endows freedom and independence; it inspires invention, intuition and revolutionary ideas. It is a planet that rules the nervous system and activates intellect. Much can be created when its energy is used wisely. Its force can be a catalyst which awakens a search for wisdom, a desire for the improvement of humanity and the planet we live on. When you tune to its rhythm and absorb its great potential, Uranus opens you to the crown chakra and the infinite possibilities of your soul. When your energy is ready to descend again, it is Saturn (planet of the root chakra) that will bring the Uranian energy down to earth, allowing you to make manifest the creative energy of Uranus.

The Sun ☉

As the earth relates to the root chakra so the sun, around which the earth revolves, realtes to the crown chakra. Both the sun and the crown chakra symbolize the masculine creative force. In Tantra yoga this force is pure consciousness, personified by Shiva. To the ancient Egyptians this creative force was known as the Sun God Ra. The triune nature of the sun, as it rises, maintains light and sets in the evening sky, gave rise to the religious trinities such as the Christian father, son and holy ghost and the Hindu creator, maintainer and destroyer.

The sun is symbolic of the very essence of all life. Our Divine essence is ever connected to the light of pure consciousness. The crown chakra embraces the sun's energy and illuminates all the chakras; it dances in duality with the moon at ajna chakra. It lends creativity to vishudda, which brings about visionary art. Its fire lights the eternal flame of love that burns in the heart chakra. At manipura chakra it fuels all activity. The waters of the soul are warmed at the sacral centre where we have the potential to glimpse the Divine Self. The Spirit of the sun shines down on the earth at the root chakra and beckons our ascension towards the light.

Deities

The crown chakra is the realm of God the creator. There is only one God, who is portrayed and named in many guises. The creator is seen as man, woman, both and neither. The Divine force is known as Olódùmárè, Amen Ra, God and Allah. In India the Goddess Aditi is infinite consciousness. Mary, I am sure, once enjoyed Supreme Goddess status. The Supreme Being is crowned creator of the sky. In African spiritual traditions, our Ancestors (Égun) are traced right back to God. We are God's children. God as Ancestor is also seen in Christianity: people pray to 'our father, who art in heaven.' In African spirituality God and Égun energies are all around us, and in Ọrun – heaven.

God the creator united with the eternal female force and created the universe and the celestial realm with its guardian angels. They created Òrìshà, deities, and messengers to communicate with humanity. At Sahasrara chakra we are invited to be with our creator; we can rest here, and create from here. If we still have questions and problems we want clarifying then we must identify the chakra that is affected and communicate with the relevant Òrìshà/deity.

Benin bronze Queen Mother bust, showing celestial images. Yorùbá women traditionally hold positions of power. Queen Mothers, like High Priestesses, are respected and held in great esteem. [Sculpture by Mr P Omo. Photograph by Dr I J Wosu.]

Of all creation, humans cause God the most concern. This is because we are blessed with free will. We often disobey the laws of nature. God gave the Òrìshàs/deities similar problems to the ones we encounter. They remain Divine but have enough love and empathy to guide us with wisdom. This leaves the creator to watch over all creation.

Mythology

THE COSMIC DANCE OF SHIVA

Shiva was originally a Dravidian triple God – creator, maintainer and destroyer. Shakti, the feminine active principle of all creation, animated him. In tantra yoga it is said that 'without Shakti, Shiva would be a corpse.' It was Shiva who taught people Tantra yoga. He was eventually relegated to the Hindu destructive God of fire. To this day, in India, Shivaism, the traditional religion of Shiva, attracts a large dedicated following of ascetics and Sadhus (holy men). Followers of Shiva are recognized by their trailing dreadlocks. Like Rastafarians they let their hair grow naturally. And like Rastas they practise herbal meditation. As part of their spiritual practice some smoke herbs which influence the pineal gland and the third eye. A vegetarian diet and a simple, natural lifestyle are also adhered to by both groups. Ethiopian ancestry is the ancient connection between Dravidians and Rastafarians.

Like the Rastaman, Shiva loves to dance. His rhythmic steps and constant movements create time and consciousness. It is at chidambaram – heart of the universe – that Shiva dances the cosmic dance. Shiva dances in the heart of all beings, his steps create the lub-dub, lub-dub, lub-dub[2] sound of your heartbeat. His rhythm keeps you alive. As long as Nataraj, as Shiva the dancer is known, continues to dance, his pulsating body keeps the universe in motion. His dance is the embodiment of the individual as well as the cosmic dance. Nataraj adds embodiment and liberation to Shiva's triple qualities. As long as Shiva is dancing we have the opportunity to live life fully. He dances in a ring of fire, showing control over natural forces. When Shiva ceases to dance and lowers his raised foot, the universe and all life will come to an end.

Nataraj is a personification of Shiva. Nataraj is seen here dancing in a Ring of Fire. When Shiva stops dancing, the world will end.

Physicists now speak of 'the dance of sub-atomic matter'. Quantum theorists postulate that matter is in a constant state of motion. What seems solid and still is on a sub-atomic level seen to dance like Shiva.

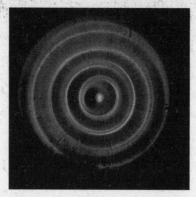

Experiments have shown that concentric circles can be created when sound excites a single drop of water. If the sound is removed, the creation disappears. The Ancients understood this natural law and taught it through mythology – hence they taught that when Shiva stops dancing and his rhythm ends, the world will cease.

The all-powerful Shiva cannot dance without the female energy of Shakti. His latent potential and her active energy combine to create Bindu, the black seed of all creation. The union and liberation of orgasm were seen to reflect the creative coupling of Shiva and Shakti. At the point of ecstasy a tantra yogi receiving *ojas* (sacred fluid) from his Shakti would call 'Shivaham' – I am Shiva. At that sacred moment he knows he is one with God. During orgasm we let go and experience a moment of sacredness.

Sri Yantra is the most significant of all Yantras. It is a symbol of involution and evolution of the cosmic forces, the unity of male and female energies – Shiva and Shakti. An infinite number of triangles make up this Yantra. Through meditation on this image, the aspirant returns to the Divine like a drop of water entering the ocean. The three-dimensional Sri Yantra is known as Mount Meru. The Yantra is seen to have three elevations, which relate to the three granthis. Prana is directed up Meru until earthly limitations are overcome and enlightenment is achieved.

Expression

The golden wings of the thousand-petalled lotus raise us way above duality. The veil of Isis lifts at Sahasrara chakra and liberated energy returns to *satya loka*, the plane of reality. Reaching this sacred destination brings expansion and peace that soars beyond understanding.

As you Open to Spirit at this level you will experience:

expansion

true letting go into *Being*

the bliss of your own inner sanctuary

contact with your inner Guru

alignment of body, mind and spirit, even if only momentarily

vision beyond the veil of Isis

awareness of your infinite potential

healing and wholeness

no fear or pain

oneness with all creation

Self-realization.

Disturbance

If you restrict the flow of energy through Sahasrara chakra you may feel:

pressure and a contraction of energy

withdrawn

depressed

longing for something more in your life

emptiness

constantly limited

ignorant when it comes to spirituality

alienated from the source of life

fragmented, as if everything is falling apart

afraid to let go into the sacred void.

Remember that we all have open crown chakras. Expression of Sahasrara will depend on the amount of energy you can process at this level, and that depends on your spiritual evolution. For some people energy flows freely, while for others it is severely restricted.

Evolved souls who Open to Spirit at Sahasrara chakra are luminous like the shining sun. Love and warmth radiate direct from their hearts. The bliss of spiritual fulfilment is seen in their eyes. Sitting in a room (*darshan*[3]) with such beings as the Dalai Lama and Mother Meera, awakens the soul and raises the vibration of everyone present.

It is also possible to meet people with strong crown chakra energy who do not consciously cultivate spirituality. I have been honoured to work among young people with Down's Syndrome and psychiatric disorders, using movement and dance. Many of the students we worked with communicated from a place of pure spirit. At times I witnessed profound energy moving through them, and felt uplifted myself. We all know people who quite naturally embody spirit.

Expression of the crown chakra can bring eternal peace or a fleeting revelation. As energy flows through Sahasrara, a poem, song or dance may arise. You sing, yet know something sang through you. You speak an unknown language or receive knowledge seemingly from nowhere. Sometimes, when we open our energy fields enough, energies move through the crown and we become channels for their expression. Much visionary art is produced in this way.

Insufficient energy vibrating at the crown maintains imbalances in the chakras below. We are bound by limitation and unable to connect with the liberated spirit. Too much crown chakra energy and it is difficult to live in this world. We literally become spaced-out and ungrounded. As long as we stay dressed in a physical body, balance between the root and crown chakras is crucial to our well-being. We should always seek to embody our divinity.

SEVEN WAYS OF OPENING TO SPIRIT AT THE CROWN CHAKRA

Altar Work

The crown chakra altar represents your ascent from gross physical matter into the realm of pure spirit. You have now completed your journey through the chakras. Although the journey up and down the chakras continues, it is time now to dwell in a place of tranquillity. Give thanks and praise to your creator. Recall the steps you have taken. Feel energy as it moves from the root chakra up to the crown. Sense the glowing, radiant, all-embracing spirit as it fills and surrounds you. You are an all-powerful sentient being full of knowledge and wisdom.

The crown chakra is about spiritual fulfilment, basking in our connection to the Divine and experiencing ourselves as whole. It is the realm of pure undifferentiated spirit, the realm of *Sat-chit-ananda* existence – knowledge and bliss absolute. No words can truly express its glory. The colour rays are violet or gold. It is symbolized by the multi-coloured thousand-petalled lotus.

For your altar use a cloth of violet or gold. The same colours can be used for your candles, or you may wish to use rainbow-coloured candles. Place water in a golden chalice or other appropriate vessel and position it on your altar. Burn the oils of lavender and spikenard to raise the vibrations of the room and still the mind. Make a mandala (sacred circle) from amethyst, clear quartz and other materials such as coloured paper, sand, stones, etc. A mandala is a sacred circular design/symbol. The Sanskrit word mandala means 'a synthesis of centre and periphery'. A mandala is a unifying image created in the round which brings apparent chaos and complexity together into a pattern of wholeness. Mandalas are used as tools for meditation and healing. Use your imagination and skills to create an altar that resonates with the pure energy of the crown chakra.

Use the sacred space you have created simply to Be. Be one with your creator. Let your entire being Open to Spirit and overflow with the Divine.

Journal-keeping

ENERGETIC REVIEW AND DESCENT

Your ascension through the chakras is now complete. You have Opened to Spirit and transformed the energy that animates your entire being. I am sure that as a result of your commitment, much has changed in your life and will continue to do so. Your connection to the Divine is everlasting. Love and wisdom are your trusted friends.

At this point you are invited to descend the chakras, moving from the crown to the root. As you journey, record in word or image your experience of each centre.

Begin by sitting upright with your eyes closed. Allow yourself to enter a meditative state. Breathe easily and relax your entire being.

1   Take your attention to your crown chakra. Focus on the colour, shape, size, element, vibration, and any other sensation present. Enter deep into the experience. Maintain your focus for at least 5 minutes.
2   What message is here for you today? See it unfold before you. What have you learned so far? What do you now know?
3   Take your journal and draw/paint your crown chakra. Write any key words. Try not to let your attention dissipate, but remain focused.
4   Repeat steps 1 – 3 at each chakra.

As you return to the root chakra, regain a sense of grounding. Feel the earth under your body as you open your whole being to the energy that floods through you. Let your body be alive and your mind quiet, feel the pulse of spirit as it speaks. The secret of life will be revealed to you. Accept the great blessing and give thanks.

Yoga Path

All paths of yoga lead us towards the crown chakra, where we can experience oneness. Here the lesson of transcendence is learned. Whichever path you choose, regular practice is the key. Continue to develop discipline in the practices you are gaining most from. Celebrate your achievements so far, be conscious of the difficulties you have encountered and the changes you have successfully made. Give thanks to your creator, knowing that you and the Divine are one.

Obstacles on the Spiritual Path

As you advance in meditation and spiritual practice, you may find that obstacles arise. I explained earlier that meditation is one of the most difficult things you can be asked to do. It gets easier with practice and some days are better than others. Swami Vishnudevananda tells us 'failures are but stepping stones to success'. We know, although the journey may be rocky, that through spiritual practice we grow, prosper and realize more of our innate potential. Others see it too; people will ask you what is it about you – you look so radiant. How have you changed your life?

Unfortunately, when you change your life and walk on the spiritual path, it does not mean problems will not continue to seek you out. They will still find you. Even with all the skills you have gained, when you feel low it may be very hard to continue your practice. This is the real test of spirit. When this happens and you feel as if you are not getting anywhere – Stop! Take a break and simply be kind to yourself. Let the universe know you need help by lighting a candle and saying a prayer.

When you feel ready, slowly introduce a simple practice. Check your diet; be sure it contains the nutrition you need. Avoid junk food, the chemicals only increase your difficulties. During the day, as you go about your business, be aware of your breath. Consciously deepen it to cleanse your system of the stress chemicals that accumulate during low times. Try to get plenty of sleep. I recognize that this can be difficult and suggest using a couple of drops of lavender on your pillow before going to bed. Rescue Remedy[4] is also helpful. The best cures I know for lack of sleep are meditation or foot massage. A short meditation that focuses on the breath and is practised before going to bed can be very effective. Foot massage is my favourite cure; it works every time. Find a professional, ask a friend or do it yourself. Of course, sometimes our own laziness and lack of discipline is to blame for our problems. If this is the case, then what can I say? It really is up to you. You have the power to make changes in your life when you are ready.

We can also overcharge our energy, becoming spaced-out and ungrounded. Sensitivity is raised and the system may feel too open. This makes it difficult for us to live in the world of pain and suffering. We choose to escape into spiritual practice. Unless you have chosen to renounce the world, then 'overcharge' is as difficult as low energy. Again the answer is to slow down or stop for a while. Pay attention to cleansing, root chakra work, diet and relaxation.

If you want to close your energy down, which some people find helpful, visualize each chakra as a flower head that opens and closes. Begin at the crown and work down to the root. See each flower very gently closing, all the petals slowly returning to the centre. Energy still passes in and out as the flowers breathe, but the central core is completely protected. Know that, with your help, the universe will always keep you safe.

As you gently Open to Spirit and allow energy to flow freely through your entire system, you will be rewarded with the peace and happiness that is your spiritual inheritance.

The universe is always asking you to grow and become your future.

Susan Taylor

Meditation

Meditation is danger for it destroys everything, nothing whatsoever is left, not even a whisper of desire, and in this vast, unfathomable emptiness there is creation and love.

J Krishnamurti[5]

Meditation at Sahasrara chakra has no need of tools. This is a place of being and not doing. In this chakra we experience Divine bliss. When we truly resonate with this centre we experience spiritual fulfilment.

Prepare for meditation as usual: cleanse and uplift your environment. Complete your pranayama practice and then sit following the natural rhythm of your breath. Eventually the mind will become quiet and still. Your experience of dharana will help you enter a deep peaceful meditation ... let go into meditation ... Allow at least half an hour for your meditation.

Vibrational Work

COLOUR

Violet is the colour of the higher Self, the colour of transcendence and grace. This fast vibratory ray resonates with the crown chakra. Red is present in violet and provides a grounding quality. Physical and spiritual energies merge in the colour violet. This explains why lavender essential oil is such a powerful remedy for both physical ailments and spiritual imbalances. It can be used to create greater alignment between the aura, the chakras and the physical body. The violet ray helps raise the spirit, making it good for depression, manic depression, schizophrenia and other disorders. Violet used in the environment, or worn next to the skin, can raise a person's vibration. It balances energy, having the ability either to energize or sedate. Visualizing violet can relieve insomnia, migraine, acute anxiety and ease pain. The blissful colour violet is used widely in colour healing.

Purple and violet are often seen at funerals to signify freedom. The Eternal Soul has finally dropped the physical vehicle and reached a place of bliss. A strong violet ray in the aura is a sign of a highly developed soul. This ray helps develop radiance and spiritual attainment.

ESSENTIAL OILS

Lavender, bay laurel, hyacinth, spikenard and valerian are all essential oils that resonate with the crown chakra. Lavender oil is an obvious choice for this chakra. Not only does its colour resonate with this level, but it also contains amazing regenerative properties, making it a great all-round healer. Hyacinth, valerian and spikenard are all hypnotic oils; they create a peaceful ambience which relaxes the nerves and acts as a tonic to the entire system. The oil that is associated with Divine wisdom and prophecy is bay laurel. This is a stimulating oil. The laurel wreath was originally sacred to Apollo, Greek God of poetry. In Britain the title 'Laureate', meaning 'the laurel-crowned one', is still given to the royal poet. Bay laurel is a powerful oil that can be used to inspire visionary art. It is best blended with other woody oils such as sandalwood and cedarwood.

GEMS

After clear quartz crystal, amethyst is a favourite healing gemstone for the crown chakra. It has many qualities. Choose an amethyst that is a rich dark purple and a suitable size to place on your body. It is also good for heart conditions, nervous complaints and stress-related disorders.

Ritual

Sahasrara chakra is the place of integration and wholeness, the pot of gold at the end of the rainbow.

In this ritual we will create a mandala. Mandalas are round images that unify diversity. These complex patterns are used in many diverse cultures as tools for meditation and healing. You will need your journal, a large sheet of card and lots of coloured pens. Paint, glitter, fabric and scrap art materials can also be used. It may take several sessions to complete your mandala.

- Create your sacred space as you want it. Cleanse, prepare your altar and call the directions (*see page 136*).
- Enter inner sacred space through meditation. Slowly raise energy up from the root chakra to the crown. Pause at each centre, tuning in to its vibration. When you reach the crown be still and focus on the thousand-petalled lotus. For a minimum of 10 minutes simply *Be*.
- Now take your journal or several small sheets of paper. Draw three separate large circles, each with a dot in the centre. The centre represents your core from which energy emanates out to the periphery.
- Begin drawing from the centre and work out. Take time to explore the space between the middle of the circle and the edge. Use symbols, lines, shapes and colours to freely express yourself. Don't censor anything, just allow the images to unfold.
- Contemplate your work. Look at the patterns and colours used. What does it say? What is the meaning in these images for you?
- You can now plan a bigger mandala on the card. Use your smaller ones as inspiration and decide what materials you will need.
- Use as little or as much time as you like. Again, draw a large circle with a dot in the centre. Then organize the mandala as you want it, working from the centre out. Let your creativity flow. Remember the process is more important than the end product.
- Your completed mandala can act as:
  - an oracle, telling you about your inner-most Self
  - medicine, a personal tool for healing
  - a focus point for meditation.
- End the ritual by thanking and releasing the directions, and giving thanks to your creator.

Remember, you are ever-loved and ever-blessed as you journey through life.

As rivers flowing into the oceans find their final peace and their name and form disappear, even so the wise become free from name and form and enter into the radiance of the Supreme Spirit who is greater than all greatness.

In truth, who knows God becomes God.

Mundaka Upanishad

———— • ————

13

DESIGN FOR

SELF-HEALING, AND

PRACTITIONER GUIDELINES

T O HEAL IS TO MAKE WHOLE, REPAIR, UNITE. HEALING, AS WITNESSED WHEN you cut yourself or break a bone, is a natural occurrence. It is extremely complex and impossible to understand fully. Yet healing is happening right now as you read. Health is more than a lack of physical disease. We may not recover from a terminal illness, yet be healed. On the other hand we can enjoy physical health and remain un-healed. Your organism prefers health and will do everything possible, using any help available, to achieve it. Each step you take on your sacred journey of life is a movement towards greater wholeness. The ups and downs, achievements and challenges are all steps on the path towards healing. Health is the harmonious symphony between body, mind and emotions. Spirit acts as a conductor, keeping everything in tune. When the conductor is ignored and the instruments are out of tune, dis-ease is the discordant result.

It is important to remember that the rhythm of health is constantly changing. Health is not static; it is a vibrational process. Your physical body changes each second, just like the mind. The rhythm of health can be reprogrammed on any level. You can change your energy, your mind, or your body. Change one and you change them all. Follow the conductor and you create harmony again. You can change the rhythm whenever you are ready.

In this chapter I offer a design for self-healing, and guidelines for practitioners. The two are closely intertwined. The trauma and fragmentation I suffered as a child caused me to search for wholeness early in life. Often the pain we suffer acts as a catalyst and propels us towards spirit. Many people are drawn to healing because of the miracles they personally encounter. This follows the law of contraction and expansion. When we are blessed with love and healing, we often want to give something to others in return.

Healing is very broad and should be recognized as such. We have planetary healers, medical healers, spiritual healers, people who heal through art, literature, music and teaching. When we put love into our work, people will be touched by it. Touch can heal. We all have the potential to aid healing for ourselves and those around us. As we learn to appreciate the gifts we carried into this world, we can begin using them for the good of the whole. We are all gifted in our own unique ways.

For those who identify a gift for spiritual healing, it is vital to stay in touch with the natural rhythms of life. The primary movement of contraction and expansion is the key to healing Self and others. Energy must flow both IN and OUT. We must inhale in order to gain the relief of exhalation. If we do not care for ourselves we will find it very difficult to positively facilitate the healing of others. To quote Ashley Montague, 'Non-swimmers should not be lifesavers.'

Healing requires training. For most of us our innate gifts will benefit from nurture. If you can sing, training strengthens your voice. Healing needs a balance of art and science. Both the left and right brain should be used in a dance of skill and intuition. The spiritual healer requires knowledge of energy principles, spiritual concepts and technical skills. They benefit greatly from knowing anatomy and physiology and enough pathology to recognize personal limitations and make appropriate referrals. Science and healing art, when blended with feeling and empathy, inform intuition. During practice you can then relax and rely on your rich intuition.

Intuition is informed by what we put in the processor. It is not a guess or a hunch, and should not be underestimated. A computer can tackle complex problems only after it has been programmed. This is how the right hemisphere works. Once we have put the data in from therapeutic training, theoretical study, intellectual analysis and personal spiritual practice, the right brain can brilliantly access the relevant information. The right brain has the potential to process information from all sources. It may connect with the client's spiritual guides – I experience this a lot in my work with individuals. The right brain can travel into the past or any realm of the aura, gathering data. It then channels that information back to you immediately. We call this complex process intuition.

After we put the necessary technical and spiritual information in, the art is to trust the unknown process. As a healer you draw energy in, let it flow freely through your vehicle and administer the appropriate technical skills, allowing intuition to guide and spirit to weave its secrets, bringing about healing.

DESIGN FOR SELF-HEALING

Design for self-healing is a seven-step assessment and healing plan. Now that you are familiar with the practices in this book, you can take an overview of where your energy is flowing and where it is blocked. This step-by-step design allows you to gauge which aspects of healing need more attention. It also provides a structure, which can be followed to enhance healing.

Seven-step Self-healing Plan

1 Self-love = Healthy Lifestyle

A commitment to yourself is essential for healing. You require as much time, energy and love as do the people around you. Respecting and loving yourself means living a healthy lifestyle. Would you nurture someone you love with cigarettes, stress and copious amounts of coffee? How would you nurture and love someone you treasure, a precious soul that the angels brought to earth and left in your care? A Divine being, who is only here because they have a valuable role to play on earth? Imagine what they need most. What they need, you deserve. We all need: time each day to connect deeply with spirit, foods that nourish, not poison the body, mind and soul, and enough exercise to keep the physical vehicle operating at its optimum. Do you love yourself enough to reassess your lifestyle and make it a healthy one?

2 Vibrational Resonance

The vibrations you are exposed to affect your health (for more on this, *see Chapter 2*). The company you keep and places you frequent interfere with your system energetically. You have the response-ability to expose yourself to positive vibrations. Whenever possible, choose environments and people who lift your energy, rather than drain and lower your vibrations.

3 Preparation

As discipline develops and you adhere to points 1 and 2, you will be well on your way to good health. At stage three you can prepare your vehicle for the increased charge of energy that is necessary for healing. This is done through cleansing, pranayama and the methods laid out in Chapter 5. You will then be prepared to raise your energetic vibration and charge your system. You can create a more healing environment by cleansing your space. Burn incense to remove negative energy and burn candles to lift the energy (*see Altar Work in Chapters 6–12 for more information*).

4 Prayer and Meditation

Prayer is asking the universe for guidance; meditation is listening to the advice given. Prayer is not the sole property of religion. We can reclaim and cleanse prayer from any negative associations it may hold for us. We have all prayed at some time in our lives. Prayer is personal and direct communication with our creator. Prayer helps us remember that we are not alone; there are natural forces in operation that are far greater than we are. Sometimes we simply need to surrender and let these forces guide us. All goals are in reach when you swim with the tide, instead of against it. Light a candle and take a moment each day to give thanks and ask for guidance. You can use the prayer below or, better still, open your heart and let your own words flow. Be mindful and open to your prayers being answered, and remember they may not be answered in exactly the way you imagined.

DAILY PRAYER: A CALL FOR GUIDANCE

> I give thanks and praise to the creator who has given me this day
> I call on the Goddess to be with me
> I ask for her peace, love and guidance
> I ask for the presence of heavenly messengers to guide me
> and for the protection and wisdom of my Ancestors.
> Let the elements and gatekeepers of the four directions light my way
> As I Open to Spirit this day show me a way
> to receive the abundant gifts and blessings that are bestowed on me.
> As I Open to Spirit this day show me a way
> to be of service to the greater good of all beings.

5 Ground, Centre and Open Your Heart

After summoning guidance in prayer, it is useful to align your vehicle in order to optimize your receptivity. Physically, grounding begins at the feet where we touch the earth – this connection helps us manifest our dreams (*see Chapter 6*). Centring begins in the sacral chakra, our centre of gravity, where we process the forces of heaven and earth, using these energies to fuel our centre. Being centred requires stillness, which allows us to access a quiet inner wisdom before moving into action (*see Chapter 7*). An open heart overflows with love, truth and compassion. Personal power opens fully when you connect to earth, draw energy into your centre and act with love and compassion. Love is central to healing.

6 Ways of Working

Many ways of working are presented in Part Two – The Chakra Workbook. They are designed to heal body, mind and spirit. Find ways that work best for you. Incorporate these methods of spiritual enhancement into your daily routines. Remember Spirit when you wake, let it guide you through the day and, before you retire, give thanks for the blessings you've received. Each day we take in breath is a blessing.

7 Open to Spirit

Opening to Spirit is to heighten awareness, extend consciousness and awaken your entire being to the energy which animates and connects you to the universe. When you truly Open to Spirit, you align yourself with the forces of the creator. You are then open to receive the great **gift of** and **d**ivinity (God) that is your birthright. Opening to Spirit is a way of being that enables healing.

GUIDELINES FOR PRACTITIONERS

A practitioner's journey starts with self-healing. Roberta Delong Miller says 'to touch someone else you must first be able to touch yourself.' Self-healing forms the foundation of the healing pyramid. When the foundations are set, those who have a gift for healing will be called by the universe to take up the responsibility of facilitating others towards wholeness. Healing is an agreement between an individual and the creator, not something you can do for someone else. As practitioners we facilitate the healing journey. Facilitate means 'to make easy'. The role of a practitioner is to empower and facilitate clients as they journey towards wholeness.

Seven-step Healing Plan for Practitioners

1 Commitment to Self, Responsibility to Others

All practitioners need a commitment to self-healing and a responsibility to others. This is fundamental. If you are not well you will be in no position to help others; working with clients will only drain your energy more. Self-healing is a continuous process, not something we finish and can then forget about. If you want to add chakra work to your practice, then you need a strong awareness of your own chakra system. In chakra work with clients, it is often necessary to mirror the energy of a blocked chakra. If your client's root chakra is depleted, it will be important for you to be grounded. If your root chakra is blocked too, not only may you not recognize the block in your client, but it will be hard for you to facilitate change.

Daily spiritual practice allows you to draw energy in and replenish your supplies after working. The support of family, friends and colleagues is invaluable if you are to maintain your health and do a good job. Many people in the caring professions suffer exhaustion because they give out constantly, without thought for themselves. Workplaces often lack adequate resources and take advantage of the caring nature of professionals. No one can continue to exhale without stopping to take a full breath in. When we overwork, the vessel becomes cloudy and grey. If this continues the energy field becomes completely blocked (burn-out) and the healer cannot work at all. This often happens because preparation and guidelines have not been adhered to, nor personal boundaries set regarding appropriate workloads. For women, healing becomes another mode through which to nurture others, when often we seek the very love and caring we put out in our work. It is vital that as a healer you ask for help and support when needed. Regular sessions, exchanges, supervision and time out are additional ways to replenish energy and avoid total depletion.

2 Principle of Resonance

Your vibration is a large part of the healing process (Chapter 2). A clear aura transmits more energy to the client. Therefore, keeping your energy as clear as possible is important. During a session, as the therapist you hold the client in your energy field. A client who feels held and safe is able to dismantle and eventually rebuild energetic patterns in the chakras, aura, mind and physical structure. People are often afraid of hospitals, not only because the procedures can be invasive, but also because it is difficult to create an energetic relationship with medical practitioners. When doctors take time to connect meaningfully with patients, feelings of safety are likely to be increased and healing enhanced.

Attention and intention go hand in hand. Intention is a powerful healer. This is evident from the placebo effect – when no real medical intervention takes place, yet a patient's health improves. Although difficult to measure, there is no doubt that presence and positive thinking create healing results.

3 Preparation

As a practitioner you are a vital tool in healing. Therefore, prepare yourself energetically before touching another Divine being. Create a safe, healing environment (SHE) where you can meet your client soul-to-soul. Be sure that your training and experience allow you to balance skill with intuition.

Healing raises the issue of cleansing and protection. Our greatest protection is to acknowledge that healing energy is channelled through us as healers, and that we are not responsible personally for healing anyone. With the grace of the creator, people heal themselves; we are privileged to accompany them on this sacred journey. As regards cleansing, it is our own egos that require cleansing. I have not known a situation where negative energy was transferred from a client to a therapist whose energy system was clear. However, I know cases where the therapist's negative energy has affected clients. In a session energy cannot penetrate our system unless we allow it to happen. Picking up a client's headache, back pain, etc. is a sign that your own energy is blocked and requires you to work on the appropriate energy centre.

I recognize that in some instances working with energy can be overwhelming. If this happens, scan your system to ascertain which chakras are affected. Ask yourself the following questions:

◎ Root	Am I grounded?
◐ Sacral	Am I centred?
◉ Solar plexus	Do I have an ego problem?
◉ Heart	Is my heart open?
◉ Throat	Am I aware of what this session is raising in me?
◌ Third eye	What is my vision and intention in this session?
◎ Crown	Am I Open to Spirit?

Once you've established where the block is, there are a lot of simple techniques you can use.

- Root – Touch the earth with your hands and take a few breaths, or use a grounding exercise (such as one on page 126).
- Sacral – Use the centring ritual on page 165. This is excellent for clearing energy. Its benefits affect all the chakras. You can also brush your hands through your aura, coming up the front from the feet and down the back from the head. Your hands and forearms can be washed in cold water and a drop of frankincense, which is a good cleanser for the aura.
- Solar plexus – Ego problems can affect us all, at times. If you identify ego as an issue, take a moment to connect with the larger scheme of things. Acknowledge the good work you are doing, but remember it comes as a blessing from the creator. Use your ability to empower, not overpower, your clients.
- Heart – Connect to the divinity in your client, then your work becomes an act of devotion and service – pure bhakti yoga. Try to work with 'loving detachment'.
- Throat – Address issues of transference and counter-transference in supervision. Often we attract clients who present issues we ourselves need to work on.
- Third eye – Structure your session so it has boundaries and space for energy to flow yet remain contained. Agree the intention with your client so you both feel safe.
- Crown – Open to Spirit and remember that you are not alone, many guides are present waiting to offer Divine assistance.

Always wash your hands and forearms in cold water after each session, to clear energy.

4 Prayer

Before beginning the day, or before each session with a client, close your eyes and say a prayer. Give thanks to the creator and ask for guidance in your work.

5 Ground, Centre and Open Your Heart

As you become more experienced at interacting with your energy fields, you will require less time to ground, centre and open your heart. Its importance, however, increases, because the amount of energy you are able to channel and work with expands with disciplined self-practice and experience. It is like making sure you are plugged in to the greater forces before you begin working. As you work, take note of your postural alignment. To maximize the movement of energy through your vehicle, keep both feet flat on the ground, not crossed. Keep your spine upright and mobile as you work, and your chest open as you breathe. Body therapists should shift the whole body towards the direction of your hands and use your back to support the work you do. Avoid twisting at the waist. Once you are aligned you can relax into your work.

6 Technique

The way you work with the chakras will depend on your primary training. Yoga teachers may advocate asanas and meditation, while some therapists will use crystals and colour, and others work hands-on. All these techniques are valuable.

Energy-charging is a simple yet powerful technique that can be used by practitioners. If you are not a therapist you will find this technique useful to relax family and friends – children are particularly receptive to the release in energy.

ENERGY-CHARGING

Begin by asking your client to lay down, facing up. Approach their energy field slowly, allowing them a moment to get comfortable before you make physical contact. Use this time to regulate your breath and focus your intention.

If your ether chakra is strong and your environment cleansed, channel healing energies from the guides and helpers of the individual being healed.

The more you can open your system and tune in to your soul purpose, the greater the healing benefits will be. Practitioners aim to tune in to, tap and harness ether energy as a medium through which healing energies are carried.

Make sure your client is comfortable, with all joints released, allowing energy to flow: no crossed ankles, heads on pillows, or folded arms. These actions indicate where energy is restricted physically. Ether energy flows through the joints, and we want to encourage clients to increase internal space. Releasing the joints starts to open the energy field. Feet should be about 12 inches (30 cm) apart, arms either side of the body, palms facing up, chin positioned slightly towards the chest to straighten the neck. Be mindful, as this sensory position, where the front of the body is open, can raise vulnerability.

Look at the body to assess energy flow. Try to observe visually the energy around and inside; look *through* the physical form. Be aware of your immediate response. You may sense an imbalance, which you can confirm with the client. Always get client feedback: chakra work is not magic, don't feel you should know what is happening in another person's energy field and body. Although you may identify a block, it is beneficial initially to treat the whole body.

Begin hands-on work at the feet – root chakra. Place your palms over the soles of your client's feet with little or no pressure. Hold for 5 minutes, feeling for energy.

Then place your right hand over the anterior sacral chakra and your left hand under the sacrum. Making sure your client is comfortable, hold for 5 minutes listening for energy.

Repeat on the solar plexus and heart chakras. Listen for energy.

On the anterior throat centre, hold your hand in the physical heat layer of the aura (approximately $1/2$ – 1 inch/2 – 3 cm away from the body) as contact may feel intrusive. Hold the back of the neck area and base of the skull with your left hand. Spend 5 minutes listening to the energy.

Charge the third eye and crown together, applying light contact over the forehead with your right hand and positioning your left hand lightly over the crown. Again hold and listen for energy.

As energy begins to flow in the chakras, particularly the head centres, you may need to raise your hands slightly to accommodate the energy expansion.

Finally, place your right hand over the sacral chakra and hold for 2 minutes, allowing energy to return to the client's centre. When you have finished ask the client to roll onto their side and rest.

Spend time listening to your client's experience, and then share what you felt.

7 Open to Spirit

The more you grow from your own healing the more effective your work will be. As you attune to your soul, miracles happen.

Miracles happen when you align with your soul purpose. Secrets are revealed and mysteries unveiled. When you are stripped of ego the door is opened for you to be dressed in grace, blessed with love and crowned with knowledge. As you embody the Divine and walk the way of wisdom, with an open heart, miracles happen.

Miracles happen when you Open to Spirit.

SANKOFA

THE NEW MILLENNIUM –

LOOKING BACK TO PROGRESS

A S I WRITE, THE YEAR 2000 IS FAST APPROACHING. THE NEW MILLENNIUM brings with it much expectation. In the yogic tradition, this present time is known as Kali Yuga, a time of turbulence. To the Mayans we are in 'the Thirteenth Heaven', a period of much change. The Mayan calendar points to 2012 as the end of the current age. The Egyptian Dendera zodiac points to the years 2004 – 2012, when due to the procession of the equinox the Piscean Age will end and the Aquarian Age will be welcomed in. This period in time holds the potential to be a major transition.

The majority of the world's cultures and spiritual traditions predate Christianity. The new millennium celebrates the two-thousandth birthday of an Enlightened Being. Christ, of course, was not the first Enlightened Being; guests at his birth included wise men from afar conferring gifts. Humans lived many thousands of years on this planet before this auspicious birth. Christianity is relatively young. As we celebrate the Christian '21st' century, if we are wise we will not forget the knowledge of times past.

The Ghanaian Sankofa symbol is a bird that looks back in order to progress. The concept of Sankofa recognizes the need to evaluate and build on the past in order to determine a prosperous future. As humans we are young, we have not been on the 4½-billion-year-old planet long. In these times of spiritual and planetary poverty we must all look back, because we need as much wisdom as we can get to propel us forward.

Ghanian Sankofa bird

We must remember that the future is not a definite reality which awaits us. It is for us to consciously create the future together. It is no coincidence that this time is a major celebration in the Western world, the very place where a lot of power is held (solar plexus energy) and change is desperately needed. The 21st century offers the opportunity for maturity. The major transition point in the chakra system lies between the solar plexus and heart chakras. The planet and her people are on this edge. We can choose power or transformation. Humanity needs to grow up and reach maturity. We need to leave the teenage years of the solar plexus and embrace adulthood – the heart chakra. The new millennium needs to act as an initiation; a 21st birthday party where humanity comes of age.

Many years ago Swami Vishnudevananda said, 'East is becoming West and West is becoming East.' The spiritually advanced nations seek technology, while the technologically developed nations are beginning to seek spirit. Our continued development would be best ensured if we try to balance technology and spirituality, utilizing all the wisdom that we have amassed through the ages.

As I suggest in Chapter 4, we need a synergy of Frazer's three stages of evolution – magic, religion and science. We also need to balance the chakras of evolutionary time. Each chakra governs a specific evolutionary time in human history. The root chakra relates to the age of magic when people lived close to the elements and moved with the earth's rhythms and cosmic laws. The age of religion is stimulated by the sacral chakra. People sought that which was sacred and spiritually uplifting. During the current age of science, ruled by the solar plexus, man tries to exercise his power over nature in a manipulative rather than harmonious way. Scientists have created the nuclear bomb, put man on the moon – exploring an alternative to earth because we have created chaos here – and Dolly, the genetically-engineered sheep, has been manufactured. What we are now capable of is frightening. The fear is not technology itself, but its divorce from sacred and universal law.

I pray that this present era of quickening and change will bring a major shift in the collective soul consciousness of humankind; moving us from the power struggles and 'scientism' of the solar plexus and granting us rebirth into our collective heart chakra of compassion and love. This will truly turn us into kind-humans. This shift to the heart chakra will mark the fourth evolutionary stage, a stage of union and synergy where we bring together the wisdom of old with that of the new. We will utilize the best of magic, religion and science and build respect for traditions that have stood the test of time.

After once repudiating ancient wisdom, science is now validating many teachings of the Ancients. What the Ancients referred to as ether is now being called the quantum vacuum. The existence of energy fields is recognized in the holographic principle. Binary systems, as used in Yorùbá and Chinese divination, form the basis of computer (digital) technology. Research shows that crystals are capable of storing information. Crystal technology has transformed our lives: we tell the time with quartz crystal clocks and watches; their reliability and precision are well known. Crystals are used in radar systems, satellites and radios – some people will remember the days when radios were actually called 'crystal radio sets'. This ability of crystals to store information has been recognized for a very long time; the Mayans stored information in crystal skulls, which are now being unearthed after thousands of years. They are thought to contain coded messages for our spiritual ascension. The vibrational energy stored in crystals was favoured by the Ancients as a tool for healing. In 1960, physicist Theodore Miaman observed the laser action of a ruby. This lead to the development of laser technology. Crystals continue to be components in some lasers. They are currently used in medicine and the military. Again we see how technology can be used positively or negatively.

As children of the earth we must prepare to make a huge leap in consciousness. We must relearn the secrets and mysteries that connect us to our mother the earth, our creator above the clouds and all the wisdom of the planets. With open hearts we must align with the forces of the cosmos. We are re-evaluating the ways of the Ancients. Healing arts, complementary medicine and spiritual awareness are all growing in popularity, bringing about greater knowledge, balance and harmony on the physical realm. The Divine nature of life on earth is known to an increasing number of people. We are recognizing the importance of embodiment and grounding spirit. As we thank the Creator, show respect to our Ancestors and listen to the Elders we will advance rapidly in our knowledge.

We are moving into global heart chakra energy. Some people have been there a long time, some of us are just arriving and many are yet to come. But like any path, be it in the bush, the city or the collective psyche, as it gets well-trodden it becomes easier for those who travel behind to advance.

We are in a time of ultimate change, you and I together are creating a path on which our children will follow. We can follow the path laid down by our sacred Ancestors.

Open to Spirit, open wide, you have nothing to fear, let your love shine out and touch those around you. Shine your bright light and make a difference in this world. You are a Divine human being, blessed with the power of creation.

As we stand at the crossroads of major change, let us unite the ancient with the new, the subjective with the objective. Let us recognize our errors and not be afraid to apologize and embrace that which was once rejected. Following the principle of Sankofa, let us go forward carrying the wisdom of times past.

REFERENCE NOTES

INTRODUCTION

1 Conversation with Femi Biko.
2 T R Blakeslee, *The Right Brain* (Papermac, 1980).
3 Swami Sivananda, *Swara Yoga: The Science of Breath* (The Divine Life Society).
4 A H Maslow, *Farther Reaches of Human Nature* (1971).
5 Now known as the Indus Valley region of Pakistan.
6 Nubia is South of Aswan in Egypt towards the Sudan. 'Nubia, the Nile's other kingdom', *Time* September 15th, 1997.

CHAPTER 1

1 Anahata chakra is the heart centre. This chakra lies in the middle of all seven chakras; it is the transition point between the personal and universal realms. Three personal chakras are below, and three universal centres above.
2 Some schools of thought utilize 8 major chakras. The extra one is *Bindu* or *Soma*.
3 Georgia Lambert Randall, *The Etheric Body* (unpublished lecture notes, 1983); Georgia Lambert Randall, *Esoteric Anatomy* (Tape series. Wrekin Trust UK, 1991).
4 Mind is all-pervading, found throughout the body. It is not limited to the brain/nervous system.
5 Those who are saying, 'I was never thought of', remember thought takes place on both conscious and unconscious levels. Nothing happens by mistake, it is all part of the greater thought process.
6 Fire and water work closely together during conception and gestation.

CHAPTER 2

1   Rosalyn Bruyere, *Wheels of Light* (Simon and Schuster, 1989)
2   Ether is the subtlest of the elements. It is the substratum that gives rise to air, fire, water and earth.
3   Fa'Lokun Fatunmbi, *Awo* (Original Publications, 1992)
4   I choose to use the word 'original' to refer to the first people of Australia and America, instead of Aboriginal, indigenous or native, as these terms have all been used in derogatory ways in the past.
5   John Matthews (ed), *The World Atlas of Divination* (Bullfinch, 1992): page 30
6   Bruyere, op cit
7   The words layer, sheath and body are each used interchangeably to describe energetic fields of energy.
8   Constitution: 'This is the structure, state of health of a person's body, temperament, disposition' (*Penguin English Dictionary*)
9   The skin's seven layers are made up of: the Five Epidermal layers – 1. Stratum germinativum, 2. Stratum spinosum, 3. Stratum granulosum, 4. Stratum lucidum, 5. Stratum corneum – and two layers of the Dermis – 1. Papillary layer, 2. Reticular layer.
10 Bruyere, op cit.
11 Ancestors are available to offer worldly help, advice and guidance.
12 Ramurti S Mishra (Saraswati Shri Brahmananda), *Fundamentals of Yoga* (Harmony Books, 1987).
13 Kemit (Land of Blacks), is the original name of Egypt.
14 *Coming Forth by Day* is the correct translation of the title of the book once commonly known as *The Egyptian Book of the Dead*.
15 The Òrìshà have Priests, Priestesses, initiates and children who call on them to receive spiritual guidance and assistance.
16 Dr Karliss at the American society of psychical research, in Gerber, *Vibrational Medicine* (Bear & Co, 1988: page 141).

CHAPTER 3

1   Yorùbá describes one of the civilizations of Nigeria, and the Benin Republic.
2   Olumide Lucas, *The Religion of The Yorubas ... especially In relation to Ancient Egypt* (Athelia Henrietta Press, 1996 [first published 1948].
3   The Hermetic tradition is named after the Greek God 'Hermes Trimegestus'. Hermes is a representation of 'Thoth or Tehuti' meaning the 'thrice-great master.' Thoth was a powerful Egyptian scribe, lord of wisdom, knowledge, speech and calculation. Much Greek knowledge was gained during the Ptolmeic period when the Greeks, who studied with Egyptian scholars in Alexandrian temple universities, ruled Egypt.
4   Dravidians are ancient Indian people, descended from the first people in India, who were Ethiopian blacks known as Negritos. The Dravidian linguistic group includes Tamil, Telegu, Khond and Oraon languages. These Africans (Negritos) are found in many parts of Asia. For further information, see Rashidi, Runoko and Van Sertima, Ivan (eds). *African Presence in Early Asia* (Transaction Press 10th anniversary edition, 1995).
5   Nagas are an ancient people of India. Many Nagas were ascetics living a spiritual life. The Sadhus continue this ascetic lifestyle in India today. Naga is also the Divine serpent.

     Nago is an original name for the Yorùbá people. It is still widely used in the Benin Republic today.

6   The original land of Kush was thought to be in Ethiopia. However, recent research suggests that the heart of the 'Kingdom of Kush' was founded in what is now the Sudan, as early as 3200 BC. David Keys, 'Ancient African Kingdom discovered in Sudan', *The Independent* August 1992.

7   Mircea Eliade, *Yoga Immortality and Freedom* (Pantheon 1958; reprint Arkana, 1989).

    Wayne Chandler, 'The Jewel in the Lotus: The Ethiopian Presence in Indus Valley Civilisation', in Rashidi and Sertima, op cit.

8   The word al-chem-y comes from *kemit*, which is the original name of Egypt. Alchemy and the beginnings of chemistry originate in ancient Egypt.

9   Polarity Therapy is a complex healing system that utilizes yoga exercises, diet and nutrition, hands-on bodywork and counselling in accordance with the five elements, to return a natural flow of energy and therefore health.

10   Bradley Whitmore, *Astronomy* (Microsoft Encarta 95).

11   Hinduism today embraces many matriarchal beliefs drawn from the ancient traditions. It therefore has both patriarchal and matriarchal qualities.

CHAPTER 4

1   Indus Khamit-Kush, *What They Never Told You in History Class* (Luxor Publications, 1983).

2   'DNA researches trace all humans to a single women in Ancient Africa', *New York Times* March 30th, 1986.

3   John G Jackson, *Man, God and Civilisation* (Citadell Press, 1972 – 1990): page 29.

4   Quoted by Professor Ben-Jochannan, in Khamit-Kush, op cit.: page 145.

5   Mircea Eliade. *Yoga Immortality and Freedom* (Pantheon 1958; reprint Arkana, 1989).

6   Mircea Eliade, op cit: page 236.

7   'Negro is a demeaning term used to suggest a savage race existed different from the Ethiopian who was cultured', in John G Jackson, *Man, God and Civilisation* (Citadell Press, 1972): page 213.

8   Swami Satyananda Saraswati (trans). *A Systematic Course in Ancient Tantric Techniques of Yoga and Kriyas* (Bihar School of Yoga, 1981 [written by Swami Nishchalanada]).

9   Kundalini is the Divine serpent Goddess. A power that resides in us all that can unleashed through the practice of yoga.

10   For more information see: 'Yoga and Aboriginal India', chapter 8 of Mircea Eliade, op cit.

11   Ethiopian was the name given to all blacks in ancient times by the Greeks. Ethios = Black, Ops = face. Oral teaching from Femi Biko, scholar in African Studies.

12   Muata Ashby, *Egyptian Yoga* (Cruzian Mystic Books, 1995).

13   Jackson, op cit.: page 247.

14   Wayne B. Chandler 'The Jewel in the Lotus: The Ethiopian Presence in Indus Valley Civilisation', in Rashidi and Sertima (eds), *African Presence in Early Asia* (Transaction Press 10th anniversary edition, 1995).

15   *Rider Encyclopedia of Eastern Philosophy and Religion* (Rider, 1986).

16   'By the second century BC Shiva had acquired a separate identity, usurping many of Rudra's fierce characteristics, and he continued to grow in importance. Numerous folk deities and lesser Gods were absorbed by him, adding to his stature and creating a complex, even paradoxical deity, as is reflected in his 1008 names, all representing different aspects of his personality. Eventually he was elevated to the highest position in the Hindu pantheon, forming part of the trinity Brahma –

Vishnu – Shiva as the God of destruction.' Dolf Hartsuiker, *Sahdus Holy Men of India* (Thames and Hudson, 1993).

17 V. T. Rajshekar, in Rashidi, *African Classical Civilisations* (Karnak House, 1992).

18 V. T. Rajshekar 'The black untouchables of India: reclaiming our African identity and our cultural heritage', essay in Introduction to Rashidi, Runoko, *African Classical Civilisations* (Karnak House, 1992).

19 *Dalit* is the name given to India's Black population. Gandhi called them *Harijans* – 'Children of God.' Today they refer to themselves as Dalits, a Hebrew word found in the traditional languages and meaning 'broken – crushed'.

20 Martin Bernal, *Black Athena* (Vintage, 1987).

21 Egypt is often thought to be outside of Africa and its people are often portrayed as white. Removing the cradle of civilization out of Africa was the work of racist historians in the early 19th and 20th centuries. Before that, Egypt's blackness was well documented. Unfortunately, a lot of our present-day learning is based on the later distorted literature.

22 Gerald Massey's Appendix in *Ancient Egypt the Light of the World* (2 vols; T Fisher Unwin, 1907; reprinted Samuel Weiser, 1970) details 200 parallels between the Jesus legend and that of Horus.

23 Lusiah Teish, *Jambalaya* (Harper & Row, 1985).

24 Santeria is the name given to this synchronization in Cuba;

    Bahia is the name given to this synchronization in Brazil.

    Voudoun in Haiti and New Orleans Caribbean.

    Lucmi in Cuba and Puerto Rico.

25 Wayne Chandler '365 Days of Black History' (a desk calendar; What's A Face Productions, 1994).

26 These Nadis are Ida, Pingala and the Shushumna.

27 Muata Ashby, *Egyptian Yoga* (Cruzian Mystic Books, 1995). Chakras, written in brackets in this quote, have been put in by this author.

28 Indus Khamit-Kush, *What They Never Told You in History Class* (Luxor Publications, 1983).

29 Higgins, Godfrey. *Anacalypsis* (2 vols; NY: University Books, 1965).

30 Seven continents, five as we know them and the missing two are Atlantis and Lemuria. 'America where we find the name Americ, signifying great mountain, (Meru) gave the continent its name.' Madame Blavatsky, *Isis Unveiled* (Theosophical Publishing, 1910).

31 Lord Rama is the seventh incarnation of Vishnu, who belongs to the Sun Dynasty.

32 In Sanskrit Sun = *Surya* and Moon = *Chandra*.

33 Apart from Monday, 'Friday' is the only feminine day and this probably explains why so much negativity and fear has been attached to it.

34 Kwanza was developed by Maulana Karenga in 1966 as a cultural and spiritual celebration of the African lifestyle for African Americans. It continues to grow in popularity.

35 Swami Satyananda Saraswati, op cit.

36 Newell S. Booth, *African Religions (God and Gods in West Africa)* (NOK, 1977).

37 Matthew 10:16.

38 Tehuti comes from the words *tehu* – to measure, and *ti* – dual. It refers to the one who guards the gates into the afterworld. Tehuti, with Maat, stands in judgement of the dead.

39 Nadi is a channel for energy, like blood vessels carry blood. Meridians are the Chinese equivalent of nadis.

40 Ayurveda is the traditional medicine of ancient India.

41   Joseph L Henderson, 'Ancient myth and modern man', in C J Jung (ed), *Man and His Symbols* (Aldus Jupiter, 1964).

42   Frazer, George James. *The Golden Bough: a study in magic and religion* (12 vols; Macmillan and Co, 1915).

CHAPTER 5

1   Dr Randolph Stone is the founder of Polarity Therapy. Polarity Therapy is a healing system that is based on ancient Kemitic (Hermetic) principles and Ayurvedic medicine. It has four main methods of interaction – Bodywork, Counselling, Diet/nutrition and Energy-based exercises. The chakras, elements, pressure points and structural adjustments are all part of Polarity Therapy. It is a truly holistic healing system.

2   A lot has been written about good purifying diets and health building regimes. If you are interested to know more about food, look out for books by Dr Randolph Stone, Leslie Kenton and Michael Van Straten. They have all written good, easy-to-follow books on diet and nutrition.

3   Olive oil. If possible use organic, cold-pressed, virgin olive oil.

4   Two antagonistic divisions make up the autonomic nervous system: the sympathetic division stimulates the body's internal organs and glands preparing the organism for action; and the parasympathetic division, which has the opposite effect, of preparing a resting phase. Ideally the two systems need to operate in balance. In today's modern world we tend to overstimulate the sympathetic division, causing the 'fight or flight' syndrome that is implicated in stress-related disorders.

5   Two hemispheres make up the cerebrum, which is the largest part of the brain. The right side has been found to function in a spatial and intuitive manner, while the left side is more linear and analytic. Due to a crossover in nerve pathways, the left side of the brain controls the right side of the body and vice versa. This relates to the ancient understanding of masculine and feminine parts of the body. The right side of the body is seen to be masculine, i.e. controlled by the left, analytic hemisphere of the brain. The left side of the body is feminine and controlled by the right, intuitive brain hemisphere. Yogis had no preference for male or female; they viewed balance as the ultimate aim. Anuloma Viloma was one method of achieving this balance.

6   Adapted from the principles of meditation by Swami Vishnudevananda, *Meditation and Mantras* (OM Lotus Publishing, 1978).

7   In many schools the solar plexus chakra is situated at the navel. You could try working here as well and see which works best for you. I work with the solar plexus fire energy below the sternum and another fire energy called the 'umbilical spiral energy' at the navel.

CHAPTER 6

1   The petals relate to the number of nadis emanating from each chakra at the vibratory frequency of the chakra.

2   The 'gunas' are three primordial states of energy that make up the entire universe. They are Sattva neutral energy, Rajas positive energy and Tamas negative energy.

3   In Polarity Therapy each of the four elements has corresponding energy triads. These are positive, negative and neutral energy relationships. For example, the Earth element relationships are:

positive pole – neck, negative pole – knees, neutral pole – large intestine. These relationships are formed at conception; they are also referred to as Foetal Triads.

4 Karma means action. We reap karma as a direct consequence of all our actions in this and previous lifetimes.

5 Auset is the original African name for the Goddess who was renamed Isis by the Greeks.

6 From the musical *Once On this Island* (Jay Productions Ltd.; Audio tape, 1994).

7 Swami Sivananda, *Kundalini Yoga* (8th edn; Divine Life Society, 1986).

8 Barbara Walker, *The Women's Encyclopedia of Myths and Secrets* (HarperCollins, 1983).

9 Odùduwà is sometimes seen as male. In oral history s/he is said to have travelled from Egypt and settled in Yorùbáland because the people there had similar rituals and beliefs.

10 Mahasamadhi is the yogic term for enlightenment, equivalent to the Buddhist word Nirvana.

11 Swami Vishnudevananda, *Meditation and Mantras* (Om Lotus Publishing, 1978; revised edition, 1981).

12 The Black Dot is an ancient African symbol of the Eternal Soul. It is the gateway that leads to one-ness with our source. Through this gate we encounter the collective unconscious and reap the knowledge of times past. To quote Dr Richard King from his book, *The African Origin of Biological Psychiatry* (UB & US Communications, 1994), 'The Black Dot is the seed of humanity, the arche-type of humanity, the black hidden doorway of historical unity with one's (African) Ancestors.' In Sanskrit the same Black Dot is known as *Bindu*.

13 Cedarwood is not to be used in pregnancy. It can be a powerful abortifacient.

CHAPTER 7

1 Mary is the name given to the ancient sea Goddess (Barbara Walker, *The Women's Encyclopedia of Myths and Secrets* HarperCollins, 1983).

2 Wilhelm Reich, *The Function of the Orgasm* (Souvenir Press, 1973)

3 Barbara Walker, op cit.

4 Ibid.

5 This is not a fixed rhythm and as women our cycles change at different times, according to the solar calender and changes in our lives, etc. Take time to watch the pattern of your own cycle.

6 Muata Ashby, *Mysticism of Ushet Rekhat* (Cruzuian Mystic Books, 1996).

7 A system similar to Tantra once existed in Egypt. The similarities (explored in Chapter 4) suggest that as the Nilotic people migrated from Egypt they took with them spiritual practices that were later developed into the yoga we know today.

8 Mudras are hand gestures designed to divert energy through specific energy pathways.

9 Swami Satyananda Saraswati (trans). *A Systematic Course in Ancient Tantric Techniques of Yoga and Kriyas* (Bihar School of Yoga, 1981 [written by Swami Nishchalanada]).

10 Shivapremananda, 'The Earth – tone and the orange robe of the Sannyasi', *Mandala Ashram Newsletter* 9 (1992).

11 Self-regulation is a term used in body-oriented psychotherapy. It relates to the body's ability to find equilibrium when given the right circumstances.

CHAPTER 8

1 Hymn acknowledging the solar energy of the serpent Goddess.

2 Rudra may predate Shiva, the Dravidian God he became associated with. Shiva was originally Creator, sustained and destroyer, before he was adopted into the Hindu trinity as a destructive God of fire. His fate was like that of many indigenous deities who found themselves incorporated into new religions, but often as demons and devils. African spirituality had no concept of the devil as is seen in Christianity. African cosmology recognizes the duality in all forces.

3 In Nigeria, the Yorùbás trace their lineage back to the first Òrìshàs, who founded the city-states of Yorùbáland. Ogun, the son of Odùduwà, left Ilé Ifé and founded Ilésha. Ilésha is my Baba Ilé (fatherland), and therefore Ogun is my Ancestral father.

4 The sympathetic nervous system is the stimulating aspect of the autonomic nervous system.

CHAPTER 9

1 Dr Maulana Karenga, *Selections from the Husia, Sacred Wisdom of Ancient Egypt* (University of Sankore Press, 1989).

2 Barbara Walker, *The Women's Encyclopedia of Myths and Secrets* (HarperCollins, 1983).

3 Recommended books include:
> Ra Un Nefer Amen, *Metu Neter*
> Starhawk, *Spiral Dance* (Harper San Francisco, 10th anniversary edition, 1989)
> Lusiah Teish, *Carnival of the Spirit*
> Lusiah Teish, *Jambalaya: The natural women's book* (Harper & Row, 1985)
> Barbara Walker, *The Women's Encyclopedia of Myths and Secrets* (HarperCollins, 1983)
> Jennifer and Roger Woolger, *The Goddess Within* (Rider, 1990)

4 Tapes can be obtained from specialist bookshops and spiritual houses.

5 Juan Mascaro (trans), *The Upanishads*, quoted from Katha Upanishad (beginning of Part Six; Penguin Classics, 1965)

CHAPTER 10

1 Hans Jenny, *Cymatics the Structure and dynamics of waves and vibrations* (2 vols; Basillius Press, 1967 and 1972).

2 The original people of Australia refer to themselves as Yolungu in the north, Anangu in the middle, and Koori in the south. There are different groups of people in each area with different languages, rites, traditions and beliefs.

3 Joachin Rodenbeck, 'A more harmonious pregnancy with Bhramari', *Bindu* 10 [periodical of The Scandinavian Yoga and Meditation School; English edition].

4 The African-American language Eubonics has coined the word edu-tainment to denote entertainment that is not just for fun but also educational.

5 More Eubonics.

CHAPTER 11

1   Hatha Yoga Pradipika, Chapter Four Verse 17 (Swami Vishnudevananda, *Commentary on Hatha Yoga Pradipika* [OM Lotus Publishing, 1987]).

2   Oral instruction from Eulinda Ince-ogiste.

3   Free radicals are highly reactive chemical compounds that have one unpaired electron. This electron can attach to other molecules and have a damaging effect. Anti-oxidants are used to neutralize free radicals.

4   J McGinness, 'A new view of pigmented neurones', *Journal of Theoretical Biology* 115 (1985): pages 475–6.

5   Serena Roney-Dougal, *Where Science and Magic Meet* (Element Books, 1991).

6   There are two kinds of melanin: one in the skin, and neuromelanin, found in the brain, which is common to all people regardless of skin colour. The locus coeruleus (top of the brain stem) and 12 sites within the brain stem, including sustantia nigra, brachialis pigmentosis and nucleus paranigralis, are highly melinated sites that make up the amenta neuro-melanin nerve tract.

7   Richard King, *The African Origin of Biological Psychiatry* (UB & US Communications, 1994); M. Maspero's *Memoires sur quelques papyrus*.

CHAPTER 12

1   Alan Oken, *Complete Astrology* (Bantam, 1980).

2   Lub-dub is the sound the heart makes as the bicuspid and tricuspid valves in the heart open and close.

3   *Darshan* is the blessing we receive from being in the company of evolved souls.

4   Rescue Remedy is a Bach Flower Essence which works on a subtle vibrational level. It is available from health food stores and chemists.

5   From Osho, *The Everyday Meditator* (Labyrinth Publishing, 1989).

BIBLIOGRAPHY

Ashby, Muta Abhaya. *Egyptian Yoga* (Cruzian Mystic Books, 1995)

—. *Temt Tchaas* (Cruzian Mystic Books, 1994)

Bernal, Martin. *Black Athena* (Vintage 1987)

Blavatsky, Eleanor. *Isis Unveiled* (Theosophical Publishing, 1910)

Booth, Newell S. *African Religions* (NOK, 1977)

Browder, Anthony T. *Nile Valley Contributions to Civilisation* (Institute of Karmic Guidance, 1996).

Bruyere, Rosalyn. *Wheels of Light* (Simon and Schuster, 1989)

Budge, Wallis. *The Gods of the Egyptians* (vols 1 & 2; Dover, 1969)

Capra, Fritjof. *The Tao of Physics* (Flamingo, 1987)

Churchward, Dr Albert. *The Origin and Evolution of the Human Race* (Allen & Unwin, 1921)

Cook, Roger. *'The Tree of Life' Image for the Cosmos* (Thames and Hudson, 1974)

Cotterell, Arthur. *Illustrated Encyclopaedia of Myths and Legends* (Cassell, 1989)

Eliade, Mircea. *Yoga Immortality and Freedom* (Pantheon 1958; reprint Arkana, 1989)

Fatunmbi, Fa'Lokun. *Awo, Ifá and the Theology of Òrìshà Divination* (Original Publications, 1992)

Frazer, George James. *The Golden Bough: a study in magic and religion* (12 vols; Macmillan and Co, 1915)

Gerber, Dr Richard. *Vibrational Medicine* (Bear & Co, 1988)

Hartsuiker, Dolf. *Sadhus Holy Men of India* (Thames and Hudson, 1993)

Higgins, Godfrey. *Anacalypsis* (2 vols; NY: University Books, 1965)

Jackson, John G. *Man, God and Civilisation* (Citadell Press, 1972)

Johari, Harish. *Chakras Energy Centres of Transformation* (Destiny Books, 1987)

Judith, Anodea. *Wheels of Light* (Llewellyn, 1987)

Jung, C J (ed). *Man and His Symbols* (Aldus Jupiter, 1964)

Karenga, Dr Maulana. *Selections from the Husia, sacred wisdom of Ancient Egypt* (University of Sankore Press, 1989)

Khamit-Kush, Indus. *What They Never Told You in History Class* (Luxor Publications, 1983)

King, Richard. *The African Origin of Biological Psychiatry* (UB & US Communications, 1994)

Knappert, Jan. *African Mythology* (Diamond, 1995)

Lucas, J. Olumide. *The Religion of the Yorubas* (Athelia Henrietta Press, 1996)

Madhu, Khanna. *Yantra – The cosmic symbol of Tantric unity* (Thames & Hudson, 1979)

Massey, Gerald. *Ancient Egypt the light of world* (2 vols; T Fisher Unwin 1907; Samuel Weiser 1970)

Matthews, John (ed). *The World Atlas of Divination* (Bulfinch, 1992)

Mishra, Ramurti S (Saraswati Shri Brahmananda). *Fundamentals of Yoga* (Harmony Books, 1987)

Montague, Ashley. *Touching* (Harper & Row, 1977)

Moore, T Owen. *The Science of Melanin* (Beckham House, 1995)

Oken, Alan. *Complete Astrology* (Bantam, 1980)

Ra un Nefer, Amen. *Metu Neter* (vol 1; Khamit Corp, 1990)

Reich, Willhelm. *The Function of the Orgasm* (Souvenir Press, 1983)

Rogers, Carl. *On Becoming a Person* (Constable, 1988)

Roney-Dougal, Serena. *Where Science and Magic Meet* (Element Books, 1991)

Rashidi, Runoko. *African Classical Civilisations* (Karnak House, 1992)

Rashidi, Runoko and Van Sertima, Ivan (eds). *African Presence in Early Asia* (Transaction Press 10th anniversary edition, 1995)

Sams, Jamie. *Native North American Divination Systems* (Thorsons, 1995)

Sarvepalli, Radhakrishnan. *Indian Philosophy* (Rider Books, 1962)

Satyananda, Swami Saraswati (trans). *A Systematic Course in Ancient Tantric Techniques of Yoga and Kriyas* (Bihar School of Yoga, 1981 [written by Swami Nishchalanada])

Sills, Franklin. *The Polarity Process* (Element Books, 1989)

Sivananda, Swami. *Kundalini Yoga* (8th edn; Divine Life Society, 1986)

—. *Science of Yoga* (vol 12, 'Science of Pranayama'; Divine Life Society)

—. *Swara Yoga* (Divine Life Society)

Stein, Diane. *The Women's Book of Healing* (Llewellyn, 1989)

Stone, Dr Randolph. *Health Building: The Conscious Art of Living Well* (CRCS, 1985)

Taylor, Susan. *Lessons in Living* (Angela Royal Publishing, 1996)

Teish, Lusiah. *Jambalaya* (Harper & Row, 1985)

Vasu, Chandra (trans). *Shiva Samhita* (India: Allahabad, 1905)

Vishnudevananda, Swami. *Commentary on Hatha Yoga Pradipika* (OM Lotus Publishing, 1987)

—. *Meditation and Mantras* (OM Lotus Publishing, 1978)

Walker, Alice. *The Temple of my Familiar* (Women's Press, 1989)

Walker, Barbara. *Women's Dictionary of Symbols* (HarperCollins, 1988)

—. *The Women's Encylopedia of Myths and Secrets* (HarperCollins, 1983)

INDEX

Caroline Shola Arewa is the founder of **Inner Visions**, centre for personal and spiritual development. Her combination of chakra work, somatic therapy, psychology and sacred ritual offers profound insight and healing. Caroline works with individuals, groups and organizations. She can be contacted at:

Inner Visions
PO Box 22032
London
SW2 2WJ
UK